I0224451

SOUTH-SEA IDYLS

BY

CHARLES WARREN STODDARD

Fredonia Books
Amsterdam, The Netherlands

South-Sea Idyls

by
Charles Warren Stoddard

ISBN: 1-4101-0777-9

Copyright © 2005 by Fredonia Books

Reprinted from the 1873 edition

Fredonia Books
Amsterdam, The Netherlands
http://www.fredoniabooks.com

All rights reserved, including the right to reproduce this book, or portions thereof, in any form.

In order to make original editions of historical works available to scholars at an economical price, this facsimile of the original edition of 1873 is reproduced from the best available copy and has been digitally enhanced to improve legibility, but the text remains unaltered to retain historical authenticity.

TO MY DEAR OLD FRIEND

ANTON ROMAN

OF

SAN FRANCISCO

ORIGINATOR AND FOUNDER OF

The Overland Monthly

INTRODUCTORY LETTER

By W. D. HOWELLS

YORKE HARBOR, August 11, 1892.

MY DEAR STODDARD:

It gives me such very great pleasure to hear you are bringing out a new edition of South Sea Idyls that I cannot help telling you of it. You knew long ago how I delighted in those things, the lightest, sweetest, wildest, freshest things that ever were written about the life of that summer ocean. I believe I was first to feel their rare quality, and I hope you won't correct me if I wasn't, for I have always been proud of it. I remember very well my joy in "A Prodigal in Tahiti," when I accepted it for the *Atlantic Monthly,* and I think, now, that there are few such delicious bits of literature in the language. The rest rise up like old memories of delight—graceful shapes, careless, beautiful, with a kind of undying youth in them, which I frankly told you, when we first met many years after they were written, I was disappointed not to find in you. You did not retort, and of course I was not reasonable. But my words should have served to show you how fast a hold your "Idyls" had kept on my fancy, and what they had taught me to expect of you. They always seemed to me of the very make of the tropic spray, which

"Knows not if it be sea or sun."

I do not see why they did not flow in rhythm under your hand, except that they found a prose there which was fluent and musical enough for them; or had had too much of your mustang humor in them to go willingly in harness.

One does these things but once, if one ever does them, but you have done them once for all; no one need ever write of the South Seas again. I am glad the public is to have another chance to know what a treasure it has in your book, for I do not think it has had a fair chance yet. Our dear Osgood (peace to his generous soul!) brought out the American edition on the eve of the great panic of '73, and so it did not count; and your London publisher defamed your delicate and charming text with illustrations so vulgar and repulsive that I do not think anyone could have looked twice inside the abominable cover. Now I hope your luck is coming, and that the whole English-reading world will recognize in your work the classic it should have known before.

Yours ever,

W. D. HOWELLS.

CONTENTS

THE COCOA-TREE

CAST on the water by a careless hand,
  Day after day the winds persuaded me :
  Onward I drifted till a coral-tree
Stayed me among its branches, where the sand
  Gathered about me, and I slowly grew,
  Fed by the constant sun and the inconstant dew.

The sea birds build their nests against my root,
  And eye my slender body's horny case.
  Widowed within this solitary place
Into the thankless sea I cast my fruit ;
  Joyless I thrive, for no man may partake
  Of all the store I bear and harvest for his sake.

No more I heed the kisses of the morn ;
  The harsh winds rob me of the life they gave ;
  I watch my tattered shadow in the wave,
And hourly droop and nod my crest forlorn,
  While all my fibres stiffen and grow numb
  Beck'ning the tardy ships, the ships that never come !

IN THE CRADLE OF THE DEEP

FORTY days in the great desert of the sea—
forty nights camped under cloud-canopies,
with the salt dust of the waves drifting over us.
Sometimes a Bedouin sail flashed for an hour upon
the distant horizon, and then faded, and we were
alone again ; sometimes the west, at sunset, looked
like a city with towers, and we bore down upon its
glorified walls, seeking a haven ; but a cold gray
morning dispelled the illusion, and our hearts sank
back into the illimitable sea, breathing a long prayer
for deliverance.

Once a green oasis blossomed before us—a garden in perfect bloom, girded about with creaming
waves ; within its coral cincture pendulous boughs
trailed in the glassy waters ; from its hidden bowers spiced airs stole down upon us ; above all
the triumphant palm-trees clashed their melodious
branches like a chorus with cymbals ; yet from the
very gates of this paradise a changeful current
swept us onward, and the happy isle was buried
in night and distance.

In many volumes of adventure I had read of sea-
perils : I was at last to learn the full interpretation
of their picturesque horrors. Our little craft, the

Petrel, had buffeted the boisterous waves for five long weeks. Fortunately, the bulk of her cargo was edible; we feared neither famine nor thirst. Moreover, in spite of the continuous gale that swept us out of our reckoning, the Petrel was in excellent condition, and, as far as we could judge, we had no reason to lose confidence in her. It was the gray weather that tried our patience and found us wanting; it was the unparalleled pitching of the ninety-ton schooner that disheartened and almost dismembered us. And then it was wasting time at sea. Why were we not long before at our journey's end? Why were we not threading the vales of some savage island, and reaping our rich reward of ferns and shells and gorgeous butterflies?

The sea rang its monotonous changes — fair weather and foul, days like death itself, followed by days full of the revelations of new life; but mostly days of deadly dulness, when the sea was as unpoetical as an eternity of cold suds and bluing.

I cannot always understand the logical fitness of things, or, rather, I am at a loss to know why some things in life are so unfit and illogical. Of course, in our darkest hour, when we were gathered in the confines of the Petrel's diminutive cabin, it was our duty to sing psalms of hope and cheer, but we didn't. It was a time for mutual encouragement: very few of us were self-sustaining, and what was to be gained by our combining in unanimous despair?

Our weather-beaten skipper—a thing of clay that seemed utterly incapable of any expression what-

ever, save in the slight facial contortion consequent
to the mechanical movement of his lower jaw—the
skipper sat, with barometer in hand, eying the
fatal finger that pointed to our doom ; the rest of
us were lashed to the legs of the centre-table, glad
of any object to fix our eyes upon, and nervously
awaiting a turn in the state of affairs, that was then
by no means encouraging.

I happened to remember that there were some
sealed letters to be read from time to time on the
passage out, and it occurred to me that one of the
times had come—perhaps the last and only—wherein I might break the remaining seals and receive a
sort of parting visit from the fortunate friends on
shore.

I opened one letter and read these prophetic
lines : "Dear child "—she was twice my age, and
privileged to make a pet of me—"dear child, I
have a presentiment that we shall never meet again
in the flesh."

That dear girl's intuition came near to being the
death of me. I shuddered where I sat, overcome
with remorse. It was enough that I had turned my
back on her and sought consolation in the treacherous bosom of the ocean ; that, having failed to find
the spring of immortal life in human affection, I
had packed up and emigrated, content to fly the ills
I had in search of change ; but that parting shot,
below the water-line as it were — that was more
than I asked for, and something more than I could
stomach. I returned to watch with the rest of our

little company, who clung about the table with a pitiful sense of momentary security, and an expression of pathetic condolence on every countenance, as though each was sitting out the last hours of the others.

Our particular bane that night was a crusty old sea-dog whose memory of wrecks and marine disasters of every conceivable nature was as complete as an encyclopædia. This "old man of the sea" spun his tempestuous yarn with fascinating composure, and the whole company was awed into silence with the haggard realism of his narrative. The cabin must have been air-tight—it was as close as possible —yet we heard the shrieking of the wind as it tore through the rigging, and the long hiss of the waves rushing past us with lightning speed. Sometimes an avalanche of foam buried us for a moment, and the Petrel trembled like a living thing stricken with sudden fear; we seemed to be hanging on the crust of a great bubble that was, sooner or later, certain to burst, and let us drop into its vast, black chasm, where, in Cimmerian darkness, we should be entombed forever.

The scenic effect, as I then considered, was unnecessarily vivid; as I now recall it, it seems to me strictly in keeping and thoroughly dramatic. At any rate, you might have told us a dreadful story with almost fatal success.

I had still one letter left, one bearing this suggestive legend: "To be read in the saddest hour." Now, if there is a sadder hour in all time than the

hour of hopeless and friendless death, I care not to
know of it. I broke the seal of my letter, feeling
that something charitable and cheering would give
me strength. A few dried leaves were stored within
it. The faint fragrance of summer bowers reassured
me : somewhere in the blank world of waters there
was land, and there Nature was kind and fruitful ;
out over the fearful deluge this leaf was borne to me
in the return of the invisible dove my heart had sent
forth in its extremity. A song was written therein,
perhaps a song of triumph. I could now silence
the clamorous tongue of our sea-monster, who was
glutting us with tales of horror, for a jubilee was at
hand, and here was the first note of its trumpets.

I read :

> "Beyond the parting and the meeting,
>   I shall be soon ;
> Beyond the farewell and the greeting,
> Beyond the pulse's fever-beating,
>   I shall be soon."

I paused. A night black with croaking ravens,
brooding over a slimy hulk, through whose warped
timbers the sea oozed—that was the sort of picture
that rose before me. I looked further for a crumb
of comfort :

> "Beyond the gathering and the strewing,
>   I shall be soon ;
> Beyond the ebbing and the flowing,
> Beyond the coming and the going,
>   I shall be soon."

A tide of ice-water seemed rippling up and down my spinal column ; the marrow congealed within my bones. But I recovered. When a man has supped full of horror and there is no immediate climax, he can collect himself and be comparatively brave. A reaction restored my soul.

Once more the melancholy chronicler of the ill-fated Petrel resumed his lugubrious narrative. I resolved to listen, while the skipper eyed the barometer, and we all rocked back and forth in search of the centre of gravity, looking like a troupe of mechanical block-heads nodding in idiotic unison. All this time the little craft drifted helplessly, "hove to " in the teeth of the gale.

The sea-dog's yarn was something like this : He once knew a lonesome man who floated about in a waterlogged hulk for three months ; who saw all his comrades starve and die, one after another, and at last kept watch alone, craving and beseeching death. It was the stanch French brig Mouette, bound south into the equatorial seas. She had seen rough weather from the first : day after day the winds increased, and finally a cyclone burst upon her with insupportable fury. The brig was thrown upon her beam-ends, and began to fill rapidly. With much difficulty her main-mast was cut away, she righted, and lay in the trough of the sea rolling like a log. Gradually the gale subsided, but the hull of the brig was swept continually by the tremendous swell, and the men were driven into the foretop cross trees, where they rigged a tent for shelter and gathered what few stores were left them from the wreck. A dozen wretched souls lay in their stormy nest for three whole days in silence and despair. By this time their scanty stores were exhausted, and not a drop of water remained; then their tongues were loosened, and they railed at the Almighty. Some wept like children, some cursed their fate. One man alone was speechless—a Spaniard, with a wicked light in his eye, and a repulsive manner that had made trouble in the forecastle more than once.

When hunger had driven them nearly to madness they were fed in an almost miraculous manner. Several enormous sharks had been swimming about the brig for some hours, and the hungry sailors were planning various projects for the capture of them. Tough as a shark is, they would willingly have risked life for a few raw mouthfuls of the same. Somehow, though the sea was still and the wind light, the brig gave a sudden lurch and dipped up one of the monsters, who was quite secure in the shallow aquarium between the gunwales. He was soon despatched, and divided equally among the crew. Some ate a little, and reserved the rest for another day; some ate till they were sick, and had little left for the next meal. The Spaniard with the evil eye greedily devoured his portion, and then grew moody again, refusing to speak with the others, who were striving to be cheerful, though it was sad enough work.

When the food was all gone save a few mouthfuls that one meagre eater had hoarded to the last, the

Spaniard resolved to secure a morsel at the risk of
his life. It had been a point of honor with the men
to observe sacredly the right of ownership, and any
breach of confidence would have been considered
unpardonable. At night, when the watch was sleeping, the Spaniard cautiously removed the last
mouthful of shark hidden in the pocket of his mate,
but was immediately detected and accused of theft.
He at once grew desperate, struck at the poor wretch
whom he had robbed, missed his blow, and fell
headlong from the narrow platform in the foretop,
and was lost in the sea. It was the first scene in
the mournful tragedy about to be enacted on that
limited stage.

There was less disturbance after the disappear-
ance of the Spaniard. The spirits of the doomed
sailors seemed broken ; in fact, the captain was the
only one whose courage was noteworthy, and it was
his indomitable will that ultimately saved him.

One by one the minds of the miserable men gave
way ; they became peevish or delirious, and then
died horribly. Two, who had been mates for many
voyages in the seas north and south, vanished mysteriously in the night ; no one could tell where they
went or in what manner, though they seemed to
have gone together.

Somehow, these famishing sailors seemed to feel
assured that their captain would be saved ; they
were as confident of their own doom, and to him
they intrusted a thousand messages of love. They
would lie around him—for few of them had strength

to assume a sitting posture—and reveal to him the story of their lives. It was most pitiable to hear the confessions of these dying men. One said : " I wronged my friend ; I was unkind to this one or to that one ; I deserve the heaviest punishment God can inflict upon me ;" and then he paused, overcome with emotion. But another took up the refrain : "I could have done much good, but I would not, and now it is too late." And a third cried out in his despair, "I have committed unpardonable sins, and there is no hope for me. Lord Jesus, have mercy !" The youngest of these perishing souls was a mere lad ; he, too, accused himself bitterly. He began his story at the beginning, and continued it from time to time as the spirit of revelation moved him ; scarcely an incident, however insignificant, escaped him in his pitiless retrospect. Oh, the keen agony of that boy's recital ! more cruel than hunger or thirst, and in comparison with which physical torture would have seemed merciful and any death a blessing.

While the luckless Mouette drifted aimlessly about, driven slowly onward by varying winds under a cheerless sky, sickness visited them. Some were stricken with scurvy ; some had lost the use of their limbs and lay helpless, moaning and weeping hour after hour ; vermin devoured them ; and when their garments were removed, and cleansed in the salt water, there was scarcely sunshine enough to dry them before night, and they were put on again, damp, stiffened with salt, and shrunken so as to crip-

ple the wearers, who were all blistered and covered
with boils. The nights were bitter cold : sometimes
the icy moon looked down upon them ; sometimes
the bosom of an electric cloud burst over them, and
they were enveloped for a moment in a sheet of flame.
Sharks lingered about them, waiting to feed upon
the unhappy ones who fell into the sea overcome
with physical exhaustion, or who cast themselves
from that dizzy scaffold, unable longer to endure
the horrors of lingering death. Flocks of sea-fowl
hovered over them ; the hull of the Mouette was
crusted with barnacles ; long skeins of sea-grass
knotted themselves in her gaping seams ; myriads
of fish darted in and out among the clinging weeds,
sporting gleefully ; schools of porpoises leaped
about them, lashing the sea into foam ; sometimes
a whale blew his long breath close under them.
Everywhere was the stir of jubilant life—everywhere but under the tattered awning stretched in
the foretop of the Mouette.

Days and weeks dragged on. When the captain
would waken from his sleep—which was not always
at night, however, for the nights were miserably
cold and sleepless—when he wakened he would
call the roll. Perhaps some one made no answer ;
then he would reach forth and touch the speechless
body and find it dead. He had not strength now
to bury the corpses in the sea's sepulchre ; he had
not strength even to partake of the unholy feast of
the inanimate flesh. He lay there in the midst of
pestilence ; and at night, under the merciful veil of

darkness, the fowls of the air gathered about him and bore away their trophy of corruption.

By and by there were but two left of all that suffering crew—the captain and the boy—and these two clung together like ghosts, defying mortality. They strove to be patient and hopeful: if they could not eat, they could drink, for the nights were dewy, and sometimes a mist covered them—a mist so dense it seemed almost to drip from the rags that poorly sheltered them. A cord was attached to the shrouds, the end of it carefully laid in the mouth of a bottle slung in the rigging. Down the thin cord slid occasional drops; one by one they stole into the bottle, and by morning there was a spoonful of water to moisten those parched lips—sweet, crystal drops, more blessed than tears, for *they* are salt; more precious than pearls. A thousand prayers of gratitude seemed hardly to quiet the souls of the lingering ones for that great charity of Heaven.

There came a day when the hearts of God's angels must have bled for the suffering ones. The breeze was fresh and fair; the sea tossed gayly its foam-crested waves; sea-birds soared in wider circles; and the clouds shook out their fleecy folds, through which the sunlight streamed in grateful warmth. The two ghosts were talking, as ever, of home, of earth, of land. Land—land anywhere, so that it were solid and broad. Oh, to pace again a whole league without turning! Oh, to pause in the shadow of some living tree! To drink of some stream whose waters flowed continually; flowed, though

you drank of them with the awful thirst of one who
has been denied water for weeks and weeks and
weeks, for three whole months—an eternity, as it
seemed to them.

Then they pictured life as it might be if God permitted them to return to earth once more. They
would pace K—— Street at noon, and revisit that
capital restaurant where many a time they had
feasted, though in those days they were unknown to
one another; they would call for coffee, and this
dish and that dish, and a whole bill of fare, the
thought of which made their feverish palates grow
moist again. They would meet friends whom they
had never loved as they now loved them ; they
would reconcile old feuds and forgive everybody
everything ; they held imaginary conversations, and
found life very beautiful and greatly to be desired ;
and somehow they would get back to the little *café*
and there begin eating again, and with a relish that
brought the savory tastes and smells vividly before
them, and their lips would move and the impalpable
morsels roll sweetly over their tongues.

It had become a second nature to scour the horizon with jealous eyes ; never for a moment during
their long martyrdom had their covetous sight fixed
upon a stationary object. But it came at last. Out
of a cloud a sail burst like a flickering flame. What
an age it was a-coming ! how it budded and blossomed like a glorious white flower, that was transformed suddenly into a bark bearing down upon
them ! Almost within hail it stayed its course, the

canvas fluttered in the wind ; the dark hull slowly rose and fell upon the water ; figures moved to and fro—men, living and breathing men ! Then the ghosts staggered to their feet and cried to God for mercy. Then they waved their arms, and beat their breasts, and lifted up their imploring voices, beseeching deliverance out of that horrible bondage. Tears coursed down their hollow cheeks, their limbs quaked, their breath failed them ; they sank back in despair, speechless and forsaken.

Why did they faint in the hour of deliverance when that narrow chasm was all that separated them from renewed life ? Because the bark spread out her great white wings and soared away, hearing not the faint voices, seeing not the thin shadows that haunted that drifting wreck. The forsaken ones looked out from their eyrie, and watched the lessening sail until sight failed them ; and then the lad, with one wild cry, leaped toward the speeding bark, and was swallowed up in the sea.

Alone in a wilderness of waters. Alone, without compass or rudder, borne on by relentless winds into the lonesome, dreary, shoreless ocean of despair, within whose blank and forbidding sphere no voyager ventures ; across whose desolate waste dawn sends no signal and night brings no reprieve ; but whose sun is cold, and whose moon is clouded, and whose stars withdraw into space, and where the insufferable silence of vacancy shall not be broken for all time.

O pitiless Nature ! thy irrevocable laws argue

sore sacrifice in the waste places of God's universe ! . . . .

The Petrel gave a tremendous lurch, that sent two or three of us into the lee corners of the cabin ; a sea broke over us, bursting in the companion-hatch, and half filling our small and insecure retreat. The swinging-lamp was thrown from its socket and extinguished ; we were enveloped in pitch darkness, up to our knees in salt water. There was a moment of awful silence ; we could not tell whether the light of day would ever visit us again ; we thought perhaps it wouldn't. But the Petrel rose once more upon the watery hill-tops and shook herself free of the cumbersome deluge ; and at that point, when she seemed to be riding more easily than usual, some one broke the silence : "Well, did the captain of the Mouette live to tell the tale ?"

Yes, he did. God sent a messenger into the lonesome deep, where the miserable man was found insensible, with eyes wide open against the sunlight, and lips shrunken apart — a hideous, breathing corpse. When he was lifted in the arms of the brave fellows who had gone to his rescue, he cried, "Good God ! am I saved ?" as though he could not believe it when it was true ; then he fainted, and was nursed through a long delirium, and was at last restored to health and home and happiness.

Our cabin-boy managed to fish up the lamp, and after a little we were illuminated ; the agile swab soon sponged out the cabin, and we resumed our tedious watch for dawn and fairer weather.

Somehow, my mind brooded over the solitary wreck that was drifting about the sea. I could fancy the rotten timbers of the Mouette clinging together by a miracle, until the Ancient Mariner was taken away from her, and then, when she was alone again, with nothing whatever in sight but blank blue sea and blank blue sky, she lay for an hour or so, bearded with shaggy sea-moss and looking about a thousand years old. Suddenly it occurred to her that her time had come—that she had outlived her usefulness, and might as well go to pieces at once. So she yawned in all her timbers, and the sea reached up over her, and laid hold of her masts, and seemed to be slowly drawing her down into its bosom. There was not an audible sound, and scarcely a ripple upon the water; but when the waves had climbed into the foretop, there was a clamor of affrighted birds, and a myriad bubbles shot up to the surface, where a few waifs floated and whirled about for a moment. It was all that marked the spot where the Mouette went down to her eternal rest.

"Ha, ha!" cried our skipper, with something almost like a change of expression on his mahogany countenance, "the barometer is rising!" and sure enough it was. In two hours the Petrel acted like a different craft entirely, and by and by came daybreak, and after that the sea went down, down, down, into a deep, dead calm, when all the elements seemed to have gone to sleep after their furious warfare. Like half-drowned flies we crawled out of the close, ill-smelling cabin to dry ourselves in the sun : there, on the steaming deck of the schooner, we found new life, and in the hope that dawned with it we grew lusty and jovial.

Such a flat, oily sea as it was then ! So transparent that we saw great fish swimming about, full fathom five under us. A monstrous shark drifted lazily past, his dorsal fin now and then cutting the surface like a knife and glistening like polished steel, his brace of pilot-fish darting hither and thither, striped like little one-legged harlequins.

Flat-headed gonies sat high on the water, piping their querulous note as they tugged at something edible, a dozen of them entering into the domestic difficulty : one after another would desert the cause, run a little way over the sea to get a good start, leap heavily into the air, sail about for a few minutes, and then drop back on the sea, feet foremost, and skate for a yard or two, making a white mark and a pleasant sound as it slid over the water.

The exquisite nautilus floated past us, with its gauzy sail set, looking like a thin slice out of a soap-bubble ; the strange anemone laid its pale, sensitive petals on the lips of the waves and panted in ecstacy ; the Petrel rocked softly, swinging her idle canvas in the sun ; we heard the click of the anchor-chain in the forecastle, the blessedest sea-sound I wot of ; a sailor sang while he hung in the ratlines and tarred down the salt-stained shrouds. The afternoon waned ; the man at the wheel struck two bells—it was the delectable dog-watch.   Down

went the swarthy sun into his tent of clouds; the
waves were of amber; the fervid sky was flushed; it
looked as though something splendid were about to
happen up there, and that it could hardly keep the
secret much longer. Then came the purplest twilight; and then the sky blossomed all over with the
biggest, ripest, goldenest stars—such stars as hang
like fruits in sun-fed orchards; such stars as lay a
track of fire in the sea; such stars as rise and set
over mountains and beyond low green capes, like
young moons, every one of them; and I conjured
up my spells of savage enchantment, my blessed islands, my reefs baptized with silver spray; I saw
the broad fan-leaves of the banana droop in the motionless air, and through the tropical night the
palms aspired heavenward, while I lay dreaming my
sea-dream in the cradle of the deep.

2

CHUMMING WITH A SAVAGE

PART I.

KÁNA-ANÁ.

THERE was a little brown rain-cloud, that blew
over in about three minutes; and Bolabola's
thatched hut was dry as a haystack in less than
half that time. Those tropical sprays are not much,
anyhow; so I lounged down into the banana-patch,
for I thought I saw something white there, something white and fluttering, moving about. I knew
pretty well what it was, and didn't go after it on an
uncertainty.

The Doctor looked savage. Whenever he slung
those saddle-bags over his left shoulder, and swung
his right arm clean out from his body, like the reg-
ulator of a steam-engine, you might know that his
steam was pretty well up. I turned to look back,
as he was strapping up his beast of burden till the
poor animal's body was positively waspish; then he
climbed into his saddle, and sullenly plunged down
the trail toward the precipice, and never said "Good-
by," or "God bless you," or any of those harmless
tags that come in so well when you don't know how
to cut off your last words.

I solemnly declare, and this without malice, the Doctor was perfectly savage.

Now, do you know what demoralized that Doctor? how we came to a misunderstanding? or why we parted company? It was simply because here was a glorious valley, inhabited by a mild, half civilized people, who seemed to love me at first sight. I don't believe I disliked them, either. Well! they asked me to stop with them, and I felt just like it. I wanted to stop and be natural; but the Doctor thought otherwise of my intentions; and that was the origin of the row.

The next thing I knew, the Doctor had got up the great precipice, and I was quite alone with two hundred dusky fellows, only two of whom could speak a syllable of English, and I the sole representative of the superior white within twenty miles. Alone with cannibals—perhaps they were cannibals. They had magnificent teeth, at any rate, and could bite through an inch and a half sugar-cane, and not break a jaw.

For the first time that summer I began to moralize a little. Was it best to have kicked against the Doctor's judgment? Perhaps not! But it is best to be careful how you begin to moralize too early; you deprive yourself of a great deal of fun in that way. If you want to do anything particularly, I should advise you to do it, and then be sufficiently sorry to make it all square.

"I'm not so sure that I was wrong, after all. Fate, or the Doctor, or something else, brought me

first to this loveliest of valleys, so shut out from
everything but itself that there were no temptations
which might not be satisfied. Well! here, as I was
looking about at the singular loveliness of the place—
you know this was my first glimpse of its abrupt
walls, hung with tapestries of fern and clambering
convolvulus; at one end two exquisite waterfalls,
rivalling one another in whiteness and airiness, at
the other the sea, the real South Sea, breaking and
foaming over a genuine reef, and even rippling the
placid current of the river that slipped quietly down
to its embracing tide from the deep basins at these
waterfalls—right in the midst of all this, before I
had been ten minutes in the valley, I saw a straw
hat, bound with wreaths of fern and *maile;* under
it a snow-white garment, rather short all around,
low in the neck, and with no sleeves whatever.

There was no sex to that garment; it was the
spontaneous offspring of a scant material and a large
necessity. I'd seen plenty of that sort of thing, but
never upon a model like this, so entirely tropical—
almost Oriental. As this singular phenomenon
made directly for me, and, having come within
reach, there stopped and stayed, I asked its name,
using one of my seven stock phrases for the purpose; I found it was called Kána-aná. Down it
went into my note-book; for I knew I was to have
an experience with this young scion of a race of
chiefs. Sure enough, I have had it. He continued
to regard me steadily, without embarrassment. He
seated himself before me; I felt myself at the

mercy of one whose calm analysis was questioning every motive of my soul. This sage inquirer was, perhaps, sixteen years of age. His eye was so earnest and so honest, I could return his look. I saw a round, full, rather girlish face; lips ripe and expressive, not quite so sensual as those of most of his race; not a bad nose, by any means; eyes perfectly glorious—regular almonds—with the mythical lashes "that sweep," etc., etc. The smile which presently transfigured his face was of the nature that flatters you into submission against your will.

Having weighed me in his balance—and you may be sure his instincts didn't cheat him; they don't do that sort of thing—he placed his two hands on my two knees, and declared, "I was his best friend, as he was mine; I must come at once to his house, and there live always with him." What could I do but go? He pointed me to his lodge across the river, saying, "There was his home and mine." By this time, my *native* without a master was quite exhausted. I wonder what would have happened if some one hadn't come to my rescue, just at that moment of trial, with a fresh vocabulary? As it was, we settled the matter at once. This was our little plan—an entirely private arrangement between Kána-aná and myself: I was to leave with the Doctor in an hour; but, at the expiration of a week we should both return hither; then I would stop with him, and the Doctor could go his way.

There was an immense amount of secrecy, and many vows, and I was almost crying, when the Doc-

tor hurried me up that terrible precipice, and we
lost sight of the beautiful valley. Kána-aná swore
he would watch continually for my return, and I
vowed I'd hurry back; and so we parted. Looking
down from the heights, I thought I could distinguish his white garment; at any rate, I knew the
little fellow was somewhere about, feeling as miserably as I felt—and nobody has any business to feel
worse. How many times I thought of him through
the week! I was always wondering if he still
thought of me. I had found those natives to be impulsive, demonstrative, and, I feared, inconstant.
Yet why should he forget me, having so little to remember in his idle life, while I could still think of
him, and put aside a hundred pleasant memories for
his sake? The whole island was a delight to me. I
often wondered if I should ever again behold such a
series of valleys, hills, and highlands in so small a
compass. That land is a world in miniature, the
dearest spot of which, to me, was that secluded valley; for there was a young soul watching for my return.

That was rather a slow week for me, but it ended
finally; and just at sunset, on the day appointed,
the Doctor and I found ourselves back on the edge
of the valley. I looked all up and down its green
expanse, regarding every living creature, in the hope
of discovering Kána-aná in the attitude of the
watcher. I let the Doctor ride ahead of me on the
trail to Bolabola's hut, and it was quite in the twilight when I heard the approach of a swift horse-

man. I turned, and at that moment there was a collision of two constitutions that were just fitted for one another; and all the doubts and apprehensions of the week just over were indignantly dismissed, for Kána-aná and I were one and inseparable, which was perfectly satisfactory to both parties!

The plot, which had been thickening all the week, culminated then, much to the disgust of the Doctor, who had kept his watchful eye upon me all these days—to my advantage, as he supposed. There was no disguising our project any longer, so I out with it as mildly as possible. "There was a dear fellow here," I said, "who loved me, and wanted me to live with him; all his people wanted me to stop, also; his mother and his grandmother had specially desired it. They didn't care for money; they had much love for me, and therefore implored me to stay a little. Then the valley was most beautiful; I was tired; after our hard riding, I needed rest; his mother and his grandmother assured me that I needed rest. Now, why not let me rest here awhile?"

The Doctor looked very grave. I knew that he misunderstood—placed a wrong interpretation upon my motives; the worse for him, I say. He tried to talk me over to the paths of virtue and propriety; but I wouldn't be talked over. Then the final blast was blown; war was declared at once. The Doctor never spoke again, but to abuse me; and off he rode in high dudgeon, and the sun kept going down on his wrath. Thereupon I renounced all the follies of this world, actually hating civilization, and feeling entirely above the formalities of society. I resolved on the spot to be a barbarian, and, perhaps, dwell forever and ever in this secluded spot. And here I am back to the beginning of this story, just after the shower at Bolabola's hut, as the Doctor rode off alone and in anger.

That resolution was considerable for me to make. I found, by the time the Doctor was out of sight and I was quite alone, with the natives regarding me so curiously, that I was very tired indeed. So Kána-aná brought up his horse, got me on to it in some way or other, and mounted behind me to pilot the animal and sustain me in my first bareback act. Over the sand we went, and through the river to his hut, where I was taken in, fed, and petted in every possible way, and finally put to bed, where Kána-aná monopolized me, growling in true savage fashion if any one came near me. I didn't sleep much, after all. I think I must have been excited. I thought how strangely I was situated : alone in a wilderness, among barbarians ; my bosom friend, who was hugging me like a young bear, not able to speak one syllable of English, and I very shaky on a few bad phrases in his tongue. We two lay upon an enormous old-fashioned bed with high posts—very high they seemed to me in the dim rushlight. The natives always burn a small light after dark ; some superstition or other prompts it. The bed, well stocked with pillows or cushions of various sizes, covered with bright-colored chintz, was hung about with numerous shawls, so that I might be dreadfully modest behind them. It was quite a grand affair, gotten up expressly for my benefit. The rest of the house—all in one room, as usual—was covered with mats, on which various recumbent forms and several individual snores betrayed the proximity of Kána-aná's relatives. How queer the whole atmosphere of the place was! The heavy beams of the house were of some rare wood, which, being polished, looked like colossal sticks of peanut candy. Slender canes were bound across this framework, and the soft, dried grass of the meadows was braided over it—all completing our tenement, and making it as fresh and sweet as new-mown hay.

The natives have a passion for perfumes. Little bunches of sweet-smelling herbs hung in the peak of the roof, and wreaths of fragrant berries were strung in various parts of the house. I found our bedposts festooned with them in the morning. O, that bed! It might have come from England in the Elizabethan era and been wrecked off the coast; hence the mystery of its presence. It was big enough for a Mormon. There was a little opening in the room opposite our bed; you might call it a window, I suppose. The sun, shining through it made our tent of shawls perfectly gorgeous in crimson light, barred and starred with gold. I lifted our bed-curtain, and watched the rocks through this window—the shining rocks, with the sea leap-

ing above them in the sun. There were cocoa-
palms so slender they seemed to cast no shadow,
while their fringed leaves glistened like frost-work
as the sun glanced over them. A bit of cliff, also,
remote and misty, running far into the sea, was
just visible from my pyramid of pillows. I wondered what more I could ask for to delight the eye.
Kána-aná was still asleep, but he never let loose his
hold on me, as though he feared his pale-faced
friend would fade away from him. He lay close by
me. His sleek figure, supple and graceful in repose,
was the embodiment of free, untrammelled youth.
You who are brought up under cover know nothing
of its luxuriousness. How I longed to take him
over the sea with me, and show him something of
life as we find it. Thinking upon it, I dropped off
into one of those delicious morning naps. I awoke
again presently ; my companion-in-arms was the occasion this time. He had awakened, stolen softly
away, resumed his single garment—said garment
and all others he considered superfluous after dark
—and had prepared for me, with his own hands, a
breakfast which he now declared to me, in violent
and suggestive pantomime, was all ready to be
eaten. It was not a bad bill of fare—fresh fish,
taro, poe, and goat's milk. I ate as well as I could,
under the circumstances. I found that Robinson
Crusoe must have had some tedious rehearsals before he acquired that perfect resignation to Providence which delights us in book form. There was
a veritable and most unexpected tablecloth for me

alone. I do not presume to question the nature of its miraculous appearance. Dishes there were— dishes, if you're not particular as to shape or completeness; forks with a prong or two—a bent and abbreviated prong or two; knives that had survived their handles; and one solitary spoon. All these were tributes of the too generous people, who, for the first time in their lives, were at the inconvenience of entertaining a distinguished stranger. Hence this reckless display of tableware. I ate as well as I could, but surely not enough to satisfy my crony; for, when I had finished eating, he sat about two hours in deep and depressing silence, at the expiration of which time he suddenly darted off on his bareback steed and was gone till dark, when he returned with a fat mutton slung over his animal. Now, mutton doesn't grow wild thereabout, neither were his relatives shepherds; consequently, in eating, I asked no questions for conscience' sake.

The series of entertainments offered me were such as the little valley had not known for years: canoe-rides up and down the winding stream; bathings in the sea and in the river, and in every possible bit of water, at all possible hours; expeditions into the recesses of the mountains, to the waterfalls that plunged into cool basins of fern and cresses, and to the orange-grove through acres and acres of guava orchards; some climbings up the precipices; goat hunting, once or twice, as far as a solitary cavern, said to be haunted—these tramps always by daylight; then a new course of bathings and sailings, interspersed with monotonous singing and occasional smokes under the eaves of the hut at evening.

If it is a question how long a man may withstand the seductions of nature, and the consolations and conveniences of the state of nature, I have solved it in one case; for I was as natural as possible in about three days.

I wonder if I was growing to feel more at home, or more hungry, that I found an appetite at last equal to any table that was offered me! Chicken was added to my already bountiful rations, nicely cooked by being swathed in a broad, succulent leaf, and roasted or steeped in hot ashes. I ate it with my fingers, using the leaf for a platter.

Almost every day something new was offered at the door for my edification. Now, a net full of large guavas or mangoes, or a sack of leaves crammed with most delicious oranges from the mountains, that seemed to have absorbed the very dew of heaven, they were so fresh and sweet. Immense lemons perfumed the house, waiting to make me a capital drink. Those superb citrons, with their rough, golden crusts, refreshed me. Cocoanuts were heaped at the door; and yams, grown miles away, were sent for, so that I might be satisfied. All these additions to my table were the result of long and vigorous arguments between the respective heads of the house. I detected trouble and anxiety in their expressive faces. I picked out a word, here and there, which betrayed their secret sorrow. No assertions, no remonstrances on my part, had the slightest effect upon the poor souls, who believed I was starving. Eat I must, at all hours and in all places; and eat, moreover, before they would touch a mouthful. So Nature teaches her children a hospitality which all the arts of the capital cannot affect.

I wonder what it was that finally made me restless and eager to see new faces! Perhaps my unhappy disposition, that urged me thither, and then lured me back to the pride of life and the glory of the world. Certain I am that Kána-aná never wearied me with his attentions, though they were incessant. Day and night he was by me. When he was silent, I knew he was conceiving some surprise in the shape of a new fruit, or a new view to beguile me. I was, indeed, beguiled; I was growing to like the little heathen altogether too well. What should I do when I was at last compelled to return out of my seclusion, and find no soul so faithful and loving in all the earth beside? Day by day this thought grew upon me, and with it I realized the necessity of a speedy departure.

There were those in the world I could still remember with that exquisitely painful pleasure that is the secret of true love. Those still voices seemed incessantly calling me, and something in my heart answered them of its own accord. How strangely idle the days had grown! We used to lie by the hour—Kána-aná and I—watching a strip of sand on which a wild poppy was nodding in the wind. This poppy seemed to me typical of their life in the quiet

valley. Living only to occupy so much space in the
universe, it buds, blossoms, goes to seed, dies, and
is forgotten.

These natives do not even distinguish the memory
of their great dead, if they ever had any. It was
the legend of some mythical god that Kána-aná told
me, and of which I could not understand a twentieth
part ; a god whose triumphs were achieved in an age
beyond the comprehension of the very people who
are delivering its story, by word of mouth, from
generation to generation. Watching the sea was a
great source of amusement with us. I discovered in
our long watches that there is a very complicated
and magnificent rhythm in its solemn song. This
wave that breaks upon the shore is the heaviest of a
series that preceded it ; and these are greater and
less, alternately, every fifteen or twenty minutes.
Over this dual impulse the tides prevail, while
through the year there is a variation in their rise
and fall. What an intricate and wonderful mechan-
ism regulates and repairs all this !

There was an entertainment in watching a particular cliff, in a peculiar light, at a certain hour, and
finding soon enough that change visited even that
hidden quarter of the globe. The exquisite perfection of this moment, for instance, is not again repeated on to-morrow, or the day after, but in its
stead appears some new tint or picture, which, perhaps, does not satisfy like this. That was the most
distressing disappointment that came upon us there.
I used to spend half an hour in idly observing the

splendid curtains of our bed swing in the light air from the sea ; and I have speculated for days upon the probable destiny awaiting one of those superb spiders, with a tremendous stomach and a striped waistcoat, looking a century old, as he clung tenaciously to the fringes of our canopy.

We had fitful spells of conversation upon some trivial theme, after long intervals of intense silence. We began to develop symptoms of imbecility. There was laughter at the least occurrence, though quite barren of humor ; also, eating and drinking to pass the time ; bathing to make one's self cool, after the heat and drowsiness of the day. So life flowed out in an unruffled current, and so the prodigal lived riotously and wasted his substance. There came a day when we promised ourselves an actual occurrence in our Crusoe life. Some one had seen a floating object far out at sea. It might be a boat adrift ; and, in truth, it looked very like a boat. Two or three canoes darted off through the surf to the rescue, while we gathered on the rocks, watching and ruminating. It was long before the rescuers returned, and then they came empty-handed. It was only a log after all, drifted, probably, from America. We talked it all over, there by the shore, and went home to renew the subject ; it lasted us a week or more, and we kept harping upon it till that log— drifting slowly, O how slowly ! from the far mainland to our island—seemed almost to overpower me with a sense of the unutterable loneliness of its voyage. I used to lie and think about it, and get very solemn, indeed; then Kána-aná would think of some fresh appetizer or other, and try to make me merry with good feeling. Again and again he would come with a delicious banana to the bed where I was lying, and insist upon my gorging myself, when I had but barely recovered from a late orgie of fruit, flesh, or fowl. He would mesmerize me into a most refreshing sleep with a prolonged and pleasing manipulation. It was a reminiscence of the baths of Stamboul not to be withstood. From this sleep I would presently be awakened by Kána-aná's performance upon a rude sort of harp, that gave out a weird and eccentric music. The mouth being applied to the instrument, words were pronounced in a guttural voice, while the fingers twanged the strings in measure. It was a flow of monotones, shaped into legends and lyrics. I liked it amazingly; all the better, perhaps, that it was as good as Greek to me, for I understood it as little as I understood the strange and persuasive silence of that beloved place, which seemed slowly but surely weaving a spell of enchantment about me. I resolved to desert peremptorily, and managed to hire a canoe and a couple of natives to cross the channel with me. There were other reasons for this prompt action.

Hour by hour I was beginning to realize one of the inevitable results of time. My boots were giving out; their best sides were the uppers, and their soles had about left them. As I walked, I could no longer disguise this pitiful fact. It was getting hard on me, especially in the gravel. Yet, regu-

larly each morning, my pieces of boot were carefully
oiled, then rubbed, or petted, or coaxed into some
sort of a polish, which was a labor of love. O Kána-
aná! how could you wring my soul with those
touching offices of friendship!—those kindnesses
unfailing, unsurpassed!

Having resolved to sail early in the morning, before the drowsy citizens of the valley had fairly
shaken the dew out of their forelocks, all that day
—my last with Kána-aná—I breathed about me silent
benedictions and farewells. I could not begin to do
enough for Kána-aná, who was more than ever devoted to me. He almost seemed to suspect our
sudden separation, for he clung to me with a sort of
subdued desperation. That was the day he took
from his head his hat—a very neat one, plaited by
his mother—insisting that I should wear it (mine
was quite in tatters), while he went bareheaded in
the sun. That hat hangs in my room now, the only
tangible relic of my prodigal days. My plan was to
steal off at dawn, while he slept; to awaken my native crew, and escape to sea before my absence was
detected. I dared not trust a parting with him before the eyes of the valley. Well, I managed to
wake and rouse my sailor boys. To tell the truth,
I didn't sleep a wink that night. We launched the
canoe, entered, put off, and had safely mounted the
second big roller just as it broke under us with terrific power, when I heard a shrill cry above the roar
of the waters. I knew the voice and its import.
There was Kána-aná rushing madly toward us; he

3

had discovered all, and couldn't even wait for that
white garment, but ran after us like one gone daft,
and plunged into the cold sea, calling my name
over and over as he fought the breakers. I urged
the natives forward. I knew if he overtook us I
should never be able to escape again. We fairly
flew over the water. I saw him rise and fall with
the swell, looking like a seal; for it was his second
nature, this surf-swimming. I believe in my heart I
wished the paddles would break or the canoe split
on the reef, though all the time I was urging the
rascals forward; and they, like stupids, took me at
my word. They couldn't break a paddle, or get on
the reef, or have any sort of an accident. Presently
we rounded the headland—the same hazy point I
used to watch from the grass house, through the
little window, of a sunshiny morning. There we
lost sight of the valley and the grass house, and
everything that was associated with the past—but
that was nothing. We lost sight of the little sea-god,
Kána-aná, shaking the spray from his forehead like
a porpoise; and this was all in all. I didn't care
for anything else after that, or anybody else, either.
I went straight home, and got civilized again, or
partly so, at least. I've never seen the Doctor since,
and never want to. He had no business to take me
there or leave me there. I couldn't make up my
mind to stay; yet I'm always dying to go back again.

So I grew tired over my husks. I arose and went
unto my father. I wanted to finish up the Prodigal
business. I ran and fell upon his neck and kissed

him, and said unto him, "Father, *if* I have sinned against Heaven and in thy sight, I'm afraid I don't care much. Don't kill anything. I don't want any calf. Take back the ring, I don't deserve it ; for I'd give more this minute to see that dear little velvet-skinned, coffee-colored Kána-aná than anything else in the wide world—because he hates business, and so do I. He's a regular brick, father, molded of the purest clay, and baked in God's sunshine. He's about half sunshine himself; and, above all others, and more than any one else ever can, he loved your Prodigal."

PART II.

How I Converted My Cannibal.

When people began asking me queer questions about my chum Kána-aná, some of them even hinting that "he might possibly have been a girl all the time," I resolved to send down for him, and settle the matter at once. I knew he was not a girl, and I thought I should like to show him some American hospitality, and perhaps convert him before I sent him back again.

I could teach him to dress, you know; to say a very good thing to your face, and a very bad one at your back; to sleep well in church, and rejoice duly when the preacher had got at last to the "Amen." I might do all this for his soul's sake; but I wanted more to see how the little fellow was getting on. I missed him so terribly—his honest way of showing likes and dislikes; his confidence in his intuitions and fidelity to his friends; and those quaint manners of his, so different from anything in vogue this side of the waters.

That is what I remarked when I got home again, and found myself growing as practical and prosy as ever. I awoke no kindred chord in the family bosom. On the contrary, they all said, "It was no use to

think of it: no good could come out of Nazareth."
The idea of a heathen and his abominable idolatry
being countenanced in the sanctity of a Christian
home was too dreadful for anything. But I believed
some good might come out of Nazareth, and I
believed that, when it did come, it was the genuine
article, worth hunting for, surely. I thought it all
over soberly, finally resolving to do a little missionary work on my own account. So I wrote to the
Colonel of the Royal Guards, who knows everybody
and has immense influence everywhere, begging him
to catch Kána-aná, when his folks weren't looking,
and send him to my address, marked C. O. D., for I
was just dying to see him. That was how I trapped
my little heathen and began to be a missionary, all
by myself.

I informed the Colonel it was a case of life and
death, and he seemed to realize it, for he managed
to get Kána-aná away from his distressed relatives
(their name is legion, and they live all over the
island), fit him out in *real* clothing—the poor little
wretch had to be dressed, you know ; we all do it in
this country—then he packed him up and shipped
him, care of the captain of the bark S——. When
he arrived I took him right to my room and began
my missionary work. I tried to make all the people
love him, but I'm afraid they found it hard work.
He wasn't half so interesting up here anyhow! I
seemed to have been regarding him through chro-
matic glasses, which glasses being suddenly removed, I found a little dark-skinned savage, whose

clothes fitted him horribly and appeared to have no
business there. Boots about twice too long, the
toes being heavily charged with wadding; in fact,
he looked perfectly miserable, and I've no doubt he
felt so. How he had been studying English on the
voyage up! He wanted to be a great linguist, and
had begun in good earnest. He said "good-
mornin'" as boldly as possible about seven P.M.,
and invariably spoke of the women of America as
"him." He had an insane desire to spell, and
started spelling-matches with everybody, at the
most inappropriate hours and inconvenient places.
He invariably spelled God, d-o-g; when duly cor-
rected—thus, G-o-d, he would triumphantly shout,
dog. He jumped at these irreverent conclusions
about twenty times a day.

What an experience I had, educating my little
savage! Walking him in the street by the hour;
answering questions on all possible topics; spelling
up and down the blocks; spelling from the centre
of the city to the suburbs and back again, and
around it; spelling one another at spelling—two
latter-day peripatetics on dress parade, passing to
and fro in high and serene strata of philosophy,
alike unconscious of the rudely gazing and insolent
citizens, or the tedious calls of labor. A spell was
over us; we ran into all sorts of people, and trod on
many a corn, loafing about in this way. Some of the
victims objected in harsh and sinful language. I
found Kána-aná had so far advanced in the acquire-
ment of our mellifluous tongue as to be very suc-

cessful in returning their salutes. I had the greatest difficulty in convincing him of the enormity of his error. The little convert thought it was our mode of greeting strangers, equivalent to their more graceful and poetic password, *Aloha*, "Love to you."

My little cannibal wasn't easily accustomed to his new restraints, such as clothes, manners, and forbidden water privileges. He several times started on his daily pilgrimage without his hat; once or twice, to save time, put his coat on next his skin; and though I finally so far conquered him as to be sure that his shirt would be worn on the inside instead of the outside of his trousers (this he considered a great waste of material), I was in constant terror of his suddenly disrobing in the street and plunging into the first water we came to—which barbarous act would have insured his immediate arrest, perhaps confinement; and that would have been the next thing to death in his case.

So we perambulated the streets and the suburbs, daily growing into each other's grace; and I was thinking of the propriety of instituting a series of more extended excursions, when I began to realize that my guest was losing interest in our wonderful city and the possible magnitude of her future.

He grew silent and melancholy; he quit spelling entirely, or only indulged in rare and fitful (I am pained to add, fruitless) attempts at spelling God in the orthodox fashion. It seemed almost as though I had missed my calling; certainly, I was hardly successful as a missionary.

The circus failed to revive him; the beauty of
our young women he regarded without interest. He
was less devout than at first, when he used to insist
upon entering every church we came to and sitting
a few moments, though frequently we were the sole
occupants of the building. He would steal away
into remote corners of the house, and be gone for
hours. Twice or three times I discovered him in a
dark closet, *in puris naturalibus*, toying with a singular shell strung upon a feather chain. The feathers
of the chain I recognized as those of a strange bird
held as sacred among his people. I began to suspect the occasion of his malady : he believed himself bewitched or accursed of some one—a common
superstition with the dark races. This revelation
filled me with alarm ; for he would think nothing of
lying down to die under the impression that it was
his fate, and no medicine under the heaven could
touch him further.

I began telling him of my discovery, begging his
secret from him. In vain I besought him. "It was
his trouble ; he must go back!" I told him he
should go back as soon as possible ; that we would
look for ourselves, and see when a vessel was to sail
again. I took him among the wharves, visiting, in
turn, nearly all the shipping moored there. How he
lingered about them, letting his eyes wander over
the still bay into the mellow hazes that sometimes
visit our brown and dusty hills!

His nature seemed to find an affinity in the tranquil
tides, the far-sweeping distances, the alluring outlines

of the coast, where it was blended with the sea-line in the ever-mysterious horizon. After these visitations he seemed loath to return again among houses and people ; they oppressed and suffocated him.

One day, as we were wending our way to the city front, we passed a specimen of grotesque carving, in front of a tobacconist's establishment. Kána-aná stood eying the painted model for a moment, and then, to the amazement and amusement of the tobacconist and one or two bystanders, fell upon his knees before it, and was for a few moments lost in prayer. It seemed to do him a deal of good, as he was more cheerful after his invocation—for that day, at least ; and we could never start upon any subsequent excursion without at first visiting this wooden Indian, which he evidently mistook for a god.

He began presently to bring tributes, in the shape of small cobble-stones, which he surreptitiously deposited at the feet of his new-found deity, and passed on, rejoicing. His small altar grew from day to day, and his spirits were lighter as he beheld it unmolested, thanks to the indifference of the tobacconist and the street contractors.

His greatest trials were within the confines of the bath-tub. He who had been born to the Pacific, and reared among its foam and breakers, now doomed to a seven-by-three zinc box and ten inches of water ! He would splash about like a trout in a saucer, bemoaning his fate. Pilgrimages to the beach were his greatest delight ; divings into the sea, so far from town that no one could possibly be

shocked, even with the assistance of an opera-glass.
He used to implore a daily repetition of these cau-
tious and inoffensive recreations, though, once in
the chilly current, he soon came out of it, shivering
and miserable.   Where were his warm sea-waves,
and the shining beach, with the cocoa-palms quivering in the intense fires of the tropical day?   How
he missed them and mourned for them, crooning
a little chant in their praises, much to the dispar-
agement of our dry hills, cold water, and careful
people !

In one of our singular walks, when he had been
unusually silent, and I had sought in vain to lift
away the gloom that darkened his soul, I was startled
by a quick cry of joy from the lips of the young
exile—a cry that was soon turned into a sharp, prolonged, and pitiful wail of sorrow and despair.   We
had unconsciously approached an art-gallery, the
deep windows of which were beautified with a few
choice landscapes in oil.   Kána-aná's restless and
searching eye, doubtless attracted by the brilliant
coloring of one of the pictures, seemed in a moment
to comprehend and assume the rich and fervent
spirit with which the artist had so successfully im-
bued his canvas.

It was the subject which had at first delighted
Kána-aná—the splendid charm of its manipulation
which so affected him, holding him there wailing in
the bitterness of a natural and uncontrollable sorrow.   The painting was illuminated with the mellowness of a tropical sunset.   A transparent light

seemed to transfigure the sea and sky. The artist wrought a miracle in his inspiration. It was a warm, hazy, silent sunset forever. The outline of a high, projecting cliff was barely visible in the flood of misty glory that spread over the face of it—a cliff whose delicate tints of green and crimson pictured in the mind a pyramid of leaves and flowers. A valley opened its shadowy depths through the sparkling atmosphere, and in the centre of this veiled chasm the pale threads of two waterfalls seemed to appear and disappear, so exquisitely was the distance imitated. Gilded breakers reeled upon a palm-fringed shore ; and the whole was hallowed by the perpetual peace of an unbroken solitude.

I at once detected the occasion of Kána-aná's agitation. Here was the valley of his birth—the cliff, the waterfall, the sea, copied faithfully, at that crowning hour when they are indeed supernaturally lovely. At that moment, the promise to him of a return would have been mockery. He was there in spirit, pacing the beach, and greeting his companions with that liberal exchange of love peculiar to them. Again he sought our old haunt by the river, watching the sun go down. Again he waited listlessly the coming of night.

It was a wonder that the police did not march us both off to the station-house ; for the little refugee was howling at the top of his lungs, while I endeavored to quiet him by bursting a sort of vocal tornado about his ears. I then saw my error. I said to myself, "I have transplanted a flower from

the hot sand of the Orient to the hard clay of our
more material world—a flower too fragile to be
handled, if never so kindly. Day after day it has
been fed, watered, and nourished by nature. Every
element of life has ministered to its development in
the most natural way. Its attributes are God's and
Nature's own. I bring it hither, set it in our tough
soil, and endeavor to train its sensitive tendrils in one
direction. There is no room for spreading them
here, where we are overcrowded already. It finds no
succulence in its cramped bed, no warmth in our
practical and selfish atmosphere. It withers from
the root upward ; its blossoms are falling ; it will
die ! " I resolved it should not die. Unfortunately,
there was no bark announced to sail for his island
home within several weeks. I could only devote my
energies to keeping life in that famishing soul until
it had found rest in the luxurious clime of its na-
tivity.

At last the bark arrived. We went at once to see
her ; and I could hardly persuade the little home-
sick soul to come back with me at night. He who
was the fire of hospitality and obliging to the utter-
most, at home, came very near to mutiny just then.

It was this civilization that had wounded him, till
the thought of his easy and pleasurable life among
the barbarians stung him to madness. Should he
ever see them again, his lovers ? ever climb with the
goat-hunters among the clouds yonder? or bathe,
ride, sport, as he used to, till the day was spent and
the night come ?

Those little booths near the wharves, where shells, corals, and gold-fish are on sale, were Kána-aná's favorite haunts during the last few days he spent here. I would leave him seated on a box or barrel by one of those epitomes of Oceanica, and return two hours later, to find him seated as I had left him, and singing some weird *méle*—some legend of his home. These musical diversions were a part of his nature, and a very grave and sweet part of it, too. A few words, chanted on a low note, began the song, when the voice would suddenly soar upward with a single syllable of exceeding sweetness, and there hang trembling in bird-like melody till it died away with the breath of the singer.

Poor, longing soul! I would you had never left the life best suited to you—that liberty which alone could give expression to your wonderful capacities. Not many are so rich in instincts to read Nature, to translate her revelations, to speak of her as an orator endowed with her surpassing eloquence.

It will always be a sad effort, thinking of that last night together. There are hours when the experiences of a lifetime seem compressed and crowded together. One grows a head taller in his soul at such times, and perhaps gets suddenly gray, as with a fright, also.

Kána-aná talked and talked in his pretty, broken English, telling me of a thousand charming secrets; expressing all the natural graces that at first attracted me to him, and imploring me over and over to return with him and dwell in the antipodes. How near I came to resolving, then and there, that I *would go*, and take the consequences—how very near I came to it! He passed the night in coaxing, promising, entreating; and was never more interesting or lovable. It took just about all the moral courage allotted me to keep on this side of barbarism on that eventful occasion; and in the morning Kána-aná sailed, with a face all over tears, and agony, and dust.

I begged him to select something for a remembrancer; and of all that ingenuity can invent and art achieve he chose a metallic chain for his neck—chose it, probably, because it glittered superbly, and was good to string charms upon. He gave me the greater part of his wardrobe, though it can never be of any earthly use to me, save as a memorial of a passing joy in a life where joys seem to have little else to do than be brief and palatable.

He said he "should never want them again;" and he said it as one might say something of the same sort in putting by some instrument of degradation—conscious of renewed manhood, but remembering his late humiliation, and bowing to that remembrance.

So Kána-aná, and the bark, and all that I ever knew of genuine, spontaneous, and unfettered love sailed into the west, and went down with the sun in a glory of air, sea, and sky, trebly glorious that evening. I shall never meet the sea when it is bluest without thinking of one who is its child and master. I shall never see mangoes and bananas without thinking of him who is their brother born and brought up with them. I shall never smell cassia, or clove, or jessamine, but a thought of Kána-aná will be borne upon their breath. A flying skiff, land in the far distance rising slowly, drifting sea-grasses, a clear voice burdened with melody, all belong to him, and are a part of him.

I resign my office. I think that, perhaps, instead of my having converted the little cannibal, he may have converted me. I am sure, at least, that if we two should begin a missionary work upon one another, I should be the first to experience the great change. I sent my convert home, feeling he wasn't quite so good as when I first got him ; and I truly wish him as he was.

·   ·   ·   ·   ·

I can see you, my beloved, sleeping, naked, in the twilight of the west. The winds kiss you with pure and fragrant lips. The sensuous waves invite you to their embrace. Earth again offers you her varied store. Partake of her offering, and be satisfied. Return, O troubled soul! to your first and natural joys ; they were given you by the Divine hand that can do no ill. In the smoke of the sacrifice ascends the prayer of your race. As the incense fadeth and is scattered upon the winds of heaven, so shall your people separate, nevermore to assemble among the nations. So perish your superstitions, your necromancies, your ancient arts of war, and the unwritten epics of your kings.

Alas, Kána-aná! As the foam of the sea you love,

as the fragrance of the flower you worship, shall
your precious body be wasted, and your untrammelled soul pass to the realms of your fathers!

Our day of communion is over. Behold how
Night extends her wings to cover you from my sight!
She may, indeed, hide your presence; she may
withhold from me the mystery of your future; but
she cannot take from me that which I have; she
cannot rob me of the rich influences of your past.

Dear comrade, pardon and absolve your spiritual
adviser, for seeking to remould so delicate and
original a soul as yours; and, though neither
prophet nor priest, I yet give you the kiss of peace
at parting, and the benediction of unceasing love.

PART III.

Barbarian Days.

WE had been watching intently the faint, shadowy outline along the horizon, and wondering whether it were really land, or but a cloudy similitude of it; while we bore down upon it all the afternoon in fine style, and the breeze freshened as evening came on. It was all clear sailing, and we were in pretty good spirits, which is not always the case with landsmen at sea.

Sitting there on the after-deck, I had asked myself, more than once, If life were made up of placid days like this, how long would life be sweet? I gave it up every time; for one is not inclined to consider so curiously as to press any problem to a solution in those indolent latitudes.

Perhaps it was Captain Kidd who told me he had sailed out of a twelve-knot breeze on a sudden— slipping off the edges of it, as it were—and found his sails all aback as he slid into a dead calm. There rocking in still weather, he saw another bark, almost within hail, blown into the west and out of sight, like a bird in a March gale.

I wonder what caused me to think of Kidd's experiences just then? I can't imagine, unless it was

4

some prescient shadow floating in my neighborhood—the precursor of the little event that followed. Such things do happen, and when we least
expect it ; though, fortunately, they don't worry us
as a general thing. I didn't worry at all, but sat
there by myself, while some of my fellow-passengers
took a regular "constitutional" up and down the
deck, and over and over it, until the nervous woman
below in the cabin "blessed her stars," and wished
herself ashore.

I preferred sitting and pondering over the cloud
that seemed slowly to rise from the sea, assuming
definite and undeniable appearances of land.

I knew very well what land it must be : one of a
group of islands every inch of which I had traversed
with the zeal of youthful enthusiasm ; but which of
them, was a question I almost feared to have answered. Yet, what difference could it make to me !
The land was providentially in our course, but not
on our way-bill. If we were within gunshot of its
loveliest portion, we must needs pass on as frigidly
as though it were Charybdis, or something equally
dreadful ; and I began to think it might be something of the sort, because of its besetting temptations.

There was not the slightest doubt as to the cer-
tainty of its being land, when we went down to
supper ; and at sunset we knew the dark spots were
valleys, and the bright ones hills. I fancied a hundred bronze-hued faces were turned toward us, as
we seemed to twinkle away off in their sunset sea
like a fallen star, or something of that sort. I

thought I could almost hear the sea beating upon the crusts of the reef in the twilight; but perhaps I didn't, for the land was miles away, and night hid it presently, while the old solitude of the ocean impressed us all as though we were again in the midst of its unbroken, circular wastes. Then they played whist in the cabin—all but me. I hung over the ship's side, resolved to watch all night for the lights on shore—the flickering watch-fires in the mountain camps; for I knew I should see them, as we were bound to pass the island before morning.

The night was intensely dark; clouds muffled the stars, and not a spark of light was visible in any direction over the waters. A shower could easily have quenched the beacons I was seeking, and my vigil soon became tedious; so presently I followed the others and turned in, rather disconsolate and disgusted.

Toward midnight the wind fell rapidly, and within half an hour we found ourselves in a dead calm, when the moan of the breakers was quite audible on our starboard quarter. The captain was nervous and watchful; the currents in the channel were strong, and he saw by the variation in the compass, that the vessel was being whirled in a great circle around a point of the island.

Fortunately it began to get light before the danger grew imminent. At three o'clock we were within soundings, and shortly after we plumped the anchor into the rough coral at the bottom of a pretty little harbor, where, the captain informed us, we must ride all day and get out with the land-breeze, that would probably come down at night. I rushed up in the gray dawn, and bent my gaze upon the shore. I think I must have turned pale or trembled a little, or done something sensational and appropriate, though no one observed it; whereat I was rather glad, on the whole, for they could not have understood it if I had done my best to explain—which I had not the least idea of doing, however, for it was none of their affair.

I knew that place the moment I saw it—the very spot of all I most desired to see; and I resolved, in my secret soul, to go ashore, there and then; amicably if I might, forcibly if I must.

The captain was not over-genial that morning, either; he hated detention, and was a trifle nervous about being tied up under the lee of the land for twelve or twenty hours. So he growled if anyone approached him all that day, and positively refused to allow the ship's boat to be touched, unless we drifted upon the rocks, broadside—which, he seemed to think, was not entirely out of question. I was sure there would be a canoe—perhaps several—alongside by sunrise; so I said nothing, but waited in silence, determined to desert when the time came; and the captain might whistle me back if he could.

Presently the time came. We were rocking easily on the swell, directly to the eastward of a deep valley. The sky was ruddy; the air fresh and invigorating, but soft as the gales of Paradise. We were in the tropics. You would have known it with your eyes shut; the whole wonderful atmosphere confessed it. But, with your eyes open, those white birds, sailing like snow-flakes through the immaculate blue heavens, with tail-feathers like our pennant; the floating gardens of the sea, through which we had been ruthlessly ploughing for a couple of days back; the gorgeous sunrises and sunsets—all were proofs positive of our latitude.

What a sunrise it was on that morning! Yet I stood with my back to it, looking west; for there I saw, firstly, the foam on the reef—as crimson as blood—falling over the wine-stained waves; then it changed as the sun ascended, like clouds of golden powder, indescribably magnificent, shaken and scattered upon the silver snow-drifts of the coral reef, dazzling to behold, and continually changing.

Beyond it, in the still water, was reflected a long, narrow strip of beach; above it, green pastures and umbrageous groves, with native huts, like great birds'-nests, half hidden among them; and the weird, slender cocoa-palms were there—those exclamation-points in the poetry of tropic landscape. All this lay slumbering securely between high walls of verdure; while at the upper end, where the valley was like a niche set in the green and glorious mountains, two waterfalls floated downward like smoke-columns on a heavy morning. Angels and ministers of grace! do you, in your airy perambulations, visit haunts more lovely than this?—as lovely as that undiscovered country from whose bourn the traveller would rather not look back, pre-

mising that the traveller were as singularly constituted as I am ; which is, peradventure, not probable.

They knew it was morning almost as soon as we
did, though they lived a few furlongs farther west,
and had no notion of the immediate proximity of a
strange craft—by no means rakish in her rig, however ; only a simple merchantman, bound for Auck-
land from San Francisco, but the victim of circumstances, and, in consequence, tied to the bottom of
the sea when half-way over.

They knew it was morning. I saw them swarming out of their grassy nests, brown, sleek-limbed,
and naked. They regarded with amazement our
floating home. The news spread, and the groves
were suddenly peopled with my dear barbarians,
who hate civilization almost as much as I do, and
are certainly quite as idolatrous and indolent as I
ever aspire to be.

I turned my palms outward toward them ; I lifted
up my voice and cried, "Hail, my brothers! We
hasten with the morning ; we follow after the sun.
Greetings to you, dwellers in the West!"

Nobody heard me. I looked again. Down they
came upon the shore, wading into the sea. Then
such a carnival as they celebrated in the shallow
water was a novelty for some of my cabin friends ;
but I knew all about it. I'd done the same thing
often enough myself, when I was young, and free,
and innocent, and savage. I knew they were asking
themselves a thousand questions as to our sudden
appearance in their seas, and would rather like to

know who we were, and where we were going, but scorned to ask us. They had once or twice been visited by the same sort of whitish-looking people, and they had found those colorless faces uncivil, and the bleached-out skins by no means to be trusted with those whom they considered their inferiors. They didn't know that it is one of the Thirty-nine Articles of Civilization to bully one's way through the world. Then I prayed that they might be moved to send out a canoe, so that I could debark and go inland for the day. I prayed very earnestly, and out she came—one of their tiny, fragile canoes, looking like a deserted chrysalis, with the invisible wings of the spiritual, tutelary butterfly wafting it over the waves. In this chrysalis dugout sat a tough little body, with a curly head, which I recognized in a minute as belonging to a once friend and comrade in my delightful exile, when I was a successful prodigal, and wasted my substance in the most startling and effectual manner, and enjoyed it a great deal better than if I had kept it in the bank, as they advised me to do. On he came, beating the sea with his broad paddle, alternately by either side of the canoe, and regarding us with a commendable degree of suspicion. I greeted him in his peculiar dialect. The gift of tongues seemed suddenly to have descended upon me, for I found little difficulty in saying everything I wanted to say, in a remarkably brief space of time.

"Hail, little friend!" said I; "great love to you. How is it on shore now?"

He replied that it was decidedly nice on shore now, and that his love for me was as much as mine for him, and more too, and that consequently he was prepared to conduct me thither, regardless of expense.

I went with that lovely boy on shore. The captain could not resist my persuasive appeals for a short leave of absence, and so I went. Perhaps it would not have been advisable for him to have suppressed me; and he made a courteous virtue of necessity.

I had leave to stop till evening, unless I heard a signal-gun, upon hearing which I was to return immediately on board, or suffer the consequences.

Now, I am free to confess, that the consequences didn't appall me as we swung off from the vessel, where I had been an uneasy prisoner for many days; and I fell to chatting with Niga, my dusky friend, in a sort of desperate joy.

Niga was a regular trump. He had more than once piled on horseback behind me, in the sweet days when we used to ride double—yea, and even treble, if necessary. There was usually a great deal more boy than horse on the premises; hence this questionable economy in our cavalry regulations. Niga told me many things as we drew near the reef: he talked of nearly everybody and everything; but of all that he told me, he said nothing of the one I most longed to hear about. Yet, somehow or other, I could not quite bring myself to ask him, out and out, this question. You know, sometimes it is hard to shape words just as you want them shaped, and the question is never asked in consequence.

The reef was growling tremendously. We were drawing nearer to it every moment. I thought the chances were against us ; but Niga was self-possessed, and, as he had crossed it once that morning —and in the more dangerous direction of the two, that is, against the grain of the waves—I concluded there was no special need of my making a scene ; and in the next moment we were poised on a terrific cataract of glittering and rushing breakers, snatched up and held trembling in mid-air, with the canoe half filled with water, and I perfectly blind with spray.

It was a memorable moment in a very short voyage ; and the general verdict on board ship, where they were watching us with some interest, was, that it served me right.

When my eyes were once more free of the water, I found myself in the midst of the natives, who had been waiting just inside of the reef to receive us ; and, as they recognized me, they laid a hand on the canoe, as many as could crowd about it, fairly lifting it out of the water on our way to the shore, all the while wailing at the top of their voices their mournful and desolate wail.

It was impossible for me to decide whether that chant of theirs was an expression of joy or sorrow, the nature of it is precisely the same, in either case.

So we went on shore in our little triumphal procession, and there I was embraced in a very emphatic manner by savages of every conceivable sex, age, and color. Having mutely submitted to their genuine expressions of love, I was conducted—a willing and bewildered captive—along the beach, around the little point that separates the river from the sea, and thence by the river-bank to the house I knew so well. I believe I looked at every dusky face in that assemblage, two or three times over, but saw not the one I sought.

What could it mean? Was he hunting in the mountains, or fishing beyond the headland, or sick, or in prison, that he came not to greet me? Surely, something had befallen him—something serious and unusual—or he would have been the first to welcome me home to barbarism!

A strange dread clouded my mind; it increased and multiplied as we passed on toward the house that had been home to me. Then, having led me to the outer door, the people all sat there upon the ground, and began wailing piteously.

I hastily crossed the narrow outer room, lifted the plaited curtain, and entered the inner chamber, where I had spent my strange, wild holiday long months before. I looked earnestly about me, while my eyes gradually became familiar with the dull light. Nothing seemed changed. I could point at once to almost every article in the room. It seemed but yesterday that I had stolen away from them in the gray dawn, and repented my desertion too late.

I soon grew accustomed to the sombre light of the room. I saw sitting about me, in the corners, bowed figures, with their faces hidden in grief. There was no longer any doubt as to the nature of their emotion. It was grief that had stricken the household, and the grief that death alone occasions. I counted every figure in the room; I recognized each, the same that I had known when I dwelt among them; he alone was absent.

I don't know what possessed me at that moment. I felt an almost uncontrollable desire to laugh, as though it were some *masque* gotten up for my amusement. Then I wished they would cease their masking, for I felt too miserable to laugh. Then I was utterly at a loss to know what to do; so I walked to the old-fashioned bed—our old-fashioned bed—in the corner, looking just as it used to. I think the same old spider was there still, clinging to the canopy; the very same old fellow, in his harlequin tights, that we used to watch, and talk about, and wonder what he was thinking of, to stop so still, day after day, and week after week, up there on the canopy. I threw myself upon the edge of the bed, my feet resting upon the floor; and there I tried to think of everything but that one dreadful reality that would assert itself, in spite of my efforts to deny it.

Where was my friend? Where could he be, that these, his friends, were so bowed with sorrow? The question involved a revelation, already anticipated in my mind. That revelation I dreaded as I would dread my own death-sentence. But it came at last. A woman who had been humbling herself in the dust moved toward me from the shadow that half concealed her. She did not rise to her feet; she was half reclining on the mats of the floor, her features veiled in the long, black hair of her race. One hand was extended toward me, then the other; the body followed; and so she moved, slowly and painfully, toward the bedside.

It was his mother. I knew her intuitively. Close to the bed she came, and crouched by me, upon the floor. There, with one hand clasped close over mine, the other flooded with her copious tears, and her forehead bowed almost to the floor, she poured forth the measure of her woe. The moment her voice was heard, those out of the house ceased wailing, and seemed to be listening to the elegy of the bereaved.

Her voice was husky with grief, broken again and again with sobs. I seemed to understand perfectly the nature of her story, though my knowledge of the dialect was very deficient.

The mother's soul was quickened with her pathetic theme. The frenzy of the poet inspired her lips. It was an epic she was chanting, celebrating the career of her boy-hero. She told of his birth, and wonderful childhood; of his beautiful strength; of his sublime affection, and the friend it had brought him from over the water.

She referred frequently to our former associations, and seemed to delight in dwelling upon them.

Then came the story of his death—the saddest canto of the melancholy whole.

How shall I ever forgive myself the selfish pleasure I took in striving to remodel an immortal soul? What business had I to touch so sensitive an organism; susceptible of infinite impressions, but incapable, in its prodigality, of separating and dismissing the evil, and retaining only the good—therefore fit only to increase and develop in the suitable atmosphere with which the Creator had surrounded it?

Why did I not foresee the climax?

I might have known that one reared in the nursery of Nature, as free to speak and act as the very winds of heaven to blow whither they list, could ill support the manacles of our modern proprieties. Of what use to him could be a knowledge of the artifices of society? Simply a temptation and a snare!

What was the story of his fate? That he came safely home, rejoicing in his natural freedom; that he could not express his delight at finding home so pleasant; that his days were spent in telling of the wonderful things he had seen; more sects than the gods of the South Seas; more doubters than believers; contradictions, and insults, and suspicions, everywhere. They laughed again, when they thought of us, and pitied us all the while.

But his exhilaration wore off, after a time. Then came the reaction. A restlessness; an undefined, unsatisfied longing. Life became a burden. The seed of dissension had fallen in fresh and fallow soil; it was a souvenir of his sojourn among us. He, the child of Nature, must now follow out the artificial and hollow life of the world, or die unsatisfied; for he could not return to his original sphere of trust and contentment. He had learned to doubt all things, as naturally as any of us.

For days he moaned in spirit, and was troubled; nothing consoled him; his soul was broken of its rest; he grew desperate and melancholy.

I believe he was distracted with the problem of society, and I cannot wonder at it. One day, when his condition had become no longer endurable, he stole off to sea in his canoe, thinking, perhaps, that he could reach this continent, or some other; possibly hoping never again to meet human faces, for he could not trust them.

It was his heroic exit from a life that no longer interested him. Great was the astonishment of the islanders, who looked upon him as one possessed of the Evil Spirit, and special sacrifices were offered in his behalf; but the gods were inexorable; and, after several days upon the solitary sea, a shadow, a mote, drifted toward the valley—a canoe, with a famishing and delirious voyager, that was presently tossed and broken in the surges; then, a dark body glistened for a moment, wet with spray, and sank forever, while the shining coral reef was stained with the blood of the first-born.

I heard it all in the desolate wail of the mother, yet could not weep; my eyes burned like fire.

Little Niga came for me presently, and led me in-

to the great grove of kamane-trees, up the valley.
He insisted upon holding me by the hand: it was
all he could do to comfort me, and he did that with
his whole soul.

In silence we pressed on to one of the largest of
the trees. I recognized it at once. Niga and I, one
day, went thither, and I cut a name upon the soft
bark of the tree.

When we reached it we paused. Niga pointed
with his finger; I looked. It was there yet—a simple name, carved in the rudest fashion. I read the
letters, which had since become an epitaph. They
were these:

"KÁNA-ANÁ, *Æt.* 16 *yrs.*"

Under them were three initials—my own—cut by
the hand of Kána-aná, after his return from America.

We sat down in the gloomy grove. "Tell me," I
said, "tell me, Niga, where has his spirit gone?"

"He is here, now," said Niga; "he can see us.
Perhaps, some day, we shall see him."

"You have more faith than our philosophers, for
they have reasoned themselves out of everything.
Would you like to be a philosopher, Niga?" I asked.

Niga thought, if they were going to die, body and
soul, that he wouldn't like to be anything of the
sort, and that he had rather be a first-class savage
than a fourth rate Christian, any day.

I interrupted him at this alarming assertion.
"The philosophers would call your faith a supersti-

tion, Niga; they do not realize that there is no true faith unmixed with superstition, since faith implies a belief in something unseen, and is, therefore, itself a superstition. Blessed is the man who believes blindly—call it what you please—for peace shall dwell in his soul. But, Niga," I continued, "where is God?"

"Here, and here, and here," said Niga, pointing me to a grotesque carving in the sacred grove, to a monument upon the distant precipice, and to a heap of rocks in the sea; and the smile of recognition with which the little votary greeted his idols was a solemn proof of his sincerity.

"Niga," I said, "we call you and your kind heathens. It is a harmless anathema, which cannot, in the least, affect you personally. Ask us if we love God! Of course we do. Do we love him above all things, animate or inanimate? Undoubtedly! Undoubtedly is easily said, and let us give ourselves credit for some honesty. We believe that we do love God, above all; that we have no other gods before him; yet, who of us will give up wealth, home, friends, and follow him? Not one. The God we love is a very vague, invisible, forbearing essence. He can afford to be lenient with us while we are debating whether our neighbor is serving him in the right fashion or not. We'd rather not have other gods before him: one is as many as we find it convenient to serve. The lover kisses passionately a miniature. It is not, however, an image of his Creator, nor any memorial of his Redeemer's passion, but only a portrait of his mistress. Do you blame us, Niga? It is the strongest instinct of our nature to worship something. Man is a born idolater, and not one of us is exempted by reason of any scruples under the sun. You see it daily and hourly : each one has his idols."

Little Niga, who sympathized deeply with me, seemed to have gotten some knowledge of our peculiarly mixed theories concerning God and the future state, from conversations overheard after the return of Kána-aná. He tried to console me with the assurance that Kána-aná died a devoted and unshaken adherent to the faith of his fathers.

I could not but feel that his blood was off my hands when I learned this ; and I believe I gave Niga a regular hug in that moment of joy.

Then we walked here and there, through the valley, and visited the old haunts, made memorable by many incidents in that romantic and chivalrous life of the South. Everyone we met had some word to add concerning the Pride of the Valley, dead in his glorious youth.

Over and over, they assured me of his fidelity to me, his white brother, adding that Kána-aná had, more than once, expressed the deepest regret at not having brought me back with him.

He even meditated sending for me, in the same manner that I had sent for him ; and, if he had done so it was his purpose to see that I was at once made familiar with their Articles of Faith ; for he anticipated a willing convert in me, and it was the desire

5

of his heart that I should know that perfect trust, peculiar to his people, and which is begotten of the brief gospel, so often quoted out of place : namely, that " seeing is believing."

It was a kind thought of his, and I wish he had carried it into execution, for then he might have lived. It was his susceptible nature that had come in contact with the great world, and received its death-wound. Had I been there to help him, I would have planned something to divert his mind until he had recovered himself, and was willing to submit to the monotony of life over yonder. Had he not done as much for me ? Had he not striven, day after day, to charm me with his barbarism, and come very near to success ? I should say he had. Dear little martyr ! was he not the only boy I ever truly loved—dead now in his blossoming prime !

O Kána-aná ! Little Niga and I sat talking of you, down by the sea, and we wept for you at last ; for the tears came by and by, when I began fully to realize the greatness of my loss. All your youth, and beauty, and freshness, in destruction, and your body swallowed up in the graves of the sea !

The meridian sun blazed overhead, but it made little difference to us. Afternoon passed, and evening was coming on almost unheeded ; for our thoughts were buried with him, under the waves, and life was nothing to us then.

I no longer cared to observe the lights and shaddows on the cliffs, nor the poppy nodding in the wind, nor the seaward prospect : that was spoiled by our vessel—the seclusion was broken in upon. I cared for nothing any longer, for I missed everywhere his step, patient and faithful as a dog's, and his marvellous face, that could look steadily at the sun without winking, and deluge itself with laughter all the while, for there was nothing hidden or corrupting in it.

Presently I returned into the sacred grove, touching the three letters he had carved there, and calling on his spirit to regard me as respecting his dumb idols, which were nothing but the representatives of his jealous gods—dear to him as the Garden of Gethsemane, the Mount of Olives, and the shining summits of Calvary to us. Then down I ran to the bathing-pools, and from place to place I wandered in a hurried and nervous tour, for it was growing dark. I saw the ship's lights flickering over the water, while the first cool whispers of the night-wind came down from the hills, filling me with warnings; in the midst of which there was a flash of flame, and a sudden, thunderous report—enough to awaken the dead of the valley—and I turned to go. I believe, if dear Kána-aná had been there, as I prayed he might be, I would have laughed at that signal and hastened inland to avoid discovery; for I was sick of the world. I might have had reason to regret it afterward, because friendship is not elastic, and the best of friends cannot long submit to being bored by the best of fellows. Perhaps it was just as it should be : I had no time to consider the matter there. I hurried to his mother, and she

clung to me ; others came about me and laid hold
of me, so that I feared I should be held captive until it was too late to board the vessel. Her sails
were even then shaking in the wind, and I heard
the faint click of the capstan tugging at the anchor-
chains.

With a quick impulse I broke away from them
and ran to the beach, where Niga and I entered his
canoe, and slid off from the sloping sands. Down
we drifted toward the open sea, while the natives
renewed their wailing, and I was half crazed with
sorrow. It is impossible to resist the persuasive
eloquence of their chants. Think, then, with what
a troubled spirit I heard them, as we floated on between the calm stars in the heavens and the whirling
stars in the sea.

We went out to the ship's side, and little Niga
was as noisy as any of them when I pressed upon
him a practical memorial of my visit ; and away he
drifted into the night, with his boyish babble
pitched high and shrill ; and the Present speedily
became the Past, and grew old in a moment.

Then I looked for the last time upon that faint
and cloudy picture, and seemed almost to see the
spirit of the departed beckoning to me with waving
arms and imploring looks ; and I longed for him
with the old longing, that will never release me
from my willing bondage. I blessed him in his new
life, and I rejoiced with exceeding great joy that he
was freed at last from the tyranny of life—released
from the unsolvable riddles of the ages. The night-

wind was laden with music, and sweet with the odors of ginger and cassia ; the spume of the reef was pale as the milk of the cocoanuts, and the blazing embers on shore glowed like old sacrificial fires.

Then I heard a voice crying out of the shadow— an ancient and eloquent voice—saying : " Behold my fated race ! Our days are numbered. Long have we feasted in the rich presence of a revealed deity. We sat in ashes under the mute gods of Baal ; we fled before the wrath of Moloch, the destroyer ; we were as mighty as the four winds of heaven ; but the profane hand of the Iconoclast has desecrated our temples, and humbled our majesty in the dust. O impious breakers of idols ! Why will ye put your new wines into these old bottles, that were shaped for spring waters only, and not for wine at all ! Lo ! ye have broken them, and the wine is wasted. Be satisfied, and depart ! "

So that spirit of air sang the death-song of his tribe, and the sad music of his voice rang over the waters like a lullaby.

Then I heard no more, and I said, " My asylum is the great world ; my refuge is in oblivion ; " and I turned my face seaward, never again to dream fondly of my island home ; never again to know it as I have known it ; never again to look upon its serene and melancholy beauty : for the soul of the beloved is transmitted to the vales of rest, and his ashes are sown in the watery furrows of the deep sea !

TABOO—A FETE-DAY IN TAHITI

IT was on one of those vagabond pilgrimages to nowhere in particular, such as every stranger is bound to make in a strange land, that I first stumbled upon my royal Jester, better known in Tahiti as Taboo.

Great Jove! what a night it was! A wild ravine full of banyan and pandanus trees, and of parasite climbers, and the thousand nameless leafing and blossoming creatures that intermarry to such an alarming extent in the free-loving tropics had tempted me to pasture there for a little while. I was wandering on among roots and trailing branches, and under ropes upon ropes of flowers that seemed to swing suddenly across my path on purpose to keep me from finding too easily the secret heart of the mountain. I felt it was right that I should be made to realize how sacred a spot that sanctuary of Nature was, but I fretted somewhat at the persistency of those speechless sentinels who guarded its outer door so faithfully. There was a waterfall within, that I had prayed to see—one of those mysterious waterfalls that descend noiselessly from the bosom of a cloud, stealing over cushions of moss, like a ray of light in a dream, or something else equally intangible.

You never find this sort of waterfall in the common way. No one can exactly point it out to you; but you must search for it yourself, and listen for its voice—and usually listen in vain—till, suddenly, you come upon it in a moment, almost as if by accident; and its whole quivering length glitters and glistens with jewels, where it hangs, like a necklace, on the bosom of a great cliff. It is the only visible chain that binds earth to heaven; and no wonder you gaze at it with questioning eyes!

Well, while I was looking about me, expecting every moment to feel the damp breath of the waterfall upon my forehead, night came down. Where was I? In the midst of a pathless forest; between cliffs whose sleek, mossy walls were so steep as to forbid even the goat's sharp hoof. Down the hollow of the ravine, among round, slippery rocks, and between trellises of giant roots, tumbled a mountain torrent. No human form visible, probably none to be looked for on that side of the inaccessible dome of the mountain; yet fearlessly I toiled on, knowing that food and shelter were on every side, and that no hand, whose clasp was as fervent as the clasp of the vine itself, would be raised against me; and, thank Heaven! outsiders were scarce.

In the midst of the narrowing chasm, with the night thickening, and the wood growing more and more objectionable, I heard a sound as of stumbling feet before me. My first thought was of *color!* I

would scarcely trust a White Man in that predica-
ment. What well-disposed White would be prowl-
ing, like a wild animal, alone in a forest at night?
It occurred to me that I was white, or had passed as
such; but I know and have always known that, in-
wardly, I am purple-blooded, and supple-limbed,
and invisibly tattooed after the manner of my lost
tribe! I was startled at the sound, and slackened
my pace to listen: the footsteps paused with mine.
I plunged forward, accusing the Echoes of playing
me false. Again the mysterious one rushed awkwardly on before me, with footfalls that were not
like mine, nor like any that I could trace: they were
neither brute nor human, but fell clumsily among
the roots and stones, out of time with me; therefore, no echo, and beyond my reckoning entirely.

At this hour the moon, of a favorable size, looked
over the cliff, flooding the chasm with her soft light.
I rejoiced at it, and hoped for a revelation of the
Unknown, whose tottering steps had mocked mine
for half an hour.

We were in the midst of a dense grove of bread-
fruit-trees. Scarcely a ray of light penetrated their
thick-woven branches; but, against the faint light
of the open distance, I marked the weird outline of
one who might once have been human, but was no
longer a tolerable image of his Maker. The figure was
like the opposite halves of two men bodily joined
together in an amateur attempt at human graft-
ing. The trunk was curved the wrong way; a great
shoulder bullied a little shoulder, and kept it decid-

edly under ; a long leg walked right around a short
leg that was perpetually sitting itself down on invisible seats, or swinging itself for the mere pleasure of
it. One arm clutched a ten-foot bamboo about three
inches in diameter, and wielded it as though it were
a bishop's crook, and something to be proud of ; the
other arm—it must have belonged to a child when
it stopped growing—was hooked up over one ear,
looking as though it had been badly wired by some
medical student, and was worn as a lasting reproach
to him. A shaggy head was set on the down-slope
of the big shoulder, and seemed to be continually
looking over the little shoulder and under the little
arm for some one always expected, but who was very
long in coming.

Upon this startling discovery I turned to flee, but
the figure immediately followed. It was evidently
too late to escape an interview, and, taking heart, I
walked toward it, when, to my amazement, it hastily
staggered away from me, looking always over its
shoulder, quickening its pace with mine, slackening
its speed with me, and keeping, or seeking to keep,
within a certain distance of me all the while. My
curiosity was excited, and, as I saw it bore me no
ill-will, I made a quick plunge forward, hoping to
capture it. With an energetic effort it strove to
escape me ; but, with the head turned the wrong
way, it stumbled blindly into a bit of jungle, where
it lay whining piteously. I assisted it to its feet,
with what caution and tenderness I could, and, finding it still wary, walked on slowly, leading the way

to the edge of the grove, where the moonlight was almost as radiant as the dawn. It followed me like a dog, and was evidently grateful for my company. I walked slowly that it might not stumble, and, as we emerged from the shadow of the breadfruits, I manœuvred so as to bring its face toward the moonlight, and I saw — a hideous visage, with all its features sliding to one corner ; and nothing but the two soft, sleepy-looking eyes saved me from yielding to the disgust that its whole presence awakened. As it was, I involuntarily started back with a shudder, and a slight exclamation that attracted its attention. "Taboo! Taboo!" moaned the poor creature, half in introduction, half in apology and explanation.

He was well named the "forbidden one:" set apart from all his fellows ; incapable of utterance ; maimed in body ; an outcast among his own people ; homeless, yet at home everywhere ; friendless, though welcomed by all for his entertaining and ludicrous simplicity ; feeding, like the birds, from Nature's lap, and, like the birds, left to the winds and waters for companionship.

Somehow I felt that Taboo could lead me at once to the waterfall ; and I tried to seek out the small door to his brain, and impress him with my anxiety to reach the place. Oh, what darkness was there, and what doubts and fears seemed to cloud the hidden portals of his soul! He made an uncouth noise for me. Perhaps he meant it as music : it was frightful to hear it up there in the mountain solitudes. He got me fruits and a little water in the palm of his hand, which he expected me to drink with a relish. He lay down at my feet in a broken heap of limbs, crooning complacently. He was playful and thoughtful alternately ; at least, he lost himself in long silences from time to time, while his eyes glowed with a deep inward light, that almost made me hope to startle his reason from its dreadful sleep ; but a single word broke the spell, and set him to laughing as though he would go all to pieces ; and his joy was more pitiful than his sorrow.

In one of his silent moods he suddenly staggered to his feet, and shambled into a narrow trail to one side of the gorge. I wondered at his unexpected impulse, and feared that he had grown tired of me already, preferring the society of his feathered comrades, a few of whom sounded their challenge-note, that soared like silver arrows in the profound stillness of the ravine. It seemed not, however : in a few moments he returned, and signalled me with his expressive grunt, and I followed him. Through thickets of fern, arching high over our heads, down spongy dells, and over rims of rock jutting from the base of the mountain, Taboo and I clambered in the warm moonlight. Anon we came upon a barricade of bamboos, growing like pickets set one against another. I know not how broad the thicket might have been—possibly as broad as the ravine itself— but into the thick of it Taboo edged himself ; and close upon his heels I followed. In a few moments we had crushed our way through the midst of the bamboos, that clashed together after us so that a bird might not have tracked us, and lo ! a crystal pool in the heart of a wonderful garden ; and to it, silently, from heaven itself descended that mysterious waterfall whose actual existence I had seriously begun to question. It lay close against the breast of the mountain, strangely pale in the full glow of the moon, while, like a vein of fire, it seemed to throb from end to end ; or, like a shining thread with great pearls slipping slowly down its full length, taking the faint hues of the rainbow as they fell, playing at prisms, until my eyes, weary of watching, closed of their own accord. I sank down by Taboo, who was sleeping soundly in the hollow of a great tree ; and the one cover for both of us was the impenetrable shadow that is never lifted from that silent sanctuary of the Most High.

The sky was as saffron when we woke from our out-of-door sleep, and the whole atmosphere was less poetical and impressive than on the night previous. Stranger than all else, there was no visible trace of the mysterious waterfall. I even began to question my own senses, and thought it possible that I had been dreaming. Yet there sat Taboo in his frightful imperfection, as happy and indifferent as possible. Of course, he could tell me nothing of the magical waters. He had doubtless already forgotten the episode of the hour previous. He lived for the solitary moment, and his mind seemed unable to grasp the secrets of ten seconds on either side of his narrow present. In fact, he was playing with a splendid lizard when I returned from my brief and fruitless reconnoissance; and as I came up he wondered at me, as he never ceased to wonder, with fresh bewilderment, whenever I came back to him, after never so brief an absence.

I soon learned to play upon Taboo's one stop; to point a finger at him, and bore imaginary auger-holes right into him anywhere; for he always winced and whined, like a very baby, and yielded at once to my pantomimic suggestion. But what a wreck was here! A delicate instrument, full of rifts and breakages, with that single key readily answerable to the slightest touch of my will. I have often wished that it had been a note more deep, profound, or sympathetic. It was simply merry and shrill, and incapable of any modulation whatever. Point a finger at him, make a few coils in the air that grow to a focus as they draw nearer to him, and he would run over with uncontrollable jollity that was at times a little painful in its boisterousness.

I knew well enough that I had sucked the honey from that particular cell in the mountain, and that I might as well resume my pilgrimage. There was to be a *Fête Napoléon* in Papeete. We hadn't heard, up to that hour, of the wreck of the great Empire, and, being in a loyal French colony, it behooved us to have the very best time possible. Said I to myself, "Taboo will find sufficient food for merriment in our mode of *fêting* an emperor; therefore Taboo shall go with me to town and enjoy himself." I suggested an immediate adjournment to Papeete with the tip of my forefinger, whereat Taboo doubled up,

as usual, and in his own fashion implored me to
stop being so funny. We at once started; returning through the bamboo-brakes, fording the stream
in some awkward way, and slowly working our passage back to town.

The Tahitians have but one annual holiday. As
this, however, is seventy-two hours in length, while
everything relating to it is broad in proportion, it is
about as much as they can conscientiously ask for.

Taboo and I entered the town on the eve of the
first day, together with multitudes from the neighboring districts, flocking thither in their best clothes.
The lovely bay of Papeete was covered with fleets of
canoes, hailing from all the seaside villages on the
island, and many of them from Moorea, and islands
even more distant. No sea is too broad to be com-
passed by an ambitious Kanack, who scents a festival from afar.

Along the crescent shores of the bay the canoes
were heaped, tier upon tier. It was as though a
whole South Sea navy had been stranded, for the
town was crowded with canoe-boys and all manner
of natives, in gala dress. The incessant rolling of
drums, the piping of bamboo-flutes, and the choruses of wandering singers began early in the dawn
of August 14th, and were expected to continue,
uninterruptedly, to the evening of the 16th. Taboo
regarded it all with singular indifference. Everybody seemed to know him, and to take particular
delight in greeting him. His sleepy disregard of
them was considered extremely laughable, and they

went their way roaring with merriment, that contrasted strongly with the grave, listless face of the simple one, who was apparently oblivious of everything.

The morning after we appeared in Papeete was Sunday, according to the calendar. The little Cathedral, with banana-leaves rustling in the open windows, was thronged with worshippers of all colors, doubly devout in the excessive heat. Various choirs relieved one another during mass, and some diminutive fellows, under ten years of age, chanted Latin hymns in a pleasingly plaintive voice, led by a friar in long clothes and a choker. Taboo crouched by the open door during service, raking the gravel-walk with his crooked fingers, and hitching about with indefatigable industry. After the last gospel, we all went into the middle of the street—for there were no sidewalks—and got our boots very dusty. Little knots of friends seemed to sit down in the way wherever they pleased, and to talk as long as they liked; while everybody else accommodatingly turned out for them, or paused and listened to the conversation, without embarrassment on either side. Liquor was imbibed on the sly; some eyes were beginning to swim perceptibly, and some tongues to wag faster and looser than ever. The Admiral's flagship was one pyramid of gorgeous bunting, and his band delighted a great audience, gathered upon the shore, with a *matinée* gratis. At sunset the imperial batteries belched their sulphurous thunder, that came as near to breaking the Sabbath as possible. In the evening more music, up at the Governor's garden—waltzes, polkas, and quadrilles, so brilliantly executed that the listeners were half mad with delight; and you couldn't for the life of you tell what day it had been, nor what night it was, but Sunday was positively set down against it in the calendar. At 10 P.M. a signal-gun says "Good-night" to the citizens of Papeete, and it behooves all those who are dark-skinned to retire instantly, on pain of arrest and a straw-heap in the calaboose.

In the midst of our Sunday festival, while yet the streets were hilarious, slap-bang went this impudent piece of ordnance, and at once the crowd began to disperse in the greatest confusion. Taboo, who had been an inanimate spectator during the day's diversions, seemed to comprehend the necessity of hasty flight to some quarter or other; and, with a confusion of ideas peculiar to him, he began careering in great circles through the swaying multitudes, and continued to revolve around an uncertain centre, until I seized him and sought to pilot him to some convenient place of shelter. I thought of the great market that, like those ancient cities of refuge, was always open to the benighted wanderer; and thither we hastened. A lofty roof, covering a good part of a block, kept the rain from a vast enclosure, stored with stalls, tables, and benches. It was simply shelter of the barest kind, but sufficient for all needs in that charitable climate. There was a buzzing of turbulent throngs as we edged our way toward the centre of the market-place; you would think that

all the bees of Tahiti were swarming in unison, from
the noise thereof. The commotion was long in
quieting. It had to subside like the sea at flood-
tide. Every little while a brace of *gendarmes* strut-
ted past the premises, feeling mighty fine in their
broad white pantaloons, like a ship with studding-sails
out, and with those comical bobtails sprouting out
of the small of their backs. I know that Taboo and
I, having laid ourselves on somebody's counter,
listened and nudged each other for two or three
hours, and that it began to feel like morning before
there was sleep enough to go entirely around the
establishment.

The man who is the first to wake in Papeete
lights his lamp and goes to market. As soon as he
makes his untimely appearance, the community begins to stir; a great clatter of drowsy voices and
dozens of yawns are the symptoms of returning day;
and in ten minutes the market is declared open,
though it is still deep and tranquil starlight overhead, with not a trace of dawn as yet visible.

When the market opens before 3 A.M.—and the
hour happens to be the blackest of the four-and-
twenty—it is highly inconvenient for any foreigner
and his royal jester who may be surreptitiously
passing the night upon one of the fruit counters, but
there is no help for them; sleepy heads give way to
fresh-gathered bread-fruits and nets of fragrant oranges; bananas are swung up within tempting reach
of everybody; all sorts of natives come in from the
four quarters of the Papeetean globe, with back-

6

loads of miscellaneous viands, a mat under one arm,
and a flaming torch in hand. Rows upon rows of
girls sell fruits and flowers to the highest bidder ;
withering old women haggle over the prices of their
perfumed and juicy wares ; solitary men offer their
solitary strings of fish for a *real* each, and refuse to
be beaten down by any wretch of a fellow who dares
to insinuate that the fish are a trifle too scaly ; boys
sit demurely over their meagre array of temptations
in the shape of six tomatoes, three eggs, a dozen or
so of guavas, and one cucumber. These youngsters
usually sit with a passionless countenance that forbids any hope of a bargain at reduced prices, and
they pass an hour or two with scarce a suggestion of
custom ; but it is suddenly discovered that they
have something desirable, and a dozen purchasers
begin quarrelling for it, during which time some
one else quietly makes his purchase from one corner
of the boy's mat ; and, having closed out his stock
in less than ten minutes, he quickly pockets his *reales*,
and departs without having uttered a syllable.

Taboo and I went from one mat to another,
eying the good things for breakfast. I offered him
the best that the market afforded ; and I could easily do so, for in no land is the article cheaper or
better. Taboo, having made the circuit of the entire establishment, upon mature deliberation concluded to take nothing. At every point he was
greeted uproariously by the noisy and good-
natured people, who were willing to give him anything he might choose to take. They probably

felt that it was worth more than the price of the article to see the sublime scorn on the poor fellow's face as he declined their limes, *feis*, mangoes, or whatever delicious morsel it might have been. As for me, I couldn't resist those seductions. I made my little purchases and withdrew to the seaside, where I could break my fast by sunrise, and enjoy comparative quiet. Taboo grinned in the market-place till he was weary of the applause showered upon him by the ungodly, who made light of his irreparable misfortune and took pleasure in his misery. He hunted me up, or, rather, stumbled upon me again, and stayed by me, amusing himself by pelting the fish that sported, like sunbeams and prisms, in the sea close at our feet.

It was *fête*-day in Tahiti. I sat, at sunrise, by the tideless margin of a South Sea lagoon, bristling with coral and glittering with gem-like fish; in either hand I held a mango and banana. I raised the mango to my lips. What a marvel it was! A plump vegetable egg, full of delusion, and stuffed with a horny seed nearly as large as itself. It had a fragrance as of oils and syrups; it purged sweet-scented and resinous gums. Its hide was, perhaps, too tough for convenience, but its inner lusciousness tempted me to persevere in the consumption of it. With much difficulty I broke the skin. Honey of Hymettus! It seemed as though the very marrow of the tropics were about to intoxicate my palate. Alas, for the hopes of youthful inexperience! What was so fair to see proved but a meagre mouthful of

saturated wool ; that colossal and horny seed as-
serted itself everywhere.   The more I strove to
handle it with caution, the more slippery and un-
manageable it became.   It shot into my beard, it
leaped lightly into my shirt-bosom, and skated over
the palms of both hands.   Small rivulets of liquor
trickled down my sleeves, making disagreeable pud-
dles at both elbows.   My fingers were webbed together in a glutinous mass.   My whole front was in
a shocking state of smear.   My teeth grew weary of
combing out the beguiling threads of the fruit.
The thing seemed, to my imagination, a small, flat
head, covered with short, blond hair, profusely saturated with some sweet sort of ointment, that I had
despaired of feasting on ; and I was not sorry when
the slippery stone sprang out of my grasp, and peppered itself with sea-sand.

I knew that there still remained to me a morsel
that was of itself fit food for the gods.   I poised
aloft, with satisfaction, the rare-ripe banana, beautiful to the eye as a nugget of purest gold.   The
pliant petals were pouting at the top of the fruit.   I
readily turned them back, forming an unique and
convenient gilded salver for the column of flaky
manna that was, as yet, swathed in lace-like folds.
These gauzy ribbons fell from it almost of their own
accord, and hung in fleecy festoons about it.

Here was a repast of singularly appropriate
mould, being about the size of a respectable mouth,
and containing just enough mouthfuls to satisfy temporarily the appetite.   Not a morsel of it but was

full of mellowness and sweet flavor and fragrance. Not an atom of it was wasted ; for, no sooner had I thrown aside the cool, clean, flesh-like case, than it was made way with by a fowl, that had, no doubt, been patiently awaiting that abundant feast.

Mangoes and bananas ! Their very names smack of shady gardens, that know no harsher premonition of death than the indolent and natural decay of all things. The nostril is excited with the thought of them ; the palate grows moist and yearns for them ; and the soul feasts itself, for a moment, with a memory of mangoes and bananas past, whose perfection was but another proof of immortality, since it is impossible ever to forget them individually. Mangoes and bananas ! the prime favorites at Nature's most bountiful board ; the realization of a dream of the orchards of the Hesperides ; alike excellent, yet so vastly dissimilar in their excellences, it seems almost incredible that the same beneficent Providence can have created the two fruits !

It was the memorable 15th of August, 1870 ; but I have reason to believe the bananas were no better on that particular occasion than almost always in their own latitude. The 15th of August—where was the Emperor then ? I forget ; I know that we rejoiced in the blissful confidence that we were to have a grand time at all hazards. There were guns at sunrise from ship and shore ; a grand national procession of French and Tahitians to high-mass at 10.30 ; guns—twenty-one of them—together with the ringing of bells, and a salute of flags, at the elevation of the host, so that you would have known the supreme moment had you been miles away. Then came a sumptuous public breakfast for the Frenchmen ; and for the natives, games of several sorts.

Taboo and I, having properly observed the more solemn ceremonials of the day, gave ourselves up to the full enjoyment of these latter diversions. There was a greased pole, with shining cups ; and flowing prints, both useful and ornamental, hung at the top of it. Several naked and superbly built fellows shinned up it with infinite difficulty, and were so fatigued when they got there, they were only too willing to clutch the first article within reach, which was, of course, the least desirable, and scarcely worth the trouble of getting. O, such magnificent grouping at the foot of the pole, as the athletes shouldered one another in a sort of co-operative experiment at getting up sooner ; such struggles to rise a little above the heads of the impatient climbers beneath as made the aspiring Kanack quite pale — that is, greenish yellow ; such losing of grips, and fainting of hearts, and slidings back to earth in the midst of taunts and jeers, but all in the best of humors and the hottest of suns ! such novelties as these were a very great delight to Taboo and myself. He, however, didn't deign to laugh heartily ; he merely smiled in a superior manner that seemed to imply that he knew of something that was twice as much fun and not half the trouble, but he didn't choose to disclose it. He nearly always seemed to

know as much as any ten of us ; and it was like an
assumption of innocence, that queer, vacant expression of his face. I'm not sure that he was not
possessed of some rare instinct beyond our comprehension, which was to him an abundant compensation for the fragmentary body he was obliged to
trundle about.

Early in the afternoon there were fresh arrivals
in the bay : two mammoth double war-canoes, of
fifty paddles each, came in from a remote sea-dis-
trict ; they were the very sort of water-monsters
that went out to greet my illustrious predecessor,
Captain Cook, nearly a century ago. Taboo and
I were only too glad to sit meekly among the
ten thousand spectators that blackened the great
sweep of the shore, while these savages matched
their prowess. With one vigorous plunge of the
paddles the canoes sprang from the beach into the
watery arena. How strange they looked ! Long,
low sides, scarce eight inches above water, and
stained like fish-scales ; big yawning jaws in their
snakelike heads, and the tail of the dragon in their
wakes ; every man of the hundred stripped to the
skin and bareheaded ; their brawny bodies glistening in the sun as though they had been oiled, while,
with mechanical accuracy, the crews beat the water
with their paddles, and chanted their guttural
chants, with the sea flashing and foaming under
them. The race was a tie ; perhaps it was fortunate that it proved so. I fear if one crew had beaten
the other crew the breadth of a paddle, that other

would have lain to and eaten that one right under
our very eyes. They had their songs of triumph,
both sounding the chorus, during which they
drummed with their paddles on the sides of their
canoes, till the frail things shivered and groaned
in genuine misery. Then they renewed the race,
because they couldn't possibly be still for a moment ;
and they looked like a brace of mastodon centipedes trying to get out of the water, with death
hissing in their throats.

The evening of the great day was drawing to a
close. Taboo and I again went out into the narrow,
green lanes of Papeete, seeking what we might devour with all our eyes and ears. They were very
charming, those long arbors of densely leaved trees,
with little tropical vignettes set in the farther end
of them. It was almost like getting a squint through
the wrong end of a telescope, pointed toward some
fairy-land or other. As it grew dark, a thousand
ready hands began illuminating the avenues that
lead to the Governor's house. Up and down its
deep veranda swung ropes of lanterns ; and as the
guards at the garden-gate presented arms at the approach of the Admiral or some distinguished and
decorated foreigner, the strains of Strauss, deli-
ciously played, filled the illuminated grove with an
air of romance that was very Oriental in its mellowness, and quickened every foot that was so happy as
to touch the soil of Tahiti in so fortunate an hour.
On every part of the public lawns the revels were
conducted after the native fashion. Bands of singers

and dancers sang and danced in the streets, and were frequently rewarded with liberal potations. Taboo looked on as amiably as usual, and for some time as passively also ; but there was something intoxicating in the air, and it began to have a visible effect upon him. It was not long before he strove to emulate the singers. St. Cecilia ! what a song was his ! To hear that royal Jester striving to tune his inharmonious voice to the glib, though monotonous, Tahitian madrigals was beyond my power of musical endurance. I walked away by myself, or rather went into another part of the village, and sought a change of scene ; for there was no seclusion to be hoped for on a *fête*-night.

From the Governor's halls came the entrancing harmony of flutes and harps ; from every lane and alley the piping of nose-fifes and droning of nasal chorals ; from the sea rolled in the deep, hoarse booming of the reef, the rhythmical plash of oars, or the clear, prolonged cry of some one in the watery distance hailing some one close at hand. Even so savage and picturesque a spectacle as this grew wearisome after a time, and I turned my steps toward a place of shelter, and suggested to myself sleep.

In one lane was a throng of natives, wilder in their demonstrations of joy than all the others. My curiosity was excited, and I hastened to join them. Having with some difficulty wedged my way into the front row of spectators, I beheld the subject of their riotous applause. In the centre of a small ring was an ungainly figure, writhing in grotesque contortions; tom-toms were being beaten with diabolical energy and wildness; flutes and shrill voices were chiming in rapid and bewildering chromatics; the audience — the half-crazed and utterly inhuman audience — gloated over the shocking spectacle with devilish delight. In one moment I comprehended all: Taboo, overcome by the general and unusual excitement, had succumbed to its depraving influences; and, unable longer to control himself, he was broadly burlesquing, in his helplessness, one of the national dances. Music had at last reached his impenetrable soul, awakened his long-slumbering sympathies, and found him her willing slave. A pity that some diviner strain had not first led him captive, that he might have been spared this disgrace!

I saw his unhappy body ambling to the shame of all. I saw those pitiful, unshapen shoulders undulating in vain attempts at passional expression; the helpless arm waving at every movement of the body, while the withered hand spun like a whirligig above his ears; his eyes, having lost their accustomed mild light, stared distractedly about, seeking rescue and protection, as I thought. In a few moments I attracted his notice, though he seemed but partly to recognize me. There was his usual uncertain recognition grown more doubtful—nay, even hopeless— as his face betrayed. Again I caught his eye: I felt that but one course was left me, and at once I aimed my finger at him. He winced in his delirious

dance. I coiled it round and round, weaving airy
circle within circle ; quicker and quicker I wove my
spell, and at last shot the whole hand at him, as
though I would run him through. He doubled, like
one struck with a fatal blow, and went to the ground
all of a senseless heap. There was a disturbance in
the audience. Some of them thought I had bewitched Taboo ; and it behooved me to go at once,
rather than seek to make explanation of the singular
result of my presence there. I went, and spent a dull
night, accusing myself of being the possible spiritual
murderer of Taboo. I had no business to bring him
to the metropolis at that unfortunate season ; I had
no right to leave him with his traducers : and that
was the whole statement of the case.

The last day of the *fête* was, of course, less joyous
to me. A score of nameless nags were to be ridden
by light - weights in breech - cloths ; and I sought
consolation in the prospect of seeing some bewitching horsemanship. The track, in use but once
every twelvemonth, and yielding annually a young
orchard of guava-trees, presented to the astonished
gaze of the foreign sporting-gentleman who happened to be on the ground—if, indeed, there was
such a one present—a half-mile course, with numerous stones and hollows relieving its surface,
while the rope that enclosed it kept giving way
every few moments, letting in a mixed multitude
among the half-broken horses.

The Queen was present at the races—Pomare,
whose life has been one long, sorrowful romance ;

the Admiral was also there; and many a petty officer, with abundant gilt and tinsel. At a signal from the trumpeter the horses were entered unannounced, and everybody fell to betting wildly. One little African jockey, mounted upon the cleverest piece of flesh and blood in the field, called for the larger stakes; and he would certainly have won, but for an unavoidable accident: the little African was pressing in on the home-stretch, and everything looked lovely for the winning mare, when, unluckily, she put her nigh leg in a crab-hole, and snapped her shin-bone square off. The undaunted little African tried his best to finish the heat on his own responsibility, and went off into the air in fine style, but missed his calculation, and burrowed about three lengths from the goal. His neck was driven in nearly up to the ears, and the mare had to be shot; but the races went mercilessly on until a tremendous thunder-storm flooded the track and washed the population back to town. Dance after dance consumed the afternoon hours; and song upon song, eternally reiterated, finally failed to create any special enthusiasm.

I saw no further traces of Taboo. Again and again I followed knots of the curious into the larger native houses, where the lascivious dances were given with the utmost *abandon*; thither—I suspected—Taboo would most likely be impelled, for the music was wilder and the applause more boisterous and unrestrained.

The evening of the last day of the *fête* was dark-

ening; most people were growing a little weary of
the long-drawn festivities; many had succumbed to
their fatigue, and slept by the wayside, or, it may
be, they had known too well the nature of the
Tahitian juices, such as no man may drink and not
fall!

The palace of Pomare—a great, hollow, incom-
plete shell, whose windows have never been glazed,
and whose doors have never been hung—was the
scene of the concluding ceremonials of the season.
The long verandas were thickly hung with numberless paper-lanterns, swinging continually in the soft
night-winds that stole down from the star-lit slopes
of Fautahua; the broad lawns in front of the palace
were blocked out in squares, like the map of a lili-
putian city. Each one of these plats was set apart
for a band of singers, and there were as many bands
as districts in Tahiti and Moorea, together with del-
egations from islands more remote. Soon the choruses began to assemble. Choirs of fifty voices each,
male and female, led by tight-headed drums and
screaming fifes, drew toward the palace-gardens,
and were formally admitted by the proper authori-
ties, who were very much swollen with the pomp of
office and, perhaps, a little sprinkle of the exhilarat-
ing accompaniments of the season. One after another the white-robed processions approached—each
fresh arrival looking more like the chorus in "Nor-
ma" than the last, though it then seemed impossible that any Druid could presume to appear more
gracefully ghostlike. Each singer wore a plume of

cocoa-leaves, whose feathers were more lovely than the downy wands of the ostrich. They were made of knots of long, slender ribbons, softer than satin, veined like clouded silver, as transparent as the clearest isinglass, and as delicate as the airiest gauze.

Out of the core of the palm-tree, in the midst of its rich, dark mass of foliage, springs a tuft of leaves as tender as the first sprouts of a lily-bulb. These budding leaves are carefully removed, split edgewise, and the enamelled sheets laid open to the sun ; then, with the thumb-nail, passed skilfully over the inner surface, a filmy membrane is separated, and spread in the air to dry. A single tree yields but a small cluster of these pale, cloud-like leaves, scarcely a handful in all, yet the tree withers when they pluck the heart of it. It is the very soul of the Southern palm, with every leaf spiritualized, and looking vapory as tangible moonlight.

The leader of the concert having challenged the choruses from the veranda of the palace, at once twenty choirs struck into their particular anthem with the utmost zeal. A discord about six acres in extent was the result. It seemed as though each choir was seeking whom it might drown out with superior vocal compass and volume. With much difficulty the several bands of singers were persuaded to await their turn for a *solo* effort that might be listened to with no small degree of pleasure. From time to time, during the entire evening, some obstreperous chorus would break loose, spite of every

precaution ; and it had always to sing itself out before order could be restored. Taboo would have
thoroughly enjoyed those two thousand singers,
each singing his or her favorite roundelay, independent of all laws of time and melody. He might
have been there, as it was, offering his inharmonious chant with the mob of contestants.

By the time the series of prize-songs had been
sung, the sky grew cloudy, and the torches began to
flicker in the increasing wind ; a few great drops of
rain spat down in the midst of the singers, and the
reef moaned loudly, like the baying of signal-guns.
It was ominous of coming storms. At the climax of
a choral revolution, in which every man's voice
seemed raised against his neighbor's, a roar as of
approaching armies was heard, mingled with the
accompanying crash of artillery. A sudden puff of
wind extinguished the major part of the torches, and
wrecked many of the lanterns in the palace porch.
It was simply a tropical shower in all its magnifi-
cence ; but it was enough ! The *fête* concluded
then and there, in the promptest manner. The narrow streets of Papeete were clogged with retreat-
ing hosts, who continually shouted a sort of general
adieu to everybody, as they gathered their skirts
about them and, with shoes in hand, turned their
bare feet homeward.

Since the end had at last come, and I had no
further claims upon the people, nor the people upon me—if, indeed, either of us were ever anything
in particular to one another — I drifted with the

majority, and soon found myself in the suburban wilderness that girdles the small capital of the queendom. I wandered on till the noise of the revellers grew more and more indistinct. They were scattering themselves over the length and breadth of the island, carrying their songs with them. Now and then a fresh gust of wind bore down to me an echo of a refrain that had grown familiar during the days of the *fête*, and will not soon be forgotten ; but the past was rapidly fading, and the necessities of the future began to present themselves with unusual boldness. Instinctively I turned to the winding trail that once before had led me toward that mysterious mountain sacristy, over whose font fell the spiritual and dreamlike rivulet whose baptismal virtues Taboo and I had sought together. I felt certain that I could find it without guidance ; for the broken clouds let slip such floods of moonlight as made day of darkness, and rendered the smallest landmark easily distinguishable.

I paused for rest in the breadfruit grove where first I met with my weird companion. Presently I resumed my pilgrimage, wending my way toward the slender path that led through fern, forest, and bamboo-jungle, to the crystal lake and waterfall. In vain I sought it ; the slightest traces of the trail seemed obliterated. I wandered up and down the winding way, till I was in despair of finding the slightest clew to the mystery. I sat down and thought how a slight accident of forgetfulness was lending a sense of enchantment to the whole valley, when I heard a stumbling step, too marked to be soon forgotten. I crept into a shadow, and awaited the approach of the solitary wanderer. How he tottered as he drew near ! He seemed to have lost part of his small skill since I last saw him. He was laughing quietly to himself while he journeyed : perhaps some memory of the *fête* still pleased him. He passed me unconscious of my presence. I ran cautiously, and followed him at a safe distance. We threaded the old path, by stream and cliff and brake, and, after a little, reached the secluded and silent borders of the lake. Once or twice he had heard me as I brushed past the bamboos or a twig snapped under foot, but those forest sounds scarcely disconcerted him ; he was too well used to them. He paused at the margin of the lake, stooped awkwardly and drank of it, went a little to one side where an outlet fed the torrent we had forded some distance down the valley, and there he bathed. Having started once or twice, as though with some remembered and definite purpose, he paused a moment or two, looked about him helplessly, and returned to the foot of the great tree where we slept the first night of our acquaintance.

There was a faint suggestion of the fall across the sombre breast of the cliff opposite, but whether it were real or a delusion, I could scarcely determine. Taboo was soon asleep among the roots of the ban-yan ; and I, weary of seeking some revelation of the island mysteries, lay down near him, and gradually sank into unconsciousness. Once in the night I

7

awoke : the clouds had blown over, and the moon was more resplendent than I ever remember to have seen it. Out on the mossy rim of the lake stood Taboo, gazing wistfully upon the mountains. Instinctively my eyes followed his, and there I beheld the waterfall in all its glory, leaping, like a ray of light, from the bosom of the sky. I could scarcely determine whether or no it really fell into the lake, for the foliage about its shores was too profuse. It flashed like handfuls of diamond-dust thrown into the light, and descended as noiselessly and airily as vapor.

The clouds soon gathered again. I slept, overcome with weariness ; and when I awoke at dawn, Taboo was missing, as well as all traces of the fall. This, however, scarcely surprised me, for I had grown to look upon it as some lunar effect that came and went with the increasing or decreasing splendor of the moon ; or it might have been the short-lived offspring of the showers that sweep over the island at uncertain intervals. It was probably the only dramatic result to be looked for in the career of Taboo. You never can depend upon one of those veering minds whose north-star has burned out in oblivion. I believe it was his destiny to disappear with that rainbow, and, perhaps, return with it when the fall should noiselessly steal down the mountain once more.

He may have had an object in secreting himself for a season ; perhaps he was renewing his youthful innocence in some more solitary spot. He may have gone apart to laugh by the hour at the folly of the foreigners who *fête* a disgraced emperor; or was he making his queer noises to hear the queerer echoes that came back to him, and all the while caring no more for life or death than a parrot or a magpie, or even a poor, half-shapen soul—one of those sacred idiots that have found worshippers before now, and never yet failed to awaken a chord of sympathy in the heart that is fashioned after the divine pattern of the Son of God!

JOE OF LAHAINA

I.

I WAS stormed in at Lahaina. Now, Lahaina is
a little slice of civilization, beached on the
shore of barbarism. One can easily stand that little
of it, for brown and brawny heathendom becomes
more wonderful and captivating by contrast. So I
was glad of dear, drowsy, little Lahaina; and was
glad, also, that she had but one broad street, which
possibly led to destruction, and yet looked lovely in
the distance. It didn't matter to me that the one
broad street had but one side to it; for the sea
lapped over the sloping sands on its lower edge, and
the sun used to set right in the face of every solitary
citizen of Lahaina, just as he went to supper.

I was waiting to catch a passage in a passing
schooner, and that's why I came there; but the
schooner flashed by us in a great gale from the
south, and so I was stormed in indefinitely.

It was Holy Week, and I concluded to go to
housekeeping, because it would be so nice to have
my frugal meals in private, to go to mass and vespers daily, and then to come back and feel quite
at home. My villa was suburban — built of dried

grasses on the model of a haystack dug out in the
middle, with doors and windows let into the four
sides thereof. It was planted in the midst of a vine-
yard, with avenues stretching in all directions under
a network of stems and tendrils.

> " Her breath is sweeter than the sweet winds
> That breathe over the grape-blossoms of Lahaina."

So the song said; and I began to think upon the
surpassing sweetness of that breath, as I inhaled the
sweet winds of Lahaina, while the wilderness of its
vineyards blossomed like the rose. I used to sit in
my veranda and turn to Joe (Joe was my private and
confidential servant), and I would say to Joe, while
we scented the odor of grape, and saw the great
banana-leaves waving their cambric sails, and heard
the sea moaning in the melancholy distance—I
would say to him, " Joe, housekeeping *is* good fun,
isn't it?" Whereupon Joe would utter a sort of
unanimous Yes, with his whole body and soul; so
that question was carried triumphantly, and we would
relapse into a comfortable silence, while the voices
of the wily singers down on the river front would
whisper to us, and cause us to wonder what they
could possibly be doing at that moment in the broad
way that led to destruction. Then we would take a
drink of cocoa-milk, and finish our bananas, and go
to bed, because we had nothing else to do.

This is the way that we began our co-operative
housekeeping: One night, when there was a riotous

sort of a festival off in a retired valley, I saw, in the excited throng of natives who were going mad over their national dance, a young face that seemed to embody a whole tropical romance. On another night, when a lot of us were bathing in the moonlight, I saw a figure so fresh and joyous that I began to realize how the old Greeks could worship mere physical beauty and forget its higher forms. Then I discovered that face on this body—a rare enough combination—and the whole constituted Joe, a young scapegrace who was schooling at Lahaina, under the eye—not a very sharp one—of his uncle. When I got stormed in, and resolved on housekeeping for a season, I took Joe, bribing his uncle to keep the peace, which he promised to do, provided I gave bonds for Joe's irreproachable conduct while with me. I willingly gave bonds—verbal ones—for this was just what I wanted of Joe: namely, to instil into his youthful mind those counsels which, if rigorously followed, must result in his becoming a true and unterrified American. This compact settled, Joe took up his bed—a roll of mats —and down we marched to my villa, and began housekeeping in good earnest.

We soon got settled, and began to enjoy life, though we were not without occasional domestic infelicities. For instance, Joe would wake up in the middle of the night, declaring to me that it was morning, and thereupon insist upon sweeping out at once, and in the most vigorous manner. Having filled the air with dust, he would rush off to the

baker's for our hot rolls and a pat of breakfast but-
ter, leaving me, meantime, to recover as I might.
Having settled myself for a comfortable hour's reading, bolstered up in a luxurious fashion, Joe would
enter with breakfast, and orders to the effect that
it be eaten at once and without delay. It was
useless for me to remonstrate with him; he was
tyrannical.

He got me into all sorts of trouble. It was Holy
Week, and I had resolved upon going to mass and
vespers daily. I went. The soft night-winds floated
in through the latticed windows of the chapel, and
made the candles flicker upon the altar. The little
throng of natives bowed in the oppressive silence,
and were deeply moved. It was rest for the soul to
be there; yet, in the midst of it, while the Father,
with his pale, sad face, gave his instructions, to
which we listened as attentively as possible—for
there was something in his manner and his voice
that made us better creatures—while we listened, in
the midst of it I heard a shrill little whistle, a sort
of chirp, that I knew perfectly well. It was Joe, sitting on a cocoa-stump in the garden adjoining, and
beseeching me to come out, right off. When service was over, I remonstrated with him for his ir-
reverence. "Joe," I said, "if you have no respect
for religion yourself, respect those who are more
fortunate than you." But Joe was dressed in his
best, and quite wild at the entrancing loveliness of
the night. "Let's walk a little," said Joe, covered
with fragrant wreaths, and redolent of cocoanut-oil.

What could I do? If I had tried to do anything to the contrary, he might have taken me and thrown me away somewhere into a well or a jungle, and then I could no longer hope to touch the chord of remorse — which chord I sought vainly, and which I have since concluded was not in Joe's physical corporation at all. So we walked a little. In vain I strove to break Joe of the shocking habit of whistling me out of vespers. He would persist in doing it. Moreover, during the day he would collect crusts of bread and banana-skins, station himself in ambush behind the curtain of the window next the lane, and, as some solitary creature strode solemnly past, Joe would discharge a volley of ammunition over him, and then laugh immoderately at his indignation and surprise. Joe was my pet elephant, and I was obliged to play with him very cautiously.

One morning he disappeared. I was without the consolations of a breakfast, even. I made my toilet, went to my portmanteau for my purse—for I had decided upon a visit to the baker—when lo! part of my slender means had mysteriously disappeared. Joe was gone, and the money also. All day I thought about it. In the morning, after a very long and miserable night, I woke up, and when I opened my eyes, there, in the doorway, stood Joe, in a brand-new suit of clothes, including boots and hat. He was gorgeous beyond description, and seemed overjoyed to see me, and as merry as though nothing unusual had happened. I was quite startled

at this apparition. "Joseph!" I said in my sever-
est tone, and then turned over and looked away
from him. Joe evaded the subject in the most delicate manner, and was never so interesting as at
that moment. He sang his specialties, and played
clumsily upon his bamboo flute—to soothe me, I suppose—and wanted me to eat a whole flat pie which
he had brought home as a peace-offering, buttoned
tightly under his jacket. I saw I must strike at
once, if I struck at all ; so I said, " Joe, what on
earth did you do with that money ?" Joe said he
had replenished his wardrobe, and bought the flat
pie especially for me. "Joseph," I said, with great
dignity, " do you know that you have been stealing,
and that it is highly sinful to steal, and may result
in something unpleasant in the world to come?"
Joe said, "Yes," pleasantly, though I hardly think
he meant it ; and then he added, mildly, " that he
couldn't lie"—which was a glaring falsehood—" but
wanted me to be sure that he took the money, and
so had come back to tell me."

"Joseph," I said, "you remind me of our noble
Washington ;" and, to my amazement, Joe was mortified. He didn't, of course, know who Washington
was, but he suspected that I was ridiculing him.
He came to the bed and haughtily insisted upon my
taking the little change he had received from his
costumers, but I implored him to keep it, as I had
no use at all for it, and, as I assured him, I much
preferred hearing it jingle in his pocket.

The next day I sailed out of Lahaina, and Joe

came to the beach with his new trousers tucked into
his new boots, while he waved his new hat violently in
a final adieu, much to the envy and admiration of a
score of hatless urchins, who looked upon Joe as the
glass of fashion, and but little lower than the angels.
When I entered the boat to set sail, a tear stood in
Joe's bright eye, and I think he was really sorry to
part with me ; and I don't wonder at it, because our
housekeeping experiences were new to him—and, I
may add, not unprofitable.

II.

SOME months of mellow and beautiful weather
found me wandering here and there among the islands, when the gales came on again, and I was
driven about homeless, and sometimes friendless,
until, by and by, I heard of an opportunity to visit
Molokai—an island seldom visited by the tourist—
where, perhaps, I could get a close view of a singularly sad and interesting colony of lepers.

The whole island is green, but lonely. As you
ride over its excellent turnpike, you see the ruins of
a nation that is passing, like a shadow, out of sight.
Deserted garden-patches, crumbling walls, and roofs
tumbled into the one state-chamber of the house,
while knots of long grass wave at halfmast in the
chinks and crannies. A land of great traditions, of
magic and witchcraft and spirits.   A fertile and
fragrant solitude. How I enjoyed it ; and yet how

it was all telling upon me, in its own way! One
cannot help feeling sad there, for he seems to be living and moving in a long revery, out of which he
dreads to awaken to a less pathetic life. I rode a day
or two among the solemn and reproachful ruins
with inexpressible complacence, and, having finally
climbed a series of verdant and downy hills, and ridden for twenty minutes in a brisk shower, came suddenly upon the brink of a great precipice, three thousand feet in the air. My horse instinctively braced
himself, and I nervously jerked the bridle square up
to my breastbone, as I found we were poised between
heaven and earth, upon a trembling pinnacle of rock.
A broad peninsula was stretched below me, covered
with grassy hills; here and there clusters of brown
huts were visible, and to the right, the white dots
of houses to which I was hastening, for that was
the leper village. To that spot were the wandering
and afflicted tribes brought home to die. Once descending the narrow stairs in the cliff under me,
never again could they hope to strike their tents and
resume their pilgrimage; for the curse was on them,
and necessity had narrowed down their sphere of
action to this compass—a solitary slope between sea
and land, with the invisible sentinels of Fear and
Fate forever watching its borders.

I seemed to be looking into a fiery furnace wherein walked the living bodies of those whom Death
had already set his seal upon. What a mockery it
seemed to be, climbing down that crag — through
wreaths of vine, and under leafy cataracts breaking

into a foam of blossoms a thousand feet below me; swinging aside the hanging parasites that obstructed the narrow way—and so entering the valley of death, and the very mouth of hell, by these floral avenues!

A brisk ride of a couple of miles across the breadth of the peninsula brought me to the gate of the keeper of the settlement, and there I dismounted and hastened into the house, to be rid of the curious crowd that had gathered to receive me. The little cottage was very comfortable, my host and hostess friends of precious memory; and with them I felt at once at home, and began the new life that everyone begins when the earth seems to have been suddenly transformed into some better or worse world, and he alone survives the transformation.

Have you never had such an experience? Then go into the midst of a community of lepers; have ever before your eyes their Gorgon-like faces; see the horrors, hardly to be recognized as human, that grope about you; listen in vain for the voices that have been hushed forever by decay; breathe the tainted atmosphere; and bear ever in mind that, while they hover about you—forbidden to touch you, yet longing to clasp once more a hand that is perfect and pure—the insidious seeds of the malady may be generating in your vitals, and your heart, even then, be drunk with death!

I might as well confess that I slept indifferently the first night; that I was not entirely free from nervousness the next day, as I passed through the various wards assigned to patients in every stage of decomposition. But I recovered myself in time to observe the admirable system adopted by the Hawaiian Government for the protection of its unfortunate people. I used to sit by the window and see the processions of the less afflicted come for little measures of milk, morning and evening. Then there was a continuous raid upon the ointment-pot, with the contents of which they delighted to anoint themselves. Trifling disturbances sometimes brought the plaintiff and defendant to the front gate, for final judgment at the hands of their beloved keeper. And it was a constant entertainment to watch the progress of events in that singular little world of doomed spirits. They were not unhappy. I used to hear them singing every evening ; their souls were singing while their bodies were falling rapidly to dust. They continued to play their games, as well as they could play them with the loss of a finger-joint or a toe, from week to week : it was thus gradually and thus slowly that they died, feeling their voices growing fainter and their strength less, as the idle days passed over them and swept them to the tomb.

Sitting at the window on the second evening, as the patients came up for milk, I observed one of them watching me intently, and apparently trying to make me understand something or other, but what that something was I could not guess. He rushed to the keeper and talked excitedly with him for a moment, and then withdrew to one side of the gate and waited till the others were served with their milk, still watching me all the while. Then the keeper entered and told me how I had a friend out there who wished to speak with me—some one who had seen me somewhere, he supposed, but whom I would hardly remember. It was their way never to forget a face they had once become familiar with. Out I went. There was a face I could not have recognized as anything friendly or human. Knots of flesh stood out upon it; scar upon scar disfigured it. The expression was like that of a mummy, stony and withered. The outline of a youthful figure were preserved, but the hands and feet were pitiful to look at. What was this ogre that knew me and loved me still?

He soon told me who he had once been, but was no longer. My little, unfortunate "Joe," my Lahaina charge. In his case the disease had spread with fearful rapidity; the keeper thought he could hardly survive the year. Many linger year after year, and cannot die; but Joe was more fortunate. His life had been brief and passionate, and death was now hastening him to his dissolution.

Joe was forbidden to come near me, so he crouched down by the fence, and, pressing his hands between the pickets, sifted the dust at my feet, while he wailed in a low voice and called me, over and over, "dear friend," "good friend," and "master." I wish I had never seen him so humbled. To think of my disreputable little *protégé*, who was wont to lord it over me as though he had been a born chief —to think of Joe as being there in his extremity, grovelling in the dust at my feet ; forbidden to climb the great wall of flowers that towered between him and his beautiful world, while the rough sea lashed the coast about him, and his only companions were such hideous forms as would frighten one out of a dream !

How I wanted to get close to him ! but I dared not ; so we sat there with the slats of the fence between us, while we talked very long in the twilight ; and I was glad when it grew so dark that I could no longer see his face—his terrible face, that came to kill the memory of his former beauty.

And Joe wondered whether I still remembered how we used to walk in the night, and go home, at last, to our little house when Lahaina was as still as death, and you could almost hear the great stars throbbing in the clear sky ! How well I remembered it, and the day when we went a long way down the beach, and, looking back, saw a wide curve of the land cutting the sea like a sickle, and turning up a white and shining swath ! Then in another place, a grove of cocoa-palms and a melancholy, monastic-looking building, with splendid palmbranches in its broad windows : for it was just after Palm Sunday, and the building belonged to a sisterhood. And I remembered how the clouds fell and the rain drove us into a sudden shelter, and we ate tamarind-jam, spread thick on thin slices of bread, and were supremely happy. In this connection I could not forget how Joe became very unruly about that time, and I got mortified, and found great difficulty in getting him home at all; and yet the memory of it would have been perfect but for this fate. O Joe! my poor, dear, terrible cobra! to think that I should ever be afraid to look into your face in my life!

Joe wanted to call to my mind one other reminiscence—a night when we two walked to the old wharf, and went out to the end of it, and sat there looking inland, watching the inky waves slide up and down the beach, while the full moon rose over the superb mountains where the clouds were heaped like wool, and the very air seemed full of utterances that you could almost hear and understand but for something that made them all a mystery. I tried then, if ever I tried in my life, to make Joe a little less bad than he was naturally, and he seemed nearly inclined to be better, and would, I think, have been so, but for the thousand temptations that gravitated to him when we got on solid earth again. He forgot my precepts then, and I'm afraid I forgot them myself. Joe remembered that night vividly. I was touched to hear him confess it; and I pray earnestly that that one moment may plead for him in the last day, if, indeed, he needs any special plea other than that Nature has published for her own.

"Sing for me, Joe," said I; and Joe, still crouching on the other side of the lattice, sang some of his old songs. One of them, a popular melody, was echoed through the little settlement, where faint voices caught up the chorus, and the night was wildly and weirdly musical. We walked by the sea the next day, and the day following that, Joe taking pains to stay on the leeward side of me—he was so careful to keep the knowledge of his fate uppermost in his mind; how could I dismiss it from my own, when it was branded in his countenance? The desolated beauty of his face pleaded for measureless pity, and I gave it, out of my prodigality, yet felt that I could not begin to give sufficient.

Link by link he was casting off his hold on life; he was no longer a complete being; his soul was prostrated in the miry clay, and waited, in agony, its long deliverance.

In leaving the leper village, I had concluded to say nothing to Joe, other than the usual "*aloha*" at night, when I could ride off in the darkness, and, sleeping at the foot of the cliff, ascend it in the first light of morning, and get well on my journey before the heat of the day. We took a last walk by the rocks on the shore; heard the sea breathing its long breath under the hollow cones of lava, with a noise like a giant leper in his asthmatic agony. Joe heard it, and laughed a little, and then grew silent; and finally said he wanted to leave the place—he hated it; he loved Lahaina dearly; how was everybody in Lahaina?—a question he had asked me hourly since my arrival.

When night came I asked Joe to sing, as usual; so he gathered his mates about him, and they sang the songs I liked best. The voices rang, sweeter than ever, up from the group of singers congregated a few rods off, in the darkness; and while they

8

sang, my horse was saddled, and I quietly bade adieu to my dear friends, the keepers, and, mounting, walked the horse slowly up the grass-grown road. I shall never see little Joe again, with his pitiful face, growing gradually as dreadful as a cobra's, and almost as fascinating in its hideousness. I waited, a little way off, in the darkness—waited and listened, till the last song was ended, and I knew he would be looking for me, to say *Good-night*. But he did not find me ; and he will never again find me in this life, for I left him sitting in the dark door of his sepulchre—sitting and singing in the mouth of his grave—clothed all in Death.

THE NIGHT-DANCERS OF WAIPIO

THE afternoon sun was tinting the snowy crest of Mauna Kea, and folds of shadow were draping the sea-washed eastern cliffs of Hawaii, as Felix and I endeavored to persuade our fagged steeds that they must go on and live, or stay and die in the middle of a lava-trail by no means inviting. As we rode, we thought of the scandal that so recently had regaled our too willing ears; here it is, in a mild solution, to be taken with three parts of disbelief:

Two venerable and warm-hearted missionaries, whose good works seemed to have found dissimilar expression, equally effective, I trust, proved their specialties to be church-building. The Rev. Mr. A seemed to think the more churches the merrier, and his pretty little meeting houses looked as though they had been baked in the lot, like a sheet of biscuits; while the Rev. Mr. B condensed his efforts into the consummation of one resplendent edifice. Mr. A was always wondering why Mr. B should waste his money in a single church, while Mr. B was nonplussed at seeing Mr. A break out in a rash of diminutive chapels. Well, Felix and I were riding northward up the coast, over dozens and dozens of

lovely ridges; through scores of deep gullies cushioned with ferns as high as our pommels, and fording numberless streams, white with froth and hurry,
eagerly seeking the most exquisite valley in the
Pacific, as some call it.   We rode till we were tired
out twenty times over; again and again we looked
forward to the bit of Mardi-life we were about to
experience in the vale of the Waipio, while now and
then we passed one of Mr. A's pretty little churches.
Once we were impatient enough to make inquiry of
a native who was watching our progress with considerable emotion; there is always some one to
watch you when you are wishing yourself at the
North Pole.   Our single spectator affected an air of
gravity, and seemed quite interested as he said, "Go
six or seven churches farther on that trail, and you'll
come to Waipio."   On we went with renewed spirits, for the churches were frequent, almost within
sight of each other.   But we faltered presently and
lost our reckoning, they were so much alike.   Again
we asked our way of a solitary watcher on a hill-top,
who had had his eye upon us ever since we rose
above the rim of the third ridge back; he revealed
to us the glad fact that we were only two churches
from Paradise!   How we tore over the rest of that
straight and narrow way with the little life left to
us, and came in finally all of a foam, fairly jumping
the last mite of a chapel that hung upon the brink
of the beautiful valley like a swallow's nest!   And
down we dropped into fifty fathoms of the sweetest
twilight imaginable—so sweet it seemed to have

been born of a wilderness of the night-blooming cereus and fed forever on jasmine buds.

There were shelter and refreshment for two hungry souls, and we slid out of our saddles as though we had been boned expressly for a cannibal feast.

By this time the rosy flush on Mauna Kea had faded, and its superb brow was pale with an unearthly pallor. "Come in," said the host; and he led us under the thatched gable, that was fragrant as new-mown hay. There we sat, "in," as he called it, though there was never a side to the concern thicker than a shadow.

A stream flowed noiselessly at our feet. Canoes drifted by us, with dusky and nude forms bowed over the paddles. Each occupant greeted us, being guests in the valley, just lifting their slumberous eyelids—masked batteries that made Felix forget his danger; they seldom paused, but called back to us from the gathering darkness with inexpressibly tender contralto voices.

Thereupon we were summoned to dinner in another apartment, screened with vines. The faint flicker of the tapers suggested that what breath of air might be stirring came from the mountain, and it brought with it a message from the orangery up the valley. "How will you take your oranges?" queried Felix; "in pulp, liquid, or perfume?"—and such a dense odor swept past us at the moment, I thought I had taken them in the triple forms. "You are just in time," said our host. "Why, what's up?" asked I. "The moon will be up presently, and after moonrise you shall see the *hula-hula*."

Felix desired to be enlightened as to the nature of the what-you-call-it, and was assured that it was worth seeing, and would require no explanatory chorus when its hour came.

It was at least a mile to the scene of action ; a tortuous stream wound thither, navigable in spots, but from time to time the canoe would have to take to the banks for a short cut into deeper water.

"I can never get there," growled Felix ; "I'm full of needles and pins ;" to which the host responded by excusing himself for a few moments, leaving Felix and me alone. It was deathly still in the valley, though a thousand crickets sang, and the fish smacked their round mouths at the top of the water. Evening comes slowly in those beloved tropics, but it comes so satisfactorily that there is nothing left out.

A moonlight night is a continuous festival. The natives sing and dance till daybreak, making it all up by sleeping till the next twilight. Nothing is lost by this ingenious and admirable arrangement. Why should they sleep, when a night there has the very essence of five nights anywhere else, extracted and enriched with spices till it is so inspiring that the soul cries out in triumph, and the eyes couldn't sleep if they would ?

At this period, enter to us the host, with several young native girls, who seat themselves at our feet, clasping each a boot-leg encasing the extremities of Felix and myself.

Felix kicked violently, and left the room with some embarrassment, and I appealed to the hospitable gentleman of the house, who was smiling somewhat audibly at our perplexity.

He assured me that if I would throw myself upon the mats in the corner, two of these maids would speedily relieve me of any bodily pain I might at that moment be suffering with.

I did so : the two proceeded as set down in the verbal prospectus ; and whatever bodily pain I may have possessed at the beginning of the process speedily dwindled into insignificance by comparison with the tortures of my novel cure. Every limb had to be unjointed and set over again. Places were made for new joints, and I think the new joints were temporarily set in, for my arms and legs went into angles I had never before seen them in, nor have I since been able to assume those startling attitudes. The stomach was then kneaded like dough. The ribs were crushed down against the spine, and then forced out by well-directed blows in the back. The spinal column was undoubtedly abstracted, and some mechanical substitute now does its best to help me through the world. The arms were tied in bow-knots behind, and the skull cracked like the shell of a hard-boiled egg, worked into shape again, and left to heal.

By this time I was unconscious, and for an hour my sleep promised to be eternal. I must have lain flat on the matting, without a curve in me, when Nature, taking pity, gradually let me rise and assume my own proportions, as though a little leaven had been mixed in my making over.

The awakening was like coming from a bath of the elements. I breathed to the tips of my toes. Perfumes penetrated me till I was saturated with them. I felt a thousand years younger ; and as I looked back upon the old life I seemed to have risen from, I thought of it much as a butterfly must think of his grub-hood, and was in the act of expanding my wings, when I saw Felix just recovering, a few feet from me, apparently as ecstatic as myself. I never dared to ask him how he was reduced to submission, for I little imagined he could so far forget himself. There are some sudden and inexplicable revolutions in the affairs of humanity that should not be looked into too closely, because a chaotic chasm yawns between the old man and the new, which no one has ever yet explored. Felix sprang to his feet like Prometheus unbound, and embraced me with fervor, as one might after a hair-breadth escape, exclaiming, "Did you ever see anything like it, Old Boy?" to which the Old Boy, thus familiarly addressed (O. B. is a pet monogram of mine, designed and frequently executed by Felix), responded, "There wasn't much to see, but my feelings were past expression." "What's its name?" asked Felix. "I think they call it *lomi-lomi*," said I. "Pass *lomi-lomi!*" shouted Felix; and then we both roared again, which summoned the host, who congratulated us and invited us to his canoe.

Felix again endeavored to fathom the mysteries of

the *hula-hula*. Was it something to eat?—did they keep it tied in the daytime?—what was its color? etc., till the amused gentleman who was conducting us to an exhibition of the great Unknown nearly capsized our absurdly narrow canoe in the very deepest part of the creek. Bands of fishermen and fisherwomen passed us, wading breast-high in the water, beating it into a foam before them, and singing at the top of their voices as they drove the fish down stream into a broad net a few rods below. Grasshouses, half buried in foliage, lined the mossy banks; while the dusky groups of women and children, clustering about the smouldering flames that betokened the preparation of the evening meal, added not a little to the poetry of twilight in the tropics.

Felix thought he would like to turn Kanaka on the spot; so we beached the canoe, and approached the fire, built on a hollow stone under a tamarind-tree, and were at once offered the cleanest mat to sit on, and a calabash of *poi* for our refreshment. How to eat paste without a spoon was the next question. The whole family volunteered to show us; drew up around the calabash in a hungry circle, and dipped in with a vengeance. Six right hands spread their first and second fingers like sign-boards pointing to a focus in the very centre of that *poi*-paste; six fists dove simultaneously, and were buried in the luscious mass. There was a spasmodic working in the elbows, an effort to come to the top, and in a moment the hands were lifted aloft in triumph, and seemed to be tracing half a dozen capital

O's in the transparent air, during which manœuvre the mass of *poi* adhering to the fingers assumed fair proportions, resembling, to a remarkable degree, large, white swellings; whereupon they were immediately conveyed to the several mouths, instinctively getting into the right one, and, having discharged freight, reappeared as good as ever, if not better than before.

"Disgusting!" gasped Felix, as he returned to the water-side. I thought him unreasonable in his harsh judgment, assuring him that our own flour was fingered as often before it came, at last, to our lips in the form of bread. "Moreover," I added, "this *poi* is glutinous: the moment a finger enters it, a thin coating adheres to the skin, and that finger may wander about the calabash all day without touching another particle of the substance. Therefore, six or sixteen fellows fingering in one dish for dinner are in reality safer than we, who eat steaks that have been mesmerized under the hands of the butcher and the cook."

Felix scorned to reply, but breathed a faint prayer for a safe return to Chicago, as we slid into the middle of the stream, and resumed our course.

The boughs of densely leaved trees reached out to one another across the water. We proceeded with more caution as the channel grew narrow; and, pressing through a submerged thicket of reeds, we routed a flock of water-fowls that wheeled overhead on heavy wings, filling the valley with their clamor.

Two or three dogs barked sleepily off somewhere

in the darkness, and the voice of some one calling floated to us as clear as a bird's note, though we knew it must be far away. We strode through a cane-field, its smoky plumes just tipped with moonlight, and saw the pinnacle of Mauna Kea, as spacious and splendid as the fairy pavilion that Nourgihan brought to Pari-Banou, illuminated as for a festival. To the left, a stream fell from the cliff, a ribbon of gauze fluttering noiselessly in the wind.

"O, look!" said Felix, who had yielded again to the influences of Nature. Looking, I saw the moon resting upon the water for a moment, while the dew seemed actually to drip from her burnished disk. Again Felix exclaimed, or was on the point of exclaiming, when he checked himself in awe. I ran to him and was silent with him, while we two stood worshipping one stately palm that rested its glorious head upon the glowing bosom of the moon, like the Virgin in the radiant aureola.

"Well," said our host, "supposing we get along!" We got along, by land and water, into a village in an orange-grove. There was a subdued murmur of many voices. I think the whole community would have burst out into a song of some sort at the slightest provocation. On we paced, in Indian file, through narrow lanes, under the shining leaves. Pale blossoms rained down upon us, and the air was oppressively sweet. Groups of natives sat in the lanes, smoking and laughing. Lovers made love in the face of heaven, utterly unconscious of any human presence. Felix grew nervous, and proposed withdrawing; but whither, O Felix, in all these islands, wouldst thou hope to find love unrequited, or lovers shamefaced withal? Much Chicago hath made thee mad!

Through a wicket we passed, where a sentinel kept ward. Within the bamboo paling, a swarm of natives gathered about us, first questioning the nature of our visit, which having proved entirely satisfactory, we were welcomed in real earnest, and offered a mat in an inner room of a large house rather superior to the average, and a disagreeable liquor—brewed of oranges, very intoxicating when not diluted, and therefore popular.

We were evidently the lions of the hour, for we sat in the centre of the first row of spectators who were gathered to witness the *hula-hula.* We reclined as gracefully as possible upon our mats, supported by plump pillows, stuffed with dried ferns. Slender rushes—strong with *kukui*-nuts, about the size of chestnuts, and very oily — were planted before us like foot-lights, which, being lighted at the top, burned slowly downward, till the whole were consumed, giving a good flame for several hours.

The great mat upon the floor before us was the stage. On one side of it a half-dozen muscular fellows were squatted, with large calabashes headed with tightly drawn goat-skins. These were the drummers and singers, who could beat nimbly with their fingers, and sing the epics of their country, to the unceasing joy of all listeners. "It's an opera!"

shouted Felix, in a frenzy of delight at his discovery.
A dozen performers entered, sitting in two lines,
face to face—six women and six men. Each bore a
long joint of bamboo, slit at one end like a broom.
Then began a singularly intricate exercise, called
pi-ulu. Taking a bamboo in one hand, they struck
it in the palm of the other, on the shoulder, on the
floor in front, to left and right; thrust it out before
them, and were parried by the partners opposite;
crossed it over and back, and turned in a thousand
ways to a thousand metres, varied with chants and
pauses. "Then it's a pantomime," added Felix,
getting interested in the unusual skill displayed.
For half an hour or more the thrashing of the bamboos was prolonged, while we were hopelessly con-
fused in our endeavors to follow the barbarous harmony, which was never broken nor disturbed by the
expert and tireless performers.

During the first rest, liquor was served in gourds.
Part of the company withdrew to smoke, and the
conversation became general and noisy. Felix was
enthusiastic, and drank the health of some of the
younger members of the *troupe* who had offered him
the gourd.

A rival company then repeated the *pi-ulu*, with
some additions; the gourds were again filled and
emptied. "Now for the *hula-hula*," said the host,
who had imbibed with Felix, though he reserved
his enthusiasm for something less childish than *pi-
ulu*. It is the national dance, taught to all children
by their parents, but so difficult to excel in that the

few who perfect themselves can afford to travel on this one specialty.

There was a murmur of impatience, speedily checked, and followed by a burst of applause, as a band of beautiful girls, covered with wreaths of flowers and vines, entered and seated themselves before us. While the musicians beat an introductory overture upon the tom-toms, the dancers proceeded to bind shawls and scarfs about their waists, turban-fashion. They sat in a line, facing us, a foot or two apart. The loose sleeves of their dresses were caught up at the shoulder, exposing arms of almost perfect symmetry, while their bare throats were scarcely hidden by the necklaces of jasmines that coiled about them.

Then the leader of the band, who sat, grayheaded and wrinkled, at one end of the room, throwing back his head, uttered a long, wild, and shrill guttural—a sort of invocation to the goddess of the *hula-hula*. There had, no doubt, been some sort of sacrifice offered in the early part of the evening—such as a pig or a fowl—for the dance has a religious significance, and is attended by its appropriate ceremonies. When this clarion cry had ended, the dance began, all joining in with wonderfully accurate rhythm, the body swaying slowly backward and forward, to left and right; the arms tossing, or rather waving, in the air above the head, now beckoning some spirit of light, so tender and seductive were the emotions of the dancers, so graceful and free the movements of the wrists; now, in violence and fear, they seemed to repulse a host of devils that hovered invisibly about them.

The spectators watched and listened breathlessly, fascinated by the terrible wildness of the song and the monotonous thrumming of the accompaniment. Presently the excitement increased. Swifter and more wildly the bare arms beat the air, embracing, as it were, the airy forms that haunted the dancers, who rose to their knees, and, with astonishing agility, caused the clumsy turbans about their loins to quiver with an undulatory motion, increasing or decreasing with the sentiment of the song and the enthusiasm of the spectators.

Felix wanted to know "how long they could keep that up and live?"

Till daybreak, as we found! There was a little resting-spell — a very little resting-spell, now and then—for the gourd's sake, or three whiffs at a pipe that would poison a white man in ten minutes; and before we half expected it, or had a thought of urging the unflagging dancers to renew their marvellous gyrations, they were at it in terrible earnest.

From the floor to their knees, from their knees to their feet, now facing us, now turning from us, they spun and ambled, till the ear was deafened with cheers and boisterous, half-drunken, wholly passionate laughter.

The room whirled with the reeling dancers, who seemed encircled with living serpents in the act of swallowing big lumps of something from their

throats clear to the tips of their tails, and the con-
vulsions continued till the hysterical dancers staggered and fell to the floor, overcome by unutterable
fatigue.

The sympathetic Felix fell with them, his head
sinking under one of the rush candles, that must
have burned into his brain had he been suffered to
immolate himself at that inappropriate and unholy
time and place.

This was the seductive dance still practised in
secret, though the law forbids it ; and to the Hawaiian it is more beautiful, because more sensuous,
than anything else in the world.

I proposed departing at this stage of the festival,
but Felix said it was not practicable. He felt un-
well, and suggested the efficacy of another attack
of *lomi-lomi*.

A slight variation in the order of the dances followed. A young lover, seated in the centre of the
room, beat a tattoo upon his calabash and sang a
song of love. In a moment he was answered. Out
of the darkness rose the sweet, shrill voice of the
loved one. Nearer and nearer it approached ; the
voice rang clear and high, melodiously swelling
upon the air. It must have been heard far off in
the valley, it was so plaintive and penetrating. Secreted at first behind shawls hung in the corner of
the room, some dramatic effect was produced by
her entrance at the right moment. She enacted
her part with graceful energy. To the regular and
melancholy thrumming of the calabash, she sang

her song of love. Yielding to her emotion, she did not hesitate to betray all, neither was he of the calabash slow to respond ; and, scorning the charms of goat-skin and gourd, he sprang toward her in the madness of his soul, when she, having reached the climax of desperation, was hurried from the scene of her conquest amid whirlwinds of applause.

"It's a dance, that's what it is ! " muttered Felix, as the audience began slowly to disperse. Leading him back to the canoe, we had the whole night's orgie reported to us in a very mixed and reiterative manner ; as well as several attempts at illustrating the peculiarities of the performance, which came near resulting in a watery grave for three, or an upset canoe, at any rate. Our host, to excuse any impropriety, for which he felt more or less responsible, said "it was so natural for them to be jolly under all circumstances that when they have concluded to die they make their P. P. C.'s with infinite grace, and then die on time."

Of course they are jolly ; and to prove it, I told Felix how the lepers, who had been banished to one little corner of the kingdom, and forbidden to leave there in the flesh, were as merry as the merriest, and once upon a time those decaying remnants of humanity actually gave a grand ball in their hospital. There was a general clearing out of disabled patients, and a brushing up of old finery, while the ball itself was *the* topic of conversation. Two or three young fellows, who had a few fingers left (they unjoint and drop off as the disease progresses), be-

9

gan to pick up a tune or two on bamboo flutes.
Old, young, and middle-aged took a sly turn in
some dark corner, getting their stiffened joints lim-
ber again.

Night came at last. The lamps flamed in the
death-chamber of the lazar-house. Many a rejoicing soul had fled from that foul spot, to flash its
white wings in the eternal sunshine.

At an early hour the strange company assembled.
The wheezing of voices no longer musical, the
shuffling of half-paralyzed limbs over the bare floor,
the melancholy droning of those bamboo flutes, and
the wild sea moaning in the wild night were the
sweetest sounds that greeted them. And while the
flutes piped dolorously to this unlovely spectacle,
there was a rushing to and fro of unlovely figures ;
a bleeding, half-blind leper, seizing another of the
accursed beings—snatching her, as it were, from
the grave, in all her loathsome clay—dragged her
into the bewildering maelstrom of the waltz.

Naturally excitable, heated with exertion, drunk
with the very odors of death that pervaded the hall
of revels, that mad crowd reeled through the hours
of the *fête*. Satiated, at last, in the very bitterness
of their unnatural gayety, they called for the *hula-
hula* as a fitting close.

In that reeking atmosphere, heavy with the smoke
of half-extinguished lamps, they fed on the voluptuous *abandon* of the dancers till passion itself fainted
with exhaustion.

"That was a dance of death, was it not, Felix?"

Felix lay on his mat, sleeping heavily, and evidently unmindful of a single word I had uttered.

Our time was up at daybreak, and, with an endless deal of persuasion, Felix followed me out of the valley to the little chapel on the cliff. Our horses took a breath there, and so did we, bird's-eying the scene of the last night's orgie.

Who says it isn't a delicious spot—that deep, narrow, and secluded vale, walled by almost perpendicular cliffs, hung with green tapestries of ferns and vines; that slender stream, like a thread of silver, embroidering a carpet of Nature's richest pattern; that torrent, leaping from the cliff into a garden of citrons; the sea sobbing at its mouth, while wary mariners, coasting in summer afternoons, catch glimpses of the tranquil and forbidden paradise, yet are heedless of all its beauty, and reck not the rustling of the cane-fields nor the voices of the charmers, because—because these things are so common in that latitude that one grows naturally indifferent!

As for Felix, who talks in his sleep of the *hula-hula,* and insists that only by the *lomi-lomi* he shall be saved, he points a moral, though at present he is scarcely in a condition to adorn any tale whatever; and said moral I shall be glad to furnish, on application, to any sympathetic soul who has witnessed by proxy the unlawful revels of those night-dances of Waipio.

PEARL-HUNTING IN THE POMO-TOUS

THE Great Western ducked in the heavy swell, shipping her regular deck-load of salt-water every six minutes. Now, the Great Western was nothing more nor less than a seventeen-ton schooner, two hours out from Tahiti. She was built like an old shoe, and shovelled in a head-sea as though it was her business.

It was something like sea life, wading along her submerged deck from morning till night, with a piece of raw junk in one hand and a briny biscuit in the other; we never *could* keep a fire in *that* galley, and as for hard tack, the sooner it got soaked through the sooner it was off our minds, for we knew to this complexion it must shortly come.

Two hours out from Tahiti we settled our course, wafting a theatrical kiss or two toward the gloriously green pyramid we were turning our backs on, as it slowly vanished in the blue desert of the sea.

A thousand palm-crowned and foam-girdled reefs spangled the ocean to the north and east of Tahiti. This train of lovely satellites is known as the Dangerous Archipelago, or, more commonly in that latitude, the Pomotou Islands. It's the very hot-bed of cocoanut-oil, pearls, half-famished Kanakas, shells, and shipwrecks. The currents are rapid and variable; the winds short, sharp, and equally unreliable. If you would have adventure, the real article and plenty of it, make your will, bid farewell to home and friends, and embark for the Pomotous. I started on this principle, and repented knee-deep in the deck-breakers, as we butted our way through the billows, bound for one of the Pomotous on a pearl hunt.

Three days I sat in sackcloth and salt water. Three nights I swashed in my greasy bunk, like a solitary sardine in a box with the side knocked out. In my heart of hearts I prayed for deliverance: you see there is no backing out of a schooner, unless you crave death in fifty fathoms of phosphorescent liquor and a grave in a shark's maw. Therefore I prayed for more wind from the right quarter, for a sea like a boundless mill-pond; in short, for speedy deliverance on the easiest terms possible. Notwithstanding my prayers, we continued to bang away at the great waves that crooked their backs under us and hissed frightfully as they enveloped the Great Western with spray until the fourth night out, when the moon gladdened us and promised much while we held our breath in anxiety.

We were looking for land. We'd been looking for three hours, scarcely speaking all that time. It's a serious matter raising a Pomotou by moonlight.

"Land!" squeaked a weak voice about six feet above us. A lank fellow, with his legs corkscrewed around the shrouds, and his long neck stretched to windward, where it veered like a weather-cock in a nor'wester, chuckled as he sang out "Land!" and felt himself a little lower than Christopher Columbus thereafter. "Where away?" bellowed our chunky little captain, as important as if he were commanding a grown-up ship. "Two points on the weather-bow!" piped the lookout, with the voice of one soaring in space, but unhappily choked in the last word by a sudden lurch of the schooner that brought him speedily to the deck, where he lost his identity and became a proper noun, second person, singular, for the rest of the cruise.

Now, "two points" is an indefinite term that embraces any obstacle ahead of anything; but the "weather-bow" has been the salvation of many a craft in her distress; so we gave three cheers for the "weather-bow," and proceeded to sweep the horizon with unwinking gaze. We could scarcely tell how near the land might lie; fancied we could already hear the roar of surf-beaten reefs, and every wave that reared before us seemed the rounded outline of an island. Of course we shortened sail, not knowing at what moment we might find ourselves close upon some low sea-garden nestling under the rim of breakers that fenced it in, and being morally averse to running it down without warning.

It was scarcely midnight; the moon was radiant; we were silently watching, wrapped in the deep mystery that hung over the weather-bow.

The wind suddenly abated; it was as though it

sifted through trees and came to us subdued with a whisper of fluttering leaves and a breath of spice. We knew what it meant, and our hearts leaped within us as over the bow loomed the wave-like outline of shadow that sank not again like the other waves, neither floated off cloud-like, but seemed to be bearing steadily down upon us — a great whale hungry for a modern Jonah.

What a night it was! We heard the howl of waters now; saw the palm - boughs glisten in the moonlight, and the glitter and the flash of foam that fringed the edges of the half-drowned islet.

It looked for all the world like a grove of cocoatrees that had waded out of sight of land, and didn't know which way to turn next. This was the Ultima Thule of the Great Western's voyage, and she seemed to know it, for she behaved splendidly at last, laying off and on till morning in fine style, evidently as proud as a ship-of-the-line.

I went below and dozed, with the low roar of the reef quite audible: a fellow gets used to such dream - music, and sleeps well to its accompaniment.

At daybreak we began beating up against wind and tide, hoping to work into smooth water by sunrise, which we did easily enough, shaking hands all around over a cup of thick coffee and molasses as three fathoms of chain whizzed overboard after a tough little anchor that buried itself in a dim wilderness of corals and sea-grass.

Then and there I looked about me with delighted

eyes. The Great Western rode at anchor in a shallow lake, whose crystal depths seemed never to have been agitated by any harsher breath than at that moment kissed without ruffling its surface. Around us swept an amphitheatre of hills, covered with a dense growth of tropical foliage and cushioned to the hem of the beach with thick sod of exquisite tint and freshness. The narrow rim of beach that sloped suddenly to the tideless margin of the lake was littered with numberless slender canoes drawn out of the water like so many fish, as though they would navigate themselves in their natural element, and they were, therefore, not to be trusted alone too near it. Around the shore, across the hills, and along the higher ridges waved innumerable cocoa-palms, planted like a legion of lances about the encampment of some barbaric prince.

As for the very blue sky and the very white scud that shot across it, they looked windy enough; moreover we could all hear the incoherent booming of the sea upon the reef that encircled our nest. But we forgot the wind and the waves in the inexpressible repose of that armful of tropical seclusion. It was a drop of water in a tuft of moss, on a very big scale; that's just what it was.

In a few moments, as with one impulse, the canoes took to water with a savage or two in each, all gravitating to the schooner, which was for the time being the head-centre of their local commerce; and for an hour or more we did a big business in the exchange of fish-hooks and fresh fruit.

The proportion of canoes at Motu Hilo (Crescent Island) to the natives of said fragment of Eden was as one to several ; but the canoeless could not resist the superior attraction of a foreign invader, therefore the rest of the inhabitants went head-first into the lake, and struck out for the middle, where we peacefully swung at anchor.

The place was sharky, but a heavy dirk full twenty inches tall was held between the teeth of the swimmers ; and if the smoke-colored dorsal of any devil of a shark had dared to cut the placid surface of the water that morning, he would speedily have had more blades in him than a farrier's knife. A few vigorous strokes of the arms and legs in the neighborhood, a fatal lunge or two, a vermilion cloud in a sea churned to a cream, and a dance over the gaping corpse of some monster who has sucked human blood more than once, probably, does the business in that country.

It was a sensation for unaccustomed eyes, that inland sea covered, littered, I might say, with woolly heads, as though a cargo of cocoanuts had been thrown overboard in a stress of weather. They gathered about as thick as flies at a honey-pot, all talking, laughing, and spouting mouthfuls of water into the air like those impossible creatures that do that sort of thing by the half-dozen in all high-toned and classical fountains.

Out of this amphibious mob one gigantic youth, big enough to eat half our ship's crew, threw up an arm like Jove's, clinched the deck-rail with lithe fingers, and took a rest, swinging there with the utmost satisfaction.

I asked him aboard, but he scorned to forsake his natural element; water *is* as natural as air to those natives. Probably he would have suffered financially had he attempted boarding us, for his thick black hair was netted with a kind of spacious nest and filled with eggs on sale. It was quite astonishing to see the ease with which he navigated under his heavy deck-load.

This colossal youth having observed that I was an amateur humanitarian, virtue received its instant reward (which it doesn't in all climates), for he at once offered me three of his eggs in a very winning and patronizing manner.

I took the eggs because I like eggs, and then I was anxious to get his head above water if possible; therefore I unhesitatingly took the eggs, offering him in return a fish-hook, a tenpenny nail, and a dilapidated key-ring.

These tempting *curios* he spurned, at the same moment reaching me another handful of eggs. His generosity both pleased and alarmed me. I saw with joy that his chin was quite out of water in consequence of his charity, even when he dropped back into the sea, floating for a few moments so as to let the blood circulate in his arm again; but whether this was his magnanimous gift, or merely a trap to involve me in hopeless debt, I was quite at a loss to know, and I paused with my hands full of eggs, saying to myself, There is an end to fish-hooks in the

South Pacific and dilapidated key-rings are not my staple product!

In the midst of my alarm he began making vows of eternal friendship. This was by no means disagreeable to me. He was big enough to whip any two of his fellows, and one likes to be on the best side of the stronger party in a strange land.

I reciprocated!

I leaned over the stern-rail of the Great Western in the attitude of Juliet in the balcony scene, assuring that egg-boy that my heart was his if he was willing to take it at second-hand.

He liked my sentiments, and proposed touching noses at once (a barbarous greeting still observed in the most civilized countries with even greater license, since with Christians it is allowable to touch mouths).

We touched noses, though I was in danger of sliding headlong into the sea. After this ceremonial he consented to board the Great Western, which having accomplished with my help, he deposited his eggs at my feet, offered me his nose once more, and communicated to me his name, asking in the same breath for mine.

He was known as Hua Manu, or Bird's Egg. Every native in the South Sea gets named by accident. I knew a fellow whose name was "Cockeye;" he was a standing advertisement of his physical deformity. A fellow that knew me rejoiced in the singular cognomen of "Thrown-from-a-horse." Fortunately he doesn't spell it with so many letters

in his tongue. His christening happened in this
wise: A bosom friend of his mother was thrown
from a horse and killed the day of his birth. Therefore the bereaved mother reared that child, an animated memorial, who in after years clove to me, and
was as jolly as though his earthly mission wasn't
simply to keep green the memory of his mother's
bosom friend sailing through the air with a dislo-
cated neck.

I turned to my new-found friend. "Hua Manu,"
said I, "for my sake you have made a bird's-nest of
your back hair. You have freely given me your
young affection and your eggs. Receive the sincere
thanks of yours truly, together with these fish-hooks,
these tenpenny nails, this key-ring." Hua Manu
smiled and accepted, burying the fish-hooks in his
matted forelock, and inserting a tenpenny nail and
a key-ring in either ear, thereby making himself the
envy of the entire population of Motu Hilo, and
feeling himself as grand as the best chief in the
archipelago.

So we sat together on the deck of the Great
Western, quite dry for a wonder, exchanging sheep's-
eyes and confidences, mutually happy in each other's
society. Meanwhile the captain was arranging his
plans for an immediate purchase of such pearls as
he might find in possession of the natives, and for a
fresh search for pearl oysters at the earliest possible
hour. There were no pearls on hand. What are
pearls to a man who has as many wives, children, and
cocoanuts as he can dispose of? Pearls are small

and colorless. Give him a handful of gorgeous glass beads, a stick of sealing-wax, or some spotted beans, and keep your pale sea-tears, milky and frozen and apt to grow sickly yellow and die if they are not cared for.

Motu Hilo is independent. No man has squatted there to levy tax or toll. We were each one of us privileged to hunt for pearls and keep our stores separate. I said to Hua Manu, "Let's invest in a canoe, explore the lagoon for fresh oyster-beds, and fill innumerable cocoanut shells with these little white seeds. It will be both pleasant and profitable, particularly for me." We were scarcely five minutes bargaining for our outfit, and we embarked at once, having agreed to return in a couple of days for news concerning the success of the Great Western and her probable date of sailing.

Seizing a paddle, Hua Manu propelled our canoe with incredible rapidity out of the noisy fleet in the centre of the lake, toward a green point that bounded it, one of the horns of the crescent. He knew a spot where the oyster yawned in profusion, a secret cave for shelter, a forest garden of fruits, a never-failing spring, etc. Thither we would fly and domesticate ourselves. The long, curved point of land soon hid the inner waters from view. We rose and sank on the swell between the great reef and the outer rim of the island, while the sun glowed fiercely overhead and the reef howled in our ears. Still on we skimmed, the water hissing along the smooth sides of the canoe, that trembled at

every fierce stroke of Hua Manu's industrious paddle. No chart, no compass, no rudder, no exchange
of references, no letter of introduction, yet I trusted
that wild Hercules who was hurrying me away, I
knew not whither, with an earnestness that forced
the sweat from his naked body in living streams.

At last we turned our prow and shot through a
low arch in a cliff, so low we both ducked our heads
instinctively, letting the vines and parasites trail
over our shoulders and down our backs.

It was a dark passage into an inner cave lit from
below—a cave filled with an eternal and sunless twilight that was very soothing to our eyes as we came
in from the glare of sea and sky.

"Look!" said Hua Manu. Overhead rose a
compressed dome of earth, a thick matting of roots,
coil within coil. At the side innumerable ledges,
shelves, and seams lined with nests, and never a nest
without its egg, often two or more together. Below
us, in two fathoms of crystal, sunlit and luminous
bowers of coral, and many an oyster asleep with its
mouth open, and many a prismatic fish poising
itself with palpitating gills, and gauzy fins fanning
the water incessantly.

"Hua Manu!" I exclaimed in rapture, "permit
me to congratulate you. In you I behold a regular
South Sea Monte Cristo, and no less magnificent
title can do you justice." Thereat Hua Manu
laughed immoderately, which laugh having run out
we both sat in our canoe and silently sucked eggs
for some moments.

A canoe-length from where we floated, a clear rill stole noiselessly from above, mingling its sweet waters with the sea ; on the roof of our cavern fruits flourished, and we were wholly satisfied. After such a lunch as ours it behooved us to cease idling and dive for pearls. So Hua Manu knotted his long hair tightly about his forehead, cautiously transferred himself from the canoe to the water, floated a moment, inhaling a wonderfully long breath, and plunged under. How he struggled to get down to the gaping oysters, literally climbing down head first ! I saw his dark form wrestling with the elements that strove to force him back to the surface, crowding him out into the air again. He seized one of the shells, but it shut immediately, and he tugged and jerked and wrenched at it like a young demon till it gave way, when he struck out and up for the air. All this seemed an age to me. I took full twenty breaths while he was down. Reaching the canoe, he dropped the great, ugly-looking thing into it, and hung over the out-rigger gasping for breath like a man half hanged. He was pale about the mouth, his eyes were suffused with blood, blood oozed from his ears and nostrils ; his limbs, gashed with the sharp corals, bled also. The veins of his forehead looked ready to burst, and as he tightened the cords of hair across them it seemed his only salvation.

I urged him to desist, seeing his condition and fearing a repetition of his first experience ; but he would go once more ; perhaps there was no pearl in that shell; he wanted to get me a pearl. He sank again and renewed his efforts at the bottom of the sea. I scarcely dared to count the minutes now, nor the bubbles that came up to me like little balloons with a death-message in each. Suppose he were to send his last breath in one of those transparent globes, and I look down and see his body snared in the antlers of coral, stained with his blood? Well, he came up all right, and I postponed the rest of my emotion for a later experience.

Some divers remain three minutes under water, but two or three descents are as many as they can make in a day. The ravages of such a life are something frightful.

No more pearl-hunting after the second dive that day; nor the next, because we went out into the air for a stroll on shore to gather fruit and stretch our legs. There was a high wind and a heavy sea that looked threatening enough, and we were glad to return after an hour's tramp. The next day was darker, and the next after that, when a gale came down upon us that seemed likely to swamp Motu Hilo. A swell rolled over the windward reef and made our quarters in the grotto by no means safe or agreeable. It was advisable for us to think of embarking upon that tempestuous sea, or get brained against the roof of our retreat.

Hua Manu looked troubled, and my heart sank. I wished the pearl oysters at the bottom of the sea, the Great Western back at Tahiti, and I loafing under the green groves of Papeete, never more to be deluded abroad.

I observed no visible changes in the weather after I had been wishing for an hour and a half. The swell rather increased ; our frail canoe was tossed from side to side in imminent danger of upsetting.

Now and then a heavy roller entirely filled the mouth of our cavern, quite blinding us with spray ; having spent its fury it subsided with a concussion that nearly deafened us, and dragged us with fearful velocity toward the narrow mouth of the cave, where we saved ourselves from being swept into the sea by grasping the roots overhead and within reach.

"Could I swim?" asked Hua Manu. Alas, no! That we must seek new shelter at any risk was but too evident. "Let us go on the next wave," said Hua, as he seized a large shell and began clearing the canoe of the water that had accumulated. Then he bound his long hair in a knot to keep it from his eyes, and gave me some hasty directions as to my deportment in the emergency.

The great wave came. We were again momentarily corked up in an air-tight compartment. I wonder the roof was not burst open with the intense pressure that nearly forced the eyes out of my head and made me faint and giddy. Recovering from the shock, with a cry of warning from Hua, and a prayer scarcely articulated, we shot like a bomb from a mortar into the very teeth of a frightful gale.

Nothing more was said, nothing seen. The air

10

was black with flying spray, the roar of the elements more awful than anything I had ever heard before. Sheets of water swept over us with such velocity that they hummed like circular saws in motion.

We were crouched as low as possible in the canoe, yet now and then one of these, the very *blade* of the wave, struck us on the head or shoulders, cutting us like knives. I could scarcely distinguish Hua's outline, the spray was so dense, and as for him, what could he do? Nothing, indeed, but send up a sort of death-wail, a few notes of which tinkled in my ear from time to time, assuring me how utterly without hope we were.

One of those big rollers must have lifted us clean over the reef, for we crossed it and were blown into the open sea, where the canoe spun for a second in the trough of the waves, and was cut into slivers by an avalanche of water that carried us all down into the depths.

. . . .

I suppose I filled at once, but came up in spite of it (almost everyone has that privilege), when I was clutched by Hua Manu and made fast to his utilitarian back hair. I had the usual round of experiences allotted to all half-drowned people : a panoramic view of my poor life crammed with sin and sorrow and regret; a complete biography written and read through inside of ten seconds. I was half strangled, call it two-thirds, for that comes nearer the truth; heard the water singing in my ears, which was *not* sweeter than symphonies, nor beguiling, nor in the least agreeable. I deny it! In the face of every corpse that ever was drowned I emphatically deny it!

Hua had nearly stripped me with one or two tugs at my thin clothing, because he didn't think that worth towing off to some other island, and he was willing to float me for a day or two, and run the risk of saving me.

When I began to realize anything, I congratulated myself that the gale was over. The sky was clear, the white caps scarce, but the swell still sufficient to make me dizzy as we climbed one big, green hill, and slid off the top of it into a deep and bubbling abyss.

I found Hua leisurely feeling his way through the water, perfectly self-possessed and apparently unconscious that he had a deck passenger nearly as big as himself. My hands were twisted into his hair in such a way that I could rest my chin upon my arms, and thus easily keep my mouth above water most of the time.

My emotions were peculiar. I wasn't accustomed to travelling in that fashion. I knew it had been done before. Even there I thought with infinite satisfaction of the Hawaiian woman who swam for forty hours in such a sea, with an aged and helpless husband upon her back. Reaching land at last she tenderly drew her burden to shore and found him—dead! The fact is historical, and but one of several equally marvellous.

We floated on and on, cheering each other hour

after hour; the wind continuing, the sea falling, and anon night coming like an ill omen—night, that buried us alive in darkness and despair.

I think I must have dozed, or fainted, or died several times during the night, for it began to grow light long before I dared to look for it, and then came sunrise—a sort of intermittent sunrise that gilded Hua's shoulder whenever we got to the top of a high wave, and went out again as soon as we settled into the hollows.

Hua Manu's eyes were much better than mine; he seemed to see with all his five senses, and the five told him that *there was land not far off!* I wouldn't believe him; I think I was excusable for questioning his infallibility then and there. The minute he cried out "Land!" I gave up and went to sleep, or to death, for I thought he was daft, and it was a discouraging business, and I wished I could die for good. Hua Manu, what a good egg you were, though it's the bad that usually keep atop of the water, they tell me!

Hua Manu was right. He walked out of the sea an hour later and stood on a mound of coarse sand in the middle of the ocean, with my miserable, water-logged body lying in a heap at his feet.

The place was as smooth and shiny and desolate as anybody's bald head. That's a nice spot to be merry in, isn't it? Yet he tried to make me open my eyes and be glad.

He said he knew the Great Western would be com-

ing down that way shortly; she'd pick us off the
shoal, and water and feed us.

Perhaps she might! Meantime we hungered and
thirsted as many a poor castaway had before us.
That was a good hour for Christian fortitude:
beached in the middle of the ocean; shelterless
under a sun that blistered Hua's tough skin; eyes
blinded with the glare of sun and sea; the sand
glowing like brass and burning into flesh already ir-
ritated with salt water; a tongue of leather cleaving
to the roof of the mouth, and no food within reach,
nor so much as a drop of fresh water for Christ's sake!

Down went my face into the burning sand that
made the very air *hop* above it. . . . Another
night, cool and grateful; a bird or two flapped
wearily overhead, looking like spirits in the moonlight. Hua scanned earnestly our narrow horizon,
noting every inflection in the voices of the wind and
waves—voices audible to him, but worse than dumb
to me—mocking monotones reiterated through an
agonizing eternity.

A wise monitor was Hua Manu, shaming me to silence in our cursed banishment. Toward the morning after our arrival at the shoal, an owl fluttered
out of the sky and fell at our feet quite exhausted.
It might have been blown from Motu Hilo, and
seemed ominous of something, I scarcely knew what.
When it had recovered from its fatigue, it sat regarding us curiously. I wanted to wring its short,
thick neck, and eat it, feathers and all. Hua objected; there was a superstition that gave that

bland bird its life. It might continue to ogle us
with one eye as long as it liked. How the lopsided
thing smirked! how that stupid owl-face, like a ro-
sette with three buttons in it, haunted me! It was
enough to craze anyone; and, having duly cursed
him and his race, I went stark mad and hoped I was
dying forever. . . .

There are plenty of stars in this narrative. Stars,
and plenty of them, cannot account for the oblivious
intervals, suspended animation, or whatever it was,
that came to my relief from time to time. I cannot
account for them myself. Perhaps Hua Manu
might; he seemed always awake, always on the
lookout, and ever so patient and faithful. A dream
came to me after that owl had stared me into stone
—a dream of an island in a sea of glass; soft ripples
lapping on the silver shores; sweet airs sighing in
a starlit grove; someone gathering me in his arms,
hugging me close with infinite tenderness; I was
consumed with thirst, speechless with hunger; like
an infant I lay in the embrace of my deliverer, who
moistened my parched lips and burning throat with
delicious and copious draughts. It was an elixir of
life; I drank health and strength in every drop;
sweeter than mother's milk flowed the warm tide
unchecked, till I was satisfied and sank into a deep
and dreamless sleep. . . .

The Great Western was plunging in her old style,
and I swashed in my bunk as of yore. The captain
sat by me with a bottle in his hand and anxiety in
his countenance.

"Where are we?" I asked.

"Two hours out from Tahiti, inward bound."

"How! What! When!" etc.; and my mind ran up and down the record of the last fortnight, finding many blots and some blanks.

"As soon as I got into my right mind I could hear all about it;" and the captain shook his bottle, and held on to the side of my bunk to save himself from total wreck in the lee-corners of the cabin.

"Why, wasn't I right-minded? I could tell a hawk from a hernshaw; and, speaking of hawks, where was that cursed owl?"

The captain concluded I was bettering, and put the physic into the locker, so as to give his whole attention to keeping right side up. Well, this is how it happened, as I afterward learned: The Great Western suffered somewhat from the gale at Motu Hilo, though she was comparatively sheltered in that inner sea. Having repaired, and given me up as a deserter, she sailed for Tahiti. The first day out, in a light breeze, they all saw a man apparently wading up to his middle in the sea. The fellow hailed the Great Western, but as she could hardly stand up against the rapid current in so light a wind, the captain let her drift past the man in the sea, who suddenly disappeared. A consultation of officers followed. Evidently someone was cast away and ought to be looked after; resolved to beat up to the rock, big turtle, or whatever it might be that kept that fellow afloat, provided the wind freshened sufficiently; wind immediately freshened; Great

Western put about and made for the spot where
Hua Manu had been seen hailing the schooner. But
when that schooner passed he threw himself upon
the sand beside me and gave up hoping at last, and
was seen no more.

What did he then? I must have asked for drink.
He gave it me from an artery in his wrist, severed
by the finest teeth you ever saw. That's what saved
me. On came the little schooner, beating up against
the wind and tide, while I had my lips sealed to
that fountain of life.

The skipper kept banging away with an old
blunderbuss that had been left over in his bargains
with the savages, and one of these explosions caught
the ears of Hua. He tore my lips from his wrist,
staggered to his feet, and found help close at hand.
Too late they gathered us up out of the deep and
strove to renew our strength. They transported us
to the little cabin of the schooner, Hua Manu, myself, and that mincing owl, and swung off into the
old course. Probably the Great Western never did
better sailing since she came from the stocks than
that hour or two of beating that brought her up to
the shoal. She seemed to be emulating it in the
home run, for we went bellowing through the sea in
a stiff breeze and the usual flood tide on deck.

I lived to tell the tale. I should think it mighty
mean of me not to live after such a sacrifice. Hua
Manu sank rapidly. I must have nearly drained his
veins, but I don't believe he regretted it. The captain said when he was dying, his faithful eyes were

fixed on me. Unconsciously I moved a little ; he smiled, and the soul went out of him in that smile, perfectly satisfied. At that moment the owl fled from the cabin, passed through the hatchway, and disappeared.

Hua Manu lay on the deck, stretched under a sail, while I heard this. I wondered if a whole cargo of pearls could make me indifferent to his loss. I wondered if there were many truer and braver than he in Christian lands. They call him a heathen. It *was* heathenish to offer up his life vicariously. He might have taken mine so easily, and perhaps have breasted the waves back to his own people, and been fêted and sung of as the hero he truly was.

Well, if he is a heathen, out of my heart I would make a parable, its rubric bright with his sacrificial blood, its theme this glowing text : " Greater love hath no man than this, that a man lay down his life for a friend."

A TROPICAL SEQUENCE

WE were at "high tea," on the broad veranda, munching thin, crisp slices of toast. Where one dines at 2 P.M., tea and toast naturally come in with the twilight—weak tea and well-browned, butterless toast; likewise that surprising delicacy, peculiar to the tropics, preserved carrots, for even the carrot is not without honor when it is out of its element.

We were at the water's edge; the ripples warily climbed the coral terrace below us; the sea fell bravely upon the reef with a low and soothing moan; a passion-vine that half veiled the tranquil marinorama bathed its splendid blossoms in the afterglow. Thus agreeably environed, I supped with my old friend the venerable pastor of a much-vaunted mission at the antipodes.

He was rosy with the passionless flush of a temperate second youth; his thin gray locks brushed briskly upward were streaked over a shining pate. He had fervently blessed the toast, the tea, and the preserved carrots, and had recommended us singly and in groups to the tender mercies of the All Merciful—by us, I mean the withered partner of his joys and sorrows, the three daughters in starched gingham gowns, and myself.

How restful this pastoral life, so to speak, after the tribulations of travel! Now we could talk complacently of the old days when I had found shelter under that hospitable roof, and of the changes—how few for them, how many for me!—that had occurred since my former visit; yet our table talk was as frugal as the repast, for we were never quite able to get rid of the impression that gathering about the board was a kind of solemnity, and to be observed as such. Hence the collision of cup and saucer seemed irreverent; the guilty one turned with a startled look; and as for the light laughter of the natives in the groves of the village, was it not worldly? Could I not see with half an eye that eternal vigilance was the price of the pastorate?

The white waxen bells of the floribunda swung to and fro, pouring their deadly odor upon the air; the dusk deepened rapidly; the night breeze grew moist and cool. After an embarrassing silence we gratefully withdrew to the sitting-room, where a tall astral lamp with a depressed globe stood in solitary state upon the centre-table, and the four bare walls were suffused with a soft glow-worm light.

We conversed shyly, as if none of us felt quite at home. In my mind, I ran about in search of a topic to touch upon and fill the imminent deadly breach; I looked about me, trying to nurse my interest in this reserved circle. I saw that in years change had not visited it; nothing was added, nothing was taken away. Yes, Elizabeth was absent. "Where is Elizabeth?" I asked, trying to appear unconcerned, for I had liked her.

"Elizabeth is married," said the pastor's wife, with an apologetic inflection as if it were an unmaidenly thing for the girl to follow the example of her foster-mother.

It seemed to me wise to leave Elizabeth to her fate, especially as at that moment the youngest of the slim daughters of the house rose, at a signal from the pastor, and brought from a side table several copies of the New Testament, in large type, bound in sheep—one for each of us.

We drew near the lofty lamp, six of us, in a solemn circle. The books were opened at a mark; my place was found for me by the eldest daughter. The pastor read a verse in a full round voice; the wife followed in her piping treble; then the daughters three took up the strain. With some embarrassment, I read in turn; my finger had been sealed to my allotted lines from the moment the reading began and I saw which way the tide set. I was careful not to repeat the error which distinguished me on my former visit : on that occasion we were reading a psalm, and I cried *Selah!* when it came my turn. I was innocent, I was ignorant, but I was not conscious of the fact until I saw that silence, a brief silence, followed each unutterable Selah during the rest of that memorable evening.

Having finished our devotions, we sat in spasmodic converse. Sometimes, in the intervals, there was the refreshing *frou-frou* of starched gingham ; sometimes a large moth, with brilliant ruby eyes and blood-spots on its wings, dashed through the open window, became delirious at the white sheen of the astral globe, darted in and out in a fine frenzy, and then soared to the ceiling and fluttered noisily ; all through that solemn evening did the mosquito wind his horn.

By 9 P.M. I was lighted to my room, a large apartment opening on the lawn. It was quite as I had known it of yore : the huge four-posted bed with profuse folds of netting, the broad toilet-stand, the cumbersome bureau ; a few books of a serious character lay on the table.

Presently I heard the gentle people ascend to the chambers above without fastening a door or window ; it reminded me that I was once again in a semi-civilized community, where bolts and bars are unknown.

In a few moments all was silent. I threw open the door upon the lawn ; a soft air stirred among the towering trees ; the young moon was not yet set. The beauty of the night distracted me ; I was unable to sleep. Slipping on my dressing-gown, I repaired to the veranda over the sea, and lighted a cigarette.

So Elizabeth was married ! How often we had sat as I was sitting, and looked off upon the sea. The reef sang to my ears as of old, pluming itself with spray that looked like diamond dust in the moonlight ; the oppressive perfume of the flori-

bunda freighted the soft, cool air; the moon sank
behind the sharp, black rim of the horizon: the fire-
flies slid to and fro among the shadows, like tiny
shooting stars; "Hokoolélé," the natives call them
—shooting stars! And that reminded me, Hokoolélé
was the star of her tribe. When but a child her
precocity awakened the sympathy of the pastor's
household; she was grafted upon the family tree;
reared as a daughter among the daughters of the
house; clothed, fed, bred like them. While she
was still too young to realize the loss, her parents
died. Then she was kept aloof from her own people, and weaned from all their ways. When I saw
her, at fifteen, she was a woman, and not all the
ginghams of Connecticut could spoil her sensuous beauty. Soft-eyed, low-voiced, supple, graceful,
this Hokoolélé, who doffed her name when she became a Christian and was christened Elizabeth—
this wondrous girl in gingham, with her demure
ways, her prim speeches, her obtrusive code of
morals—was an enigma that had charmed and puz-
zled me. Is it any wonder that she should have
been the first flower plucked from that garden of
girls?

My last cigarette was cold in my fingers; I was a
little chilled, for at midnight the air blew fresh from
the hills. So Elizabeth was married!

I stole back to my room and put out the candle,
which was still burning.

The next day was the Sabbath. How the spirit of
the Lord's day broods over the regenerated tribes of

the Antipodes! The solemnity of our matutinal meal was undisturbed save by the subdued murmur of the sea. In the door-yard the domestic fowls stretched lazily, as is their custom of a Sunday; occasionally some hen, filled with wisdom and experience, broke the monotony with the sharp *staccato* of her recitative. The villagers spoke in hushed voices as they passed the house, walking with that undulating motion which seems to quicken the air, and sweeten it with the fragrance of their inevitable floral accompaniment.

Family prayers were more impressive than common, as befitted the day; and we were clothed in white raiment when we marched in grave and dignified procession down the long walk to the front gate, and thence by the road around the corner to the square white meeting-house; this we invariably did, instead of stepping quietly through the side gate, a short cut, and allowable on a week day when there was no service.

We filled the pastoral pew, facing the aisles, and watched the natives as they quietly glided in. They were resplendent after their kind, in purple and fine linen. Those who had shoes for the most part bore them in their hands as far as the threshold, where they were put on with some effort; but they were put off again almost as soon as the worshippers were seated. They imagine a vain thing who think that the dispensable shoe is a luxury.

Through all of that long, long sermon the hornets buzzed in and out of the window; sometimes a fitful

gust from the sea fluttered the broad leaves in the
banana hedge, and the breeze in the dense branches
of the trees without was as the sound of a sudden
shower.

In the high, old-fashioned choir-loft the natives
sang lustily to the accompaniment of a wheezing
melodeon. How I missed the voice of Elizabeth,
that superb contralto voice which used to lead the
dusky choristers. Perhaps she was even then piping like the nightingales that thrill the bowers in the
villas of Frascati.

I grew restless in the heat of the afternoon; I began to think that the parsonage without Elizabeth
was a bore. There were old haunts to be revisited
about the island, and new spots to be discovered. I
would fly into the wilderness, and set up my taber-
ernacle in the mountain solitudes, where I could at
least escape the frequent reminders that depreciated
the frank hospitality of the pastor and his house.

It is no very difficult task to prepare for a tramp
in the tropics; your food falls like manna from the
boughs above you; your drink flows at your feet;
you have at your command a veritable bed of roses;
and as for shelter, it is an impertinence to dream of
such a thing.

Plan I had none; a bee or a bird was pilot
enough for me.

There was a formal adieu at the hospitable gate—
a ponderous and patriarchal farewell. There was a
hope expressed that we might be reunited, if not in
the serene but suffocating atmosphere of the mis-

sion house, then in that brighter world whose mysterious geography seemed as plain as day to the old pastor.

I passed out of the village saluted by the populace; all extremes meet at the antipodes. Why should they not? I saluted them again, as cordially as if I had been able to distinguish one from another, and strode onward down the wide, white road that girdles the island close upon the sea.

My heart grew light in my bosom. I sang a song of liberty, albeit I am no singer, and am never asked to sing; but somehow I bubbled over, and made the woods ring with thanksgiving and praise. I was passing southward toward Point Venus, on the Tahitian shore. On my right the clouds were pierced by the sharp needles of Fatahua. I had heard of the picturesque retreat of the warriors who, years ago, nested like young eagles among those mighty peaks, held the vultures of France at bay; why not spy out this wild haunt? At the very thought my fancy turned lightly from romance to historical research.

With the single exception of the tamarind-tree planted by Captain Cook at Point Venus, there is nothing in that part of the world of more interest to the antiquarian than Fatahua. It is a toy fort hidden away up in the mountains, by a stream that makes a clear leap of a thousand feet from under the shadow of cloud-crowned cliffs, and feeds a slender river that winds through dust and heat down a fine valley to the sea.

When Pomare, the queen, was a power, instead of

a puppet, this eyrie might have been an altar to some deity; then came the French siege, and the dismayed natives fled from the shore to the mountains. Once within the battlements of Fatahua, they could defy the elements; and they did, rejoicing like the immortals. Close at hand grew fruits in inexhaustible profusion; the wood was filled with game; a stream flowed within their gates; and there was shade and sunshine without limit in that little world above the clouds.

The one possible hope for the French in the siege of Tahiti was to gain by strategy that fort of Fatahua; with the enemy in the heart of this stronghold the submission of the Tahitians would naturally follow. Two natives, treacherous dogs from a neighboring island, were bribed; and at night, by sinuous paths, ascending the mountain on the unpeopled slope of it, the French infantry was led to a cliff commanding the little fort. At daybreak, while the young eagles were pluming their wings, a volley of hot shot was poured into their nest, and it was speedily deserted.

There is a blow which paralyzes the heart, and they received it then. The ill-fated Tahitians came down to the sea again, and cast their nets as of yore, but they have never regained their pride or power, and never will.

I resolved to take Fatahua alone and single-handed; this seemed to me a dramatic justice. I laid in rations for a twelve-hour siege, footed it along a road that threads Fatahua valley, passed a sugar-mill loading the air with saccharine steams, crossed acres of thriving cane, fought shy of some native huts scattered among the bread-fruit trees, and was always within sound of the little river that dashed onward to the sea in the jolliest mood imaginable.

Having wedged myself in among the hills that are locked at the foot of the mountain, I began ascending ; and so continued until I came to a point where three streams, beside each of which was a path, chattered forth from the dense guava jungle and ran together—as if they were in a hurry to keep an appointment at this very spot.

I paused, perplexed. A wandering native took me upon his shoulders and kindly bore me across the second of the three streams, and I resumed my stealthy march.

The middle stream and the middle path, beginning at the big pandanas, is the only key to Fatahua. It was a long pull, and a weary one ; the native had disappeared, and with him the last hope of human aid. Again my trail led me knee-deep into the riotous torrent ; with shoes and stockings in hand, I forded it, only to find that it was next to impossible to replace them, for they were moist already. My kingdom for a shoehorn !

It is but two miles to the fort from the outer edge of the jungle—two almost perpendicular and rather spongy miles ; a combination of green shadows and gushing springs with an opaque background of guava growth.

At last I climbed into the open, and paused upon the edge of a frightful chasm; on the opposite brink, sixty yards away, the little fort hung like a swallow's nest under the eaves of the cliff. The gate had fallen from its hinges, and lay rotting in the moss; the parapets were masked with vines; the bastion was a bed of roses; the mango and the wild lime marked the ruin of turret and tower; the green banners of the plantain crackled in the gale; and the sentinel lizards, watchful at their posts, surrendered and slipped out of view at the approach of the invader. Without bloodshed the fort was mine!

Leaning from the dismantled ramparts, I heard the hiss of the water as it plunged into the darksome pool a thousand feet below; I saw the birds' backs as they sped through space; I dropped a great golden lime into the pit, and saw it go out in the profound shadow, like a globe of fire.

What a sanctuary for a recluse! Why not roll a stone against the narrow threshold, and forswear the world?

The deserted magazine, overrun with roses, was shelter enough from the brief showers that fall almost hourly through the night and day, and even from the gales that sometimes visit that island of tranquil delights.

Meat and drink were there, and music and sleep. What rapture to be voluntarily cast forth and forgotten of men! A place wherein to nurse one's fancies, and to brood on the great work one is always going to do, but never does.

While I mused thus the heavens darkened ; down came the javelins of the rain in a sharp and sudden shower. I ignominiously retreated to the magazine, and threw myself upon a mat left by some earlier hermit. It was dark and chilly within that windowless habitation; there was a suggestion of mildew and of unmistakable discomfort, despite the picturesque element which ever predominates in the tropics.

On second thought, did I care to end my days in Fatahua? Suddenly the doorway was darkened by a stalwart brave, whose noiseless step had given no warning of his approach.

On his shoulder he balanced a bamboo laden with clusters of *feii*, the wild plantain, that grows abundantly on the heights, and which, when cooked, is the delight of the Tahitian palate.

He paused at the threshold until his friendly greeting had been returned ; then he entered with some diffidence, deposited his fruits in a corner, squatted upon the mat near me, and breathed audibly, for his burden was heavy, and the trail no primrose path. Except for the *pareu* that girded his loins, my visitor was quite naked.

Long we gazed at each other with an earnest, honest gaze that ended in a smile of recognition ; we had never met before, but the uncivilized and the overcivilized are brothers. He placed his hand on my shoulder and stroked me fondly. From the back of his ear he drew his tobacco pouch, and rolled a cigarette, of which we took alternate puffs in token of perpetual peace.

Presently he made a fruit offering, guavas, mangoes, limes; then a drink offering, water in a cup
formed of a folded leaf; and then—we had been
silent until now—he said, in hesitating English with
a childish accent, "I know you; you like me; you
come my house."

I nodded assent. The savage shouldered his burden, and stepped lightly down the trail, turning now
and again to give me a look or a word of encouragement; at every stream he put down his load and
bore me dry-shod to the other shore; when it
showered, as it did now at intervals, we halted under
some broad-leaved tree. Once we sat in the moss
and renewed our vow in tobacco; and thus tran-
quilly we came at last to a log smouldering by a
stream, and our tramp was ended.

It was a large log, partially decayed; it had been
fired long before, and was slowly and imperceptibly
burning, like a gigantic piece of punk. At meal
time it could be blown into a flame; a few dry twigs
and leaves heaped against it served to warm the
frugal meal. This is the national Tahitian hearth—
a cloud by day, a pillar of fire by night; it puts the
blue spurt of the lucifer match to the blush; showers cannot quench it; the gale gives it new life; it
was the one luxury in the household of my host.

I was attracted by a rude shelter close at hand,
and went thither to inspect it. Imagine a screen of
leaves, about six feet wide and eight feet high, slant-
ing against the trade-wind and supported by a
couple of unbarked saplings; the gale rushed over

jt, the rain slid down it. The sides and front were as open as the day. Three logs hedged in a bed of fine grass mats, which, like a carpet, filled the space from the low eaves in the moss, to the sapling supports in front; plump clean pillows were stowed in corners; an uncovered calabash contained articles of feminine apparel; a silver thimble and a bit of unfinished embroidery with a needle thrust through it lay on the mat; a hand-mirror was lodged among the beams of the roof. Evidently the bower was not unvisited of women. From the peak of the roof hung a cluster of ripe bananas; I filled my hands with them and returned to the blazing log.

For the most part my companion and I communed in silence. You may sit for hours by a savage without uttering a syllable, yet he will turn to you at intervals with an intelligent glance and an appreciative smile, as if he were comprehending everything you left unsaid.

While we were thus growing in grace we were startled by a sharp cry. In a moment we discovered the cause of the alarm; a goat, standing on its hind legs, with one hoof placed daintily against the support of the bower was playing havoc with the bananas.

With the cry a woman sprang from the thicket, a babe at her breast, and seizing the destroyer by the horns she lustily dragged him away. For a few moments there was a struggle, while the child screamed with fright, but with the aid of my comrade the beast was beaten into the bush, and the woman, breathless from exertion and laughter, returned to the bower, where she nestled her babe in her arms.

I was presented in an ingenuous fashion, and seating myself on the threshold with unfeigned interest I regarded the hostess. She was scantily clad; her single garment, sleeveless, and with the fastening over the bosom broken in the struggle, slipped from her well-turned shoulder; her rich locks fallen from the comb partially veiled her. Her beauty was heightened by her confusion, and she hastily sought to swathe the naked babe in the folds of her robe.

To my surprise she addressed me in English, admirable English, which flowed from her lips as freely as if it were her native tongue. This was her husband, she said, and this her home. There was something in her voice that startled me; it seemed the echo of a forgotten song.

The babe was laid to sleep upon a pillow; the mother busied herself with cookery; the father meanwhile looking on idly.

We grew communicative; dinner *al fresco* is ever a jovial meal—fish from the sea, *feii* from the mountain, bread-fruit, oranges, bananas from the wild plantations of the valley. We broke the bread of ease, and solaced ourselves with such trivial scraps of gossip as were flung about the island from lip to lip.

The woman's conversational abilities astounded me; while the man sat in statuesque indifference, she spoke of nature and her life in nature with unaffected enthusiasm. As we grew more familiar I ventured to intrude upon her confidence, and not without startling results.

This was Hokoolélé; this was the Elizabeth whom I had known some years before, when she was in gingham and abeyance at the mission house. She had not recognized me, but this was scarcely surprising; I was fagged out; I had achieved a beard; I was weatherworn, and by no means so mirthful as when she knew me in my adolescence. Moreover, at the pastor's house, almost the only guest house in the village, she saw many strangers, and was probably interested in very few of them; but finding that we were indeed old friends, she told me her story, which ran something like this:

Her fate, the bronzed fellow who piloted me to her fireside, first saw her at the church, whither he had wandered out of idle curiosity, for he was not of the elect. The love of a savage is instantaneous and overwhelming. He loved; he watched her afar off for a little time, fearful of stepping into the charmed circle that surrounded her. Their eyes had met; what the lip dares not utter in secret the eyes publish to the world. He piped to her in the twilight. He wooed her with both flute and harp —a bamboo nose-flute and a harp strung with horsehair: it is possible with this harp to say even unutterable things.

Night after night the bronzed one came out of his lair in the hills, and woke his lady from her Christian slumbers to listen to the loves of her race.

He pictured the life she had been so early weaned

from ; the divine passion inflamed him ; in his heart he caressed her. His beseeching songs grew more fervent, until they rose into threnes and lamentations, and then she yielded ; but flute and harp were not resigned until they had sounded the last strain of the epithalamium.

The pastor wedded them, because he saw that this marriage was the lesser of the two evils that threatened Elizabeth.

At long intervals she revisited her early home, but she seemed to have let fall from her, like a mantle, all the influence of domestic Puritan life. She was no longer Elizabeth, but Hokoolélé, the shooting star.

"And you prefer this life," I asked, "to any other?"

"Infinitely," she replied, in a tone of earnest conviction.

A little way down the stream stood a thatched hut ; thither I was conducted by the husband of Elizabeth, and for his sake and hers was most cordially welcomed by the master and his household.

The bronzed one bade me farewell, and vanished into the night ; I was to resume my pilgrimage to nowhere in particular on the morning following.

I had left Elizabeth standing in the firelight, bareheaded, bare-footed, bare-armed, and with a bare shift to cover her, as gentle a savage as ever drew breath or blood ; but I wondered if her wakeful eyes ever turned again to the luxury of shelter and plenty, and if the shadow of repentance never once plunged its airy dagger to her heart, and made horrible the long watches of the night.

A CANOE-CRUISE IN THE CORAL SEA

IF you can buy a canoe for two calico shirts, what will your annual expenses in Tahiti amount to? This was a mental problem I concluded to solve, and, having invested my two shirts, I began the solution in this wise: My slender little treasure lay with half its length on shore, and being quite big enough for two, I looked about me, seeking some-one to sit in the bows, for company and ballast.

Up and down the shady beach of Papeete I wandered, with this advertisement written all over my anxious face :

"WANTED—A crew about ten years of age; of a mild disposition, and with no special fondness for human flesh ; not particular as to sex. Apply immediately, at the new canoe, under the breadfruit-tree, Papeete, South Pacific."

Some young things were pitching French coppers so earnestly they didn't read my face ; some were not seafaring at that moment ; while most of them evidently ate more than was good for them, which might result disastrously in a canoe-cruise, and I set my heart against them. The afternoon was waning, and my ill-luck seemed to urge upon me the necessity of my constituting a temporary press-gang for the kidnapping of the required article.

"Who is anxious to go to sea with me?" I bawled, returning through the crowds of young gamblers, all intently disinterested in everything but "pitch and toss." Not far away a group of wandering minstrels—such as make musical the shores of Tahiti—sat in the middle of the street, chanting. One youth played with considerable skill upon a joint of bamboo, of the flute species, but breathed into from the nostrils, instead of from the lips. Three or four minor notes were piped at uncertain intervals, in an impromptu variation upon the air of the singers. Drawing near, the music was suspended, and I proposed shipping one of the melodious vagabonds; whereupon the entire chorus expressed a willingness to accompany me, in any capacity whatever, remarking, at the same time, that "they were a body bound, so to speak, by chords of harmony, and any proposal to disband them would by it be regarded as highly absurd." Then I led the solemn procession of volunteers to my canoe, and we regarded it in silence; it was something larger than a pea-pod, to be sure, but about the shape of one. After a moment of deliberation, during which a great throng of curious spectators had assembled, the orchestra declared itself in readiness to ship before the paddle for the trifling consideration of $17. I knew the vague notion that money is money, call it dollar or dime, generally enter-

tained by the innocent children of Nature ; and dazzling the unaccustomed eyes of the flutist with a new
two-franc piece he immediately embarked. The bereaved singers sat on the shore and lifted up their
voices in resounding discord, as the canoe slid off
into the still waters, and my crew with commendable fortitude, laid down the nose-flute, took up the
paddle, and we began our canoe-cruise.

The frail thing glided over the waves as though
invisible currents were sweeping her into the hereafter ; the shore seemed to recede, drawing the low,
thatched houses into deeper shadow ; other canoes
skimmed over the sea, like great water-bugs, while
the sun set beyond the sharp outlines of beautiful
Morea, glorifying it and us.

There was a small islet not far away—an islet as
fair and fragrant as a bouquet—looking, just then,
like a mote in a sheet of flame. Thither I directed
the reformed flutist, and then let myself relapse
into the all-embracing quietness that succeeds nearly
every vexation that flesh is heir to.

There was something soothing in the nature of
my crew. He sat with his back to me—a brown
back, that glistened in the sun, and arched itself,
from time to time, cat-like, as though it was very
good to be brown and bare and shiny. From the
waist to the feet fell the resplendent folds of a
pareu, worn by all Tahitians, of every possible age
and sex, and consisting, in this case, of a thin breadth
of cloth, stamped with a deep blue firmament, in
which supernaturally yellow suns were perpetually

setting in several spots. A round head topped his
chubby shoulders, and was shaven from the neck to
the crown, with a matted forelock of the blackness
of darkness falling to the eyes and keeping the sun
out of them.   One ear was enlivened with a crescent
of beaten gold, which decoration, having been won
at " pitch and toss," will probably never again, in the
course of human events, meet with its proper mate.
On the whole he looked just a little bit like a fan-
tail pigeon with his wings plucked.

At this point my crew suddenly rose in the bows
of the canoe, making several outlandish flourishes
with his broad paddle. I was about to demand the
occasion of his sudden insanity, when we began to
grate over some crumbling substance that materially
impeded our progress and suggested all sorts of
disagreeable sensations—such as knife-grinding in
the next yard, or saw-filing round the corner. It
was as though we were careering madly over a multitude of fine-tooth combs. With that caution which
is inseparable from canoe cruising in every part of
the known world, I leaned over the side of my personal property and penetrated the bewildering depths
of the coral sea.

Were we, I asked myself, suspended about two
feet above a garden of variegated cauliflowers ? Or
were the elements wafting us over a minute winter-
forest, whose fragile boughs were loaded with prismatic crystals ?

The scene was constantly changing : now it
seemed a disordered bed of roses—pink, and white,

and orange ; presently we weie floating in the air,
looking down upon a thousand-domed mosque, pale
in the glamour of the Oriental moon ; and then a
wilderness of bowers presented itself—bowers whose
fixed leaves still seemed to quiver in the slight ripple
of the sea—blossoming for a moment in showers of
buds, purple, and green, and gold, but fading almost as soon as born. I could scarcely believe my
eyes, when these tiny. though marvellously brilliant,
fish shot suddenly out from some lace-like structure,
each having the lurid and flame-like beauty of sulphurous fire, and all turning instantly, in sudden con-
sternation at finding us so near, and secreting themselves in the coral pavilion that amply sheltered
them. Among the delicate anatomy of these frozen
ferns our light canoe was crashing on its way. I
saw the fragile structures overwhelmed with a single
blow from the young savage, who stood erect, pro-
pelling us onward amid the general ruins. With my
thumb and finger I annihilated the laborious monu-
ments of centuries, and saw havoc and desolation
in our wake.

There, in one of God's reef-walled and cliff-shel-
tered *aquaria*, we drifted, while the sky and sea were
glowing with the final, triumphant gush of sunset
radiance. Fefe at last broke the silence, with an
interrogation : "Well, how you feel?" "Fefe," I
replied, "I feel as though I were some good and
faithful bee, sinking into a sphere of amber, for a
sleep of a thousand years." Fefe gave a deep-mouthed
and expressive grunt, as he laid his brown profile

against the sunset sky, thereby displaying his solitary ear-ring to the best advantage, and with evident
personal satisfaction. "And how do you feel, Fefe?"
I asked. He was mum for a moment; arched his
back like any wholesome animal when the sun has
struck clean through it; ejaculated an ejaculation
with his tongue and teeth that cannot possibly be
spelled in English, and thereupon his nostril quiv-
ered spasmodically, and was only comforted by the
immediate application of his nose-flute, through
which dulcet organ he confessed his deep and otherwise unutterable joy. I blessed him for it, though
there were but three notes, all told, and those minors
and a trifle flat.

Fefe's impassioned soul having subsided, we both
looked over to beautiful Morea, nine miles away.
How her peaks shone like steel, and her valleys
looked full of sleep! while here and there one gold-
en ray lingered for a moment to put the final touch
to a fruit it was ripening or a flower it was painting
—for they each have their perfect work allotted to
them, and they leave it not half completed.

It was just the hour that harmonizes everything
in nature, and when there is no possible discord in
all the universe. The fishes were baptizing themselves by immersion in space, and kept leaping into
the air, like momentary inches of chain-lightning.
Our islet swam before us, spiritualized—suspended,
as it were, above the sea—ready at any moment to
fade away. The waves had ceased beating upon the
reef; the clear, low notes of a bell vibrating from

the shore called us to prayer. Fefe knew it, and
was ready—so was I ; and with bare heads and souls
utterly at peace we gave our hearts to God—for the
time being !

Then came the hum of voices and the rustle of
renewed life. On we pressed toward our islet, under the increasing shadows of the dusk. A sloping
beach received us ; the young cocoa-palms embraced
one another with fringed branches. Through green
and endless corridors we saw the broad disk of the
full moon hanging above the hill.

Fefe at once chose a palm, and having ascended
to its summit cast down its fruit. Descending, he
planted a stake in the earth, and striking a nut
against its sharpened top soon laid open the fibrous
husk, with which a fire was kindled.

Taking two peeled nuts in his hands, he struck
one against the other and laid open the skull of it
—a clear sort of scalping that aroused me to enthusiasm. There is one end of a cocoanut's skull
as delicate as a baby's, and a well directed tap does
the business; possibly the same result would follow
with those of infants of the right age—twins, for
instance. Fefe agrees with me in this theory, now
first given to the public.

Then followed much talk, on many topics, over
our tropical supper—said supper consisting of sea-
weed salad, patent self-stuffing banana-sausages, and
cocoanut hash. We argued somewhat, also, but in
South Pacific fashion—which would surely spoil, if
imported ; I only remember, and will record, that

12

Fefe regarded the nose-flute as a triumph of art, and considered himself no novice in musical science, as applicable to nose-flutes in a land where there is scarcely a nose without its particular flute, and many a flute is silent forever, because its special nose is laid among the dust.

Having eaten, I proposed sleeping on the spot, and continuing the cruise at dawn. " Why should we return to the world and its cares, when the sea invites us to its isles? Nature will feed us. In that blessed land clothing has not yet been discovered. Let us away!" I cried. At this juncture voices came over the sea to us—voices chanting like sirens upon the shore. Instinctively Fefe's nose-flute resumed its *tremolo*, and I knew the day was lost. "Come!" said the little rascal, as though he were captain and I the crew, and he dragged me toward the skiff. With terrific emphasis, I commanded him to desist. " Don't imagine," I said, " that this is a modern *Bounty*, and that it is your duty to rise up in mutiny for the sake of dramatic justice. Nature never repeats herself, therefore come back to camp!"

But he wouldn't come. I knew I should lose my canoe unless I followed, or should have to paddle back alone—no easy task for one unaccustomed to it. So I moodily embarked with him; and having pushed off into deep water, he sounded a note of triumph that was greeted with shouts on shore, and I felt that my fate was sealed.

It had been my life-dream to bid adieu to the

human family, with one or two exceptions; to sever
every tie that bound me to anything under the sun;
to live close to Nature, trusting her, and getting
trusted by her.

I explained all this to the young "Kanack," who
was in a complete state of insurrection, but failed to
subdue him. Overhead the air was flooded with
hazy moonlight; the sea looked like one immeasura-
ble drop of quicksilver, and upon the summit of this
luminous sphere our shallop was mysteriously
poised. A faint wind was breathing over the ocean;
Fefe erected his paddle in the bows, placed against
it a broad mat that constituted part of my outfit for
that new life of which I was defrauded, and on we
sped like a belated sea-bird seeking its mossy
nest.

Beneath us slept the infinite creations of another
world, gleaming from the dark bosom of the sea
with an unearthly pallor, and seeming to reveal
something of the forbidden mysteries that lie beyond the grave. "La Petite Pologne," whispered
Fefe, as he arched his back for the last time, and
stepped on shore at the foot of this singular rendez-
vous—a narrow lane threading the groves of Papeete, bordered by wine-shops, bakeries, and a convent wall, lit at night by smoky lanterns hanging
motionless in the dead air of the town, and thronged
from 7 P.M. till 10 P.M. by people from all quarters
of the globe.

Fefe having resumed his profession as soon as his
bare foot was on his native heath again, the min-

strels moved in a hollow square through the centre of La Petite Pologne. They were rendering some Tahitian madrigal—a three-part song, the solo, or first part, of which being got safely through with—a single stanza—it was repeated as a duo, and so re-repeated through simple addition with a gradually-increasing chorus; the nose-flute meantime getting delirious, and sounding its *finale* in an ecstasy prolonged to the point of strangulation, when the whole unceremoniously terminated, and everybody took a rest and a fresh start. During these performances, the audience was dense and demonstrative. Fefe was in his element, sitting with his best side to the public, and flaunting his ear-ring mightily. A dance followed: a dance always follows in that land of light hearts, and as one after another was ushered into the arena and gave his or her body to the interpretation of such songs as would startle Christian ears—albeit there be some Christian hearts less tender, and Christian lips less true—to my surprise, Fefe abandoned his piping and danced before me, and then came a flash of intuition—rather late, it is true, but still useful as an explanatory supplement to my previous vexations. "Fefe!" I gasped (Fefe is the Tahitian for *Elephantiasis*), and my Fefe raised his or her skirts, and danced with a shocking leg. I really can't tell you *what* Fefe was. You never can tell by the name. He might have been a boy, or she might have been a girl, all the time. I don't know that it makes any particular difference to me what it was, but I cannot encourage elephantiasis in anything, and therefore I concluded my naval engagement with Fefe, and solemnly walked toward my chamber, scarcely a block off. The music followed me to my door with a song of some kind or other, but the real nature of which I was too sensitive definitely to ascertain.

Gazelle-eyed damsels, with star-flowers dangling from their ears, obstructed the way. The *gendarmes* regarded me with an eye single to France and French principles. Mariners arrayed in the blue of their own sea and the white of their own breakers bore down upon us with more than belonged to them. Men of all colors went to and fro, like mad creatures; women followed; children careered hither and thither. Wild shouts rent the air; there was an intoxicating element that enveloped all things. The street was by no means straight, though it could scarcely have been narrower; the waves staggered up the beach, and reeled back again; the moon leered at us, looking blear-eyed as she leaned against a cloud; and half-nude bodies lay here and there in dark corners, steeped to the toes in rum. Out of this human maelstrom, whose fatal tide was beginning to sweep me on with it, I made a plunge for my door-knob and caught it. Twenty besetting sins sought to follow me, covered with wreaths and fragrant with sandal-wood oil; twenty besetting sins rather pleasant to have around one, because by no means as disagreeable as they should be. Fefe was there also, and I turned to address him a parting word—a word calculated to do its work in a soil particularly mellow.

"Fefe," I said, "how can I help regarding it as a dispensation of Providence that your one leg is considerably bigger than your other? How can I expect you, with your assorted legs, to walk in that straight and narrow way wherein I have frequently found it inconvenient to walk myself, to say nothing of the symmetry of my own extremities? Therefore, adieu, child of the South, with your one earring and your piano-forte leg ; adieu—forever."

With that I closed my door upon the scene, and strove to bury myself in oblivion behind the white window-shade. In vain: the shadow with the mustache and goatee still pursued the shadow with the flowing locks that fled too slowly. Voices faint though audible indulged in allusions more or less profane, and with a success which would be considered highly improper in any latitude.

Thus sinking into an unquiet sleep, with a dream of canoe-cruising in a coral sea, whose pellucid waves sang sadly upon the remote shores of an ideal sphere, across the window loomed the gigantic shadow of some brown beauty, whose vast proportions suggested nothing more lovely than a new Sphinx, with a cabbage in either ear.

UNDER A GRASS ROOF

A LEAF TORN AT RANDOM FROM A TROPICAL
NOTE-BOOK.

AT Kahakuloa, under a terrific hill and close
upon a frothing tongue of the sea, I draw
rein. The act is simply a formality of mine; probably the animal would have paused here of his own
free will, for he has been rehearsing his stops a
whole hour back, during which time he limped
somewhat and reaped determinedly the few tufts of
dry grass that Nature had provided him by the trail-
side. The clouds are falling; the cliffs are festooned
with damp gauze; the air is moist and cool; a grass
hut of uncommon purity stands invitingly by. A
moon-faced youth, whose spotless garments appealed
to me as he overtook our caravan a mile back, says,
"Will you eat and sleep?" I am but human, and a
hungry and sleepy human, at that; so I tip off from
my mule's back with gratitude and alacrity. In a
moment the fine linen of mine host is hung upon its
peg, and a good study of the Nude returns to me
for further orders. I am literally famishing, and the
mule is already up to his ears in water-cress; but
then I have ridden and he has carried me. How
just, O Mother Nature, are thy judgments!

With the superb poses of a trained athlete, the Nude swings a fowl by the neck, and shortly it is plucked and potted together with certain vegetables of the proper affinities. Then he swathes a fish in succulent leaves, and buries it in hot ashes; and then he smokes his peace-pipe. Pipe no sooner lighted than mouths mysteriously gather: five, ten, a dozen of them magically assemble at the smell of smoke and take their turn at the curled shell, with a hollow stalk for a mouth piece. Dinner at last. O fish, fruit, and fowl on a mat on a floor in a grass hut at evening! How excellent are these—amen! Night —supper over—someone twanging upon a stringed instrument of rude native origin. Gossip lags— darkness and silence and a cigarette. The Nude rises haughtily and lights a lamp that looks very like a diminutive coffe-pot with a great flame in the nose of it. He hangs it against a beam already blackened with smoke to the peak of the roof. Again the peace-pipe sweeps the home-circle, and is passed out to the mouths of the neighborhood.

Guests drop down upon us and fill the one aper- ture of the hut with rows of curious, welcoming faces; assorted dogs press through the door in turn, receive a slap from each member of the family, and retreat with invisible tails; sudden impulses set all tongues wagging in unison; impulses, equally sud- den and unaccountable, enjoin protracted intervals of silence. The sea breathes heavily; there is a noise of rain-drops sliding down the thatch. Guests disperse with a kind "*aloha.*" We are alone with the

night. The spirit of repose descends upon us ; one
by one the dusky members of mine host's household
roll themselves into mummies and lie in a solemn
row along the side of the room, sleeping. I, also,
will sleep. A great bark-cloth (*kapa*), that rattles as
though it had received seven starchings, is all mine
for covering—a royal *kapa* this, of exceeding stiff-
ness. I lie with my eyes to the roof, and count the
beams that look like an arbor. What is it, as large
as my thumb, cased in brown armor? A roach !—
a melancholy procession of roaches passing from one
side of the hut, over the roof, with their backs downward, and descending on the other side by the
beams—a hundred of them, perhaps, or a thousand :
the cry is, " Still they come ! " There is a noise of
tiny feet upon the roof, and it isn't rain ; there is
a sound as of falling objects that escape before I
can catch them. My hand rests upon a cool, moist
creature that writhes under it—an animated spinal
column with four legs at one end of it. Away, thou
slimy newt ! Something runs over the matting,
making a still, small clatter as it goes—something
looking like a toy train of dirt-cars. Ha ! the ven-
omous and wily centipede ! Put out the coffee-pot,
for these sights are horrible !

Now I will sleep with my face under the *kapa*—
silence, serene silence, and darkness profound ; the
sea beating in agony at the foot of the big hill—a
time for lofty and sublime reverie. More rain outside the hut ; gusts of wind, wailing as they rush
past us. Thanks for this shelter. My pillow satu-

rated with cocoanut-oil—ah, what savage dreams
may have disturbed these sleepers! No matter.
Will get a wink of sleep before daybreak. Sleep, at
last—how refreshing art thou!

Hello! the coffee-pot in a blaze again; the Nude
smoking his peace-pipe; children eating and making merry. Daybreak? No; midnight, perchance
—darkness without, darkness once more (by request) within. "Come again, bright dream." Horror! the house shaken as by an earthquake—gnash-
ing of teeth distinctly audible; the mule undoubtedly eating up the side of the grass hut! Anon, quiet
restored. A suggestion of moonlight through the
open door; the twanging of the stringed affair: a
responsive twang in the distance. Someone steals
cautiously forth into the starlight. All is not well
in Kahakuloa. Rain over; mule vegetating elsewhere; roaches subdued; sea comparatively quiet.
Welcome, kind Nature's sweet restorer! . . .
Humming of voices; rolling of dogs about the
house; ditto of children, ditto; broad daylight, and
breakfast waiting. Mule saddled, and, with a
mouthful of roses, looking fresh and happy. Mule-
boy eager for the fray. Time up. Adieu, adieu—
O beautiful Kahakuloa! I must away.

Above the terrible hill hang clouds and shadows;
fringes of rain obscure the trail as it climbs persist-
ently to heaven; but up that trail, into and through
those clouds and shadows, I pursue my solitary pilgrimage.

MY SOUTH-SEA SHOW

HIGH in her lady's chamber sat Gail, looking with calm eyes through the budding maples across the hills of spring. Her letter was but half finished, and the village post was even then ready; so she woke out of her reverie, and ended the writing as follows :

"SPRING, ——.

"I know not where you may be at this moment—living with what South-Sea Island god, drinking the milk of cocoanut, and eating bread-fruit—but wherever you are, forget not your promise to come home again, bringing your sheaves with you."

Anon she sealed it and mailed it, and it was hurried away, over land and sea, till, after many days, it found me drinking my cocoa-milk and refreshing myself with bread-fruits.

Anon I replied to her, not on the green enamel of a broad leaf, with a thorn stylet, but upon the blank margins of Gail's letter, with my last half inch of pencil. I said to her :

"SUMMER, ——.

"By and by I will come to you, when the evenings are very long, and the valley is still. I will cross the lawn in silence, and stand knocking at the south entry. Deborah will open the door to me with fear and trembling, for I shall be sunburnt and brawny, with a baby cannibal under each arm. Then at a word a tattooed youngster shall reach her a Tahitian pearl and I will cry, 'Give it to Mistress Gail;' whereat Deborah will willingly withdraw, leaving me motionless in the dead leaves by the south entry. You will take the token, dear Gail, and know it as the symbol of my return. You will come and greet us, and lead us to the best chamber, and we will feast with you as long as you like—I and my cannibals."

I was never quite sure of what Gail said to my letter, but I knew her for a true soul ; so I gathered my cannibals under my metaphorical wings, and journeyed unto the village, and came into it at sunset, while it was autumn. We passed over the lawn in silence, and stood knocking at the south entry, in real earnest. Deborah came at last, and the little striped fellow bore aloft his pearl of Tahitian beauty, while I gave my message, and Deborah was terrified and thought she was dreaming. But she took the pearl and went, and we stood in the keen air of autumn, and my South Sea babies were very cold and moaned pitifully under my arms, and the little pearl-bearer shivered in all his stripes, and capered in the dead leaves like an imp of darkness.

Then Gail came to us and let us in, and we camped by the great fire in the sitting-room, whither Deborah brought bowls of new milk for the little ones, and was wonderfully amazed at their quaintness and beauty, but quite failed to affiliate with my striped pearl-bearer.

So I said, "Sit you down, Deborah, and hear the true story of my Zebra." Gail had already captured the bronze babies, and was helping them with their bowls of milk as they nestled at her feet, and I took my striped beauty between my knees and stroked his soft wool, and told how he saved me from a watery death, and again from the fiery stake, and was doubly dear to me forevermore :

"We were at the island of Pottobokee, getting water and fruit; had stacked the last sack of mangoes and limes in the boat, and were off for the ship, glad to escape with our scalps, when a wave took us amidships on the reef, and we swamped in the dreadful spume. Some were drowned; some clung to the boat, though it was stove badly, while relief came from the vessel as quickly as possible, and the fragments were gathered out of the waves and taken aboard.

"They thought themselves lucky to escape with the remnants, for they knew the natives for cannibals, and the shore was black and noisy within ten minutes after the accident. It looked stormy in that neighborhood, hence the caution and haste of the relief-crew, who left me for drowned, I suppose, as they never came after me, but spread everything, and went out of sight before dark that evening.

"I was no swimmer at all, but I kicked well, and was about diving the fatal dive—last of three warnings that seem providentially allotted the luckless soul in its extremity; I was just upon the third sinking, when a tough little arm gripped me under the breast, and I hung over it limp and senseless, knowing nothing further of my deliverance, until I found myself a captive in Kabala-kum—a heathenish sort of paradise, a little way back from the sea-coast.

"The natives had given up all hope of feasting upon me, for there wasn't a respectable steak in my

whole carcass, nor was my appetite promising; so
they resolved to make a bonfire of me, to get me out
of the way. But that tough little arm that saved me
from an early grave in the water was husband to a
tough little heart, that resolved I shouldn't be burnt.
I was his private and personal property; he had
fished me out of the sea; he would cook me in his
own style when he got ready, and no one else was to
have a word in the matter.

"There he showed his royal blood, Deborah, for
he was the King's son: this marvellous tattooing
proclaims his rank. Only the noble and brave are
permitted to brand these rainbows into their brown
skins.

"I was almost frightened when I first returned to
consciousness, and saw this little fellow pawing me
in his tender and affectionate way. He was lithe as
a panther, and striped all over with brilliant and
changeless stripes; so I called him my boy Zebra,
and I suppose he called me his white mouse, or
something of that sort.

"Well, he saved me at all events; and having
heard something of you and Gail from me, he wanted
to see you very much, and we made our escape together, though he had to sacrifice all his bone-
jewelry, and lots of skulls and scalps: and here he
is, and you must like him, Deborah, because he is a
little heathen, and doesn't go to Sabbath school, as a
general thing, and worships idols very badly."

Deborah did me the compliment to absorb a tear
in the broad hem of her apron, at the conclusion of

my episode, whereat my beautiful Zebra regarded
her in utter amazement, then turned his queer face
—ringed, streaked, and striped—up to mine, and
laughed his barbaric laugh. He was wonderful to
see, with his breast like a pigeon ; his round, supple,
almost voluptuous limbs, peculiar to his amphibious
tribe ; his head crowned with a turban of thick
wool, so fine and flossy, it looked as though it had
been carded : it stood two inches deep at a tangent
from his oval pate.

From his woolly crown to the soles of his feet, my
Zebra was frescoed in the most brilliant and artistic
fashion. Every color under the sun seemed pricked
into his skin (there he discounted the zebras, who
are limited in their combinations of light and
shade) ; this, together with the multiplicity of figures therein wrought, was a never-failing joy to me.
O my Zebra ! how did you ever grow so splendid
off yonder in the South Seas ?

We chatted that evening. by Gail's fire, till my
Zebra's woolly head went clean to the floor, and he
looked like some prostrate idol about to be immo-
lated on that Christian hearth ; and the baby cannibals were as funny as two little brown rabbits, with
their ears clipped, nestling at Gail's patient feet.

It was fully nine o'clock by this time, so Deborah
got the Bible, smoothed out her apron, and opened
it thereon, while she read a chapter. We sat by the
fire and listened. I heard the earnest voice of the
reader, while the autumn winds rose in gusts, and
puffed out the curtains now and then. I thought of

the chilly nights and frosty mornings we were to endure—we exiles of the South. I thought of the
snows that were to follow, and of the little idolators
sleeping through the gospel, with deaf ears while
their hearts panted high in some dream of savage
joy.

There was a big bed made up on the floor of my
room—the best Chamber at Gail's—and there I laid
out my little pets, tucking them in with infinite concern; for they looked so like three diminutive mummies, as they lay there, that I didn't know whether
they would think it worth while to wake up again
into life; and what would I be worth then, without
my wild boys?—I, who was born by some mischance
out of my tropical element, and whose birthright is
Polynesia! Gail laughed when she saw me fretting
so, and she patted the curly heads of the babies,
and stroked the Zebra's shaggy pate, and said
" Good-night " to us, as her step measured the hall,
and a door closed in the distance; whereupon, instead of freezing in the icy linen of the spare bed at
the other end of the room, I crept softly into the
nest of cannibals, and we slept like kittens until
morning.

At a seasonable hour the next day, I got my
jewels—my little inhuman jewels—into their thick,
winter clothes again, and we trotted down to breakfast, as hungry as bears. Deborah was good enough
to embrace both the little ones, but she gave the
Zebra a wide berth, and was not entirely satisfied at
leaving him loose in the house.

He was rather odd-looking, I confess. He used to curl up under the table and go to sleep, at all hours of the day—I think it was the cold weather that encouraged him in it—stretching himself, now and then, like a spaniel, and showing his sharp saw-teeth in a queer way, when he laughed in his dreams. Presently Gail came in, and we sat at table, and came near to eating her out of house and home. Deborah said grace—rather a long one, considering we were so hungry—a grace in which my babies were not forgotten, and the Zebra was made the subject of a special prayer. To my horror, Zebra was helping himself surreptitiously to the nearest dish, the while. It was a merry meal. I rose in the midst of it, and laid before Gail an enormous placard, printed in as many colors as even the Zebra could boast, and Gail read it out to Deborah:

JENKINS' HALL.
IMMENSE ATTRACTION!
FOR ONE NIGHT ONLY!
HOKY AND POKY,
A BRACE OF SOUTH-SEA BABIES, FROM THE ANCIENT RIVERS OF
KABALA-KUM,
—and—
THE WONDERFUL BOY
ZEBRA,
A CANNIBAL PRINCE, FROM THE PALMY PLAINS OF POTTOBOKEE,
IN THEIR GRAND MORAL DIVERSION.

☞ The first and only opportunity is now afforded the great public
to observe with safety how the heathen, in his blindness,
bows down to wood and stone.

☞ These are the only original and genuine representatives of the
Kabalakumists and Pottobokees that ever left
their coral strand.

ADMISSION, ——. CHILDREN, HALF PRICE.

13

Deborah was awed into silence, and Gail was apparently thinking over the possible result of this strange advertisement, for she said nothing, but took deliberate sips of coffee, and broke the dry toast between her fingers, while she looked at all four of us savages in a peculiar and ominous manner. Nothing was said, however, to disparage any further announcement of the entertainment; and, having appeased our hunger, we adjourned to the reading of another chapter, during which the South Sea babies *would* play cat's-cradles under Gail's writing-table, and the Zebra put his foot into the middle of her work-basket, and was very miserable indeed.

My hands were full of business. As an *impressario* I had to rush about all day, mustering the Great Public for the evening. Out I went, full of it, while the bronze midgets were left in charge of Gail and Deborah, and the Zebra was locked in an upper room, with plenty to eat, and no facilities for getting into mischief. I saw the leading men in town : the preacher, who was deeply interested, proposing to take up a collection on the next Sabbath for our benefit—which proposition I received with a graceful acquiescence peculiarly my own; the professor, at the Seminary, who was less affable, but whose pupils were radiant at the prospect of getting into the cannibals at reduced rates; and the editor, who desired to print full biographies of myself and cannibals, with portraits and fac-similes of autographs. He strongly urged the plausibility of this new method of winning the heart of the

Great Public, and was willing to take my note for thirty days, in consideration of his personal friendship for me, and his sympathy, as a public man and a member of the press, with the show business.

Everything worked so nicely that it really seemed quite providential that I had come as I had, like anything in the night—noiseless and unheralded. Everything was in good order, and, after our late dinner, I went out again, to finish for the evening— portioning off my charges, as before, and returning, at the last moment, to bring them up to the hall for their *début*. But judge of my horror at finding my Zebra stretched upon the floor of his room, quite insensible ; and all this time Jenkins's Hall was thronged with the Great Public, who had come to see us bow down to wood and stone.

I was greatly alarmed. What could this sudden attack mean ? He was not subject to disorders of that nature—at least I had never seen him in a similar condition. The little fellows began to cry, in their peculiar fashion, which is simply raising the voice to the highest and shrillest pitch, and then shaking to an unlimited degree. Gail was by no means charmed at these new developments, and Deborah fled from the room. In a moment the cause of our trouble was disclosed. Gail's cologne bottles were exhumed from under the bed, but quite empty. Their contents had been imbibed by the Zebra in an extemporaneous bacchanalian festival, tendered to himself by himself, in honor of the occasion.

It was useless to borrow further trouble, so I pre-

pared my apology : " The sudden indisposition peculiar to young cannibals during the early stages of
a public and Christian career had quite prostrated
the representative from many a palmy plain ; and
the South-Sea babies would endeavor to fill the vacancy caused by his absence with several new and
interesting features not set down in the bills."

I was most cordially received by the audience,
and the little midgets danced their weird and fantastic dances, in the least possible clothing imaginable, and sang their love-lyrics, and chanted their
passionate war-chants, and gave the funeral wail in
a manner that reflected the highest credit upon
their respective South-Sea papas and mammas. I
considered it an entire success, and pocketed the
proceeds with considerable satisfaction.

But to return to my poor little Zebra. His co-
logne-spree had been quite too much for him. He
was mentally and physically demoralized, and could
be of no use to me, professionally, for a week at
least. I at once saw this, and as I had two or three
engagements during that time, I begged Gail to allow him to remain with her during his convales-
cence, while I went on with the babes and fulfilled
my engagements. She consented. Deborah also
promised to be very good to him. I think she took
a deeper interest in him when she found how very
human he was—a fact she did not fully realize until
he took to drinking.

On we went, through three little villages, in three
little valleys, with crowded houses every evening.

Delighted and enthusiastic audiences wanted the midgets passed around, just as we passed the bone fish-hooks and shark's teeth combs, for inspection.

About this time I received a short and decisive epistle from Gail—an immediate summons home. The Zebra, in an unwatched moment, had got into the kerosene, and was considered no longer a welcome guest at Gail's. Deborah was praying with him daily, which didn't seem to have the desired effect, for he was growing worse and worse every hour.

There were at least seven towns anxiously awaiting my South-Sea Lecture, with the " heathen in his blindness" attachment. Yet it was out of the question to think of pressing on in my tour, thereby sacrificing my poor Zebra, and possibly Gail as well. I feared it was already too late to save him, for I knew the nature of his ailment, and foresaw the almost inevitable result. When we returned, Gail met us with tears in her eyes and furrows of care foreshadowed in her face. I felt how great a responsibility I had shifted upon her shoulders, and accused myself roundly for such selfishness. The babes rushed into her arms with the first impulse of love, and refused to allow her out of their sight again for some hours.

Deborah was, even then, wrestling with the angels up in Zebra's room, and I waited until she came down, with her eyes red and swollen ; a bottle of physic in one hand and a Bible in the other ; then I went in to my poor, thin, shadowy little Zebra, who was wild-eyed and nervous, and scarcely knew me at first, but went off into hysterics the moment he found me out, to make up for it. He had had no opportunity of speaking to anyone, save in his broken English, for several days, and he rushed into a torrent of ejaculations so violent and confusing that I was thoroughly alarmed at his condition. Presently he grew quieter, from sheer exhaustion, and then I learned how he had taken Deborah's well-intended efforts toward his spiritual conversion. *He believed her praying him to death!* Deborah knew nothing of the sensitive organism of these islanders. When moved by a spirit of revenge, they threaten one another with prayers. Incantations are performed and sacrifices offered, under which fearful spells the unhappy victim of revenge cannot think of surviving. So he lies down and dies, without pain, or any effort on his part; and all your physic is like so much water, administer it in what proportions you choose.

I went into the garden, where I saw Gail under the maples—the very maples that were budding in pink and white when she wrote me the letter bidding me come out of the South, bringing my sheaves with me. The animated sheaves were even then swinging on the clothes-lines, and taking life easily. "Gail," I said, "O Gail, the Zebra is a dead boy!" Gail was shocked and silent. I told her how useless, how hopeless it was to think of saving him. All the doctors and all the medicines in the world were a fallacy where the soul was overshadowed with a malediction. "Gail," I said, "that Zebra says he wants to be an angel, and he couldn't possibly have decided upon anything more unreasonable than this. What shall I do without my Zebra?" And I walked off by myself, and felt desperately, while Gail was wrapped in thought, and the babes continued to do inexpressible things on the clothes-lines, to the intense admiration of three small boys on the other side of the garden-fence.

The doctor had already been called, and the physic that Deborah carried about with her was a legitimate draught prescribed by him. Little did he know of the death-angel that walks hand-in-hand with a superstition as antique as Mount Ararat. So day by day the little Zebra grew more and more slender, till his frail, striped skeleton stretched itself in a hollow of the bed, and great gleaming eyes watched me as they would devour me with deathless and passionate love.

Sometimes his soul seemed to steal out of his withering body and make mysterious pilgrimages into its native clime. I heard him murmuring and muttering in a language unfamiliar to me. I remembered that the chiefs had a dialect of their own— a vocabulary so sacred and secret that no commoner ever dared to study out its meaning. This I took to be his classical and royal tongue, for he was of the best blood of the kingdom, and a King's heir.

Deborah, at the delicate suggestion of Gail, discontinued her visitations to his chamber, as it seemed to excite him so sadly; but her earnest soul never rested from prayer in his behalf till his last breath was spent, and his splendid stripes grew livid for a moment, and seemed to change like the dolphin's before their waning glories were faded out in the lifeless flesh.

One twilight I took the midgets into the darkened room. They scarcely knew the thin, drawn face, with the slender, wiry fingers locked over it, but they recognized the death-stroke with prophetic instinct, and crouching at the foot of the bed, rocked their dusky bodies to and fro, to and fro, wailing the death-wail for Zebra.

Then I longed for wings to fly away with my savage brood—away over seas and mountains, till the palms waved again their phantom crests in the mellow starlight, and the sea moaned upon the reef, and the rivulet leaped from crag to crag through silence and shadow: where death seemed but a grateful sleep; for the soul that dawned in that quiet life had never known the wear and tear of this one, but was patient, and peaceful, and ready at any hour of summons.

Dear Gail strove to comfort me in my tribulation; but the Great Public went its way, and knew nothing of the young soul that was passing in speedy death. Yet the Great Public was my guide, philosopher, and friend. I could do nothing without its sanction and co-operation. I basked in its smiles. I trembled at the thought of its displeasure; and now death was robbing me of my hard-earned riches, and annihilating my best attraction. No wonder I fretted myself, and berated my ill-fortune. Poor Gail had her hands full to keep me within bounds. I rushed to the Zebra's room, and vowed to him that if he wouldn't die just yet, I would take him home at once to his kingdom, and we'd always live there, and die there, by and by, when we were full of years.

Alas, it was too late! "I want to be an angel," reiterated my Zebra, his thin face brightening with an unearthly light; "to be an angel," whispered that faint and failing voice, while his humid eyes glowed like twin moons sinking in the far, mystical horizon of the new life he was about to enter upon. I struggled with him no longer. I bowed down by his pillow, and pressed the shadowy form of my once beautiful Zebra. "Well, be an angel, little prince," said I; "be anything you please, now, for I have done my best to save you, and failed utterly."

So he passed hence to his destiny; and his nation wept not, neither wore they ashes upon their heads, nor burned seams in their flesh; for they knew not of his fate. But there was a small grave digged in the orchard, and at dusk I carrried the coffin in my arms thither: how light it was! he could have borne me upon his brawny shoulders once—strong as a lion's. Gail cried, and Deborah cried; and I was quite beside myself. The mites of cannibals ate earth and ashes, and came nearly naked to the obsequies, refusing to wear their jackets, though the air was frosty and the night promised snow. We knelt there, to cover Zebra for the last time.

crying and shivering, and feeling very, *very* miserable.

I took a little rest from business after that; seeing, meantime, a stone cut in this manner:

> Here lies,
> In this far land,
> A PRINCE OF THE SAVAGE SOUTH,
> And the Last of his Tribe.

But life called me into the arena again. A showman has little time to waste in mourning over his losses, however serious they may be.

One frosty evening I got my brace of cannibals into the lumbering ambulance that constituted my caravan, with our boxes of war-clubs and carved whale's-teeth lashed on behind us; plenty of buffalo-robes around us, and a layer of hot bricks underfoot, and so we started for our next scene of action. The inexorable calls of the profession forbade our lingering longer under Gail's hospitable roof; and it was not without pangs of inexpressible sorrow that we turned from her door, and knew not if we were ever again to enjoy the pure influences of her household.

My heart warmed toward poor, disconsolate Deborah in that moment, and I forgave her all, which was the most Christian act I ever yet performed. As we rode down the lane, I caught a glimpse of the low mound in the orchard, and I buried my little barbarians under my great-coat, so as to spare them a fresh sorrow, while I thought how, spring after

spring, that small grave would be covered with drifts
of pale apple-blossoms, and in the long winters it
would be hidden under the paler drifts of snow—
when it should be strewn with sea-shells, and laid
away under a cactus-hedge, in a dense and fragrant
shade ; and I gathered my little ones closer to me,
and said in my soul : " O, if the August Public could
only know them as I know them, it would doubt us
less, and love us more ! The Zebra is gone, indeed,
but my babes are here, fresh souls in perfect bodies,
like rareripe fruits, untouched as yet, with the nap
and the dew upon them." The stars sparkled and
flashed in the cloudless sky, as we hurried over the
crisp ground, a little bereaved, benighted company
of South-Sea strollers, who ask your charity, and
give their best in return for it.

I have told you of my South-Sea show. You may
yet have an opportunity of judging how you like it,
provided my baby heathens don't insist upon turning into angels before their time, after the manner of
the lamented Zebra. In the meantime, the dread
of this not improbable curbing of my high career is
but one of the sorrows of a South-Sea showman.

THE HOUSE OF THE SUN

MY Hawaiian oracle, Kahéle, having posed himself in compact and chubby grace, awaited his golden opportunity, which was not long a-coming. I sat on the steps of L——'s veranda, and yawned frightfully, because life was growing tedious, and I did not know exactly what to do next. L——'s house was set in the nicest kind of climate, at the foot of a great mountain, just at that altitude where the hot air stopped dancing, though it was never cool enough to shut a door, or to think of wearing a hat for any other purpose than to keep the sun out of one's eyes. L——'s veranda ran out into vacancy as blank as cloudless sky and shadowless sea could make it ; in fact, all that the eye found to rest upon was the low hill jutting off from one corner of the house beyond a jasmine in blossom ; and under the hill a flat-sailed schooner rocking in a calm. I think there was nothing else down the slope of the mountain but tangled yellow grass, that grew brown and scant as it crept into the torrid zone, a thousand feet below us, and there it had not the courage to come out of the earth at all ; so the picture ended in a blazing beach, with warm waves sliding up and

down it, backed by blue-watery and blue-airy space
for thousands and thousands of miles.

Why should not a fellow yawn over the situation?
especially as L—— was busy and could not talk
much, and L——'s books were as old as the hills
and a good deal drier.

Having yawned, I turned toward Kahéle, and
gnashed my teeth. The little rascal looked knowing; his hour had come. He fired off in broken
English, and the effect was something like this:

"Suppose we sleep in House of the Sun—we make
plenty good sceneries!"

"And where is that?' quoth I.

Kahéle's little lump of a nose was jerked up toward the great mountain at the back of L——'s
house. "Haleakala!" * cried he, triumphantly, for
he saw he had resurrected my interest in life, and
felt that he had a thing or two worth showing, a
glimpse of which might content me with this world,
dull as I found it just then. "Haleakala—the House
of the Sun—up before us," said Kahéle.

"And to get into the Sun's House?"

"Make a good climb up, and go in from the top!"

Ha! to creep up the roof and drop in at the sky-
light: this were indeed a royal adventure. "How
long would it take?"

Kahéle waxed eloquent. That night we should
sleep a little up on the slope of the mountain, lodging with the *haolis* (foreigners) among the first

*Haleakala, an extinct crater in the Sandwich Islands,
supposed to be the largest in the world.

clouds; in the morning we should surprise the sun in the turrets of his temple; then down—down—down into the crater, that had been strewn with ashes for a thousand years. After that, out on the other side, toward the sea, where the trade-winds blew, and the country was fresh and fruitful. The youngster sweated with enthusiasm while he strove to make me comprehend the full extent of the delights pertaining to this journey; and, as he finished, he made a rapid flank movement toward the animals, staked a few rods away.

It was not necessary that I should consent to undertake this expedition. He was eager to go, and he would see that I enjoyed myself when I went; but go I must, now that he had made up my mind for me. I confess, I was as wax in that climate. Yet, why not take this promising and uncommon tour? The charm of travel is to break new paths. I ceased to yawn any further over life. Kahéle went to the beasts and began saddling them. L——'s hospitality culminated in a bottle of cold black coffee, and a hamper of delicious sandwiches, such as Mrs. L—— excels in. I had nothing to do but to go. It did look like a conspiracy; but, as I never had the moral courage to fight against anything of that sort, I got into the saddle and went.

Turning for a moment toward the brute's tail, overcome with conflicting emotions, I said:

"Adieu, dear L——, thou picture of boisterous industry! Adieu, Mrs. L——, whose light is hid under the bushel of thy lord; but, as it warms him,

it is all right, I suppose, and thy reward shall come
to thee some day, I trust! By-by, multitudes of
little L——s, tumbling recklessly in the back-
yard, crowned with youth and robust health and
plenty of flaxen curls! Away, Kahéle! for it is toward evening, and the clouds are skating along
the roof of the House of the Sun. Sit not upon
the order of your going, but strike spurs at once—
and away!"

It was thus that I relieved myself. The prospect
of fresh adventure intoxicated me. I do not believe
I could have been bought off after that enlivening
farewell. The air of the highlands was charged with
electricity. I bristled all over with new life. I
wanted to stand up in my saddle and fly.

It seemed the boy had engaged a special guide for
the crater—one accustomed to feeling his way
through the bleak hollow, where any unpractised
feet must have surely gone astray. Kahéle offered
him a tempting bonus to head our little caravan at
once, though it goes sorely against the Hawaiian
grain to make up a mind inside of three days.
Kahéle managed the financial department, whenever
he had the opportunity, with a liberality worthy
of a purse ten times as weighty as mine; but, as he
afterward assured me, that guide was a fine man,
and a friend of his whom it was a pleasure and a
privilege to serve.

Of course it was all right, since I couldn't help
myself; and we three pulled up the long slopes of
Haleakala, while the clouds multiplied as the sun

sank, and the evening grew awfully still. Somewhere up among the low-hanging mist there was a
house full of *haolis*, and there we proposed to spend
the night. We were looking for this shelter with all
our six eyes, while we rode slowly onward, having
scarcely uttered a syllable for the last half hour.
You know there are some impressive sorts of solitude
that seal up a fellow's lips; he can only look about
him in quiet wonderment, tempered with a fearless
and refreshing trust in that Providence who has
enjoined silence. Well, this was one of those times;
and right in the midst of it Kahéle sighted a smoke-
wreath in the distance. To me it looked very like
a cloud, and I ventured to declare it such; but the
youngster frowned me down, and appealed to the
special guide for further testimony. The guide
declined to commit himself in the matter of smoke
or mist, as he ever did on all succeeding occasions,
being a wise guide, who knew his own fallibility. It
was smoke !—a thin, blue ribbon of it, uncoiling
itself from among the branches of the overhanging
trees, floating up and up and tying itself into double-
bow knots, and then trying to untie itself, but
perishing in the attempt.

In the edge of the grove we saw the little white
cottage of the *haolis;* and, not far away, a camp-fire,
with bright, red flames dancing around a kettle,
swung under three stakes with their three heads
together. Tall figures were moving about the camp,
looking almost like ghosts, in the uncertain glow
of the fire; and toward these lights and shadows

we jogged with satisfaction, scenting supper from afar.

"Halloo!" said we, with voices that did not sound very loud, up in that thin atmosphere.

"Halloo!" said they, with the deepest unconcern, as though they had been through the whole range of human experience, and there was positively nothing left for them to get excited over.

Some of their animals whinnied in a fashion that drew a response from ours. A dog barked savagely until he was spoken to, and then was obliged to content himself with an occasional whine. Some animal—a sheep, perhaps—rose up in the trail before us, and plunged into the bush, sending our beasts back on their haunches with fright. A field-cricket lifted up his voice and sang; and then a hundred joined him; and then ten thousand times ten thousand swelled the chorus, till the mountains were alive with singing crickets.

"Halloo, stranger! Come in and stop a bit, won't you?" That was our welcome from the chief of the camp, who came a step or two forward, as soon as we had ridden within range of the camp-fire.

And we went in unto them, and ate of their bread, and drank of their coffee, and slept in their blankets—or tried to sleep—and had a mighty good time generally.

The mountaineers proved to be a company of California miners, who had somehow drifted over the sea, and, once on that side, they naturally enough went into the mountains to cut wood, break trails,

14

and make themselves useful in a rough, out-of-door fashion. They had for companions and assistants a few natives, who, no doubt, did the best they could, though the Californians expressed considerable contempt for the "lazy devils, who were fit for nothing but to fiddle on a jew's harp."

We ate of a thin, hot cake, baked in a frying-pan over that camp fire ; gnawed a boiled bone fished out of the kettles swung under the three sticks ; drank big bowls of coffee, sweetened with coarse brown sugar and guiltless of milk ; and sat on the floor all the while, with our legs crossed, like so many Turks and tailors. We went to our blankets as soon as the camp-fire had smothered itself in ashes, though meanwhile Jack, chief of the camp, gathered himself to windward of the flames, with his hips on his heels and his chin on his knees, smoking a stubby pipe and talking of flush times in California. He was one of those men who could and would part with his last quarter, relying upon Nature for his bed and board. He said to me, "If you can rough it, hang on a while—what's to drive you off?" I could rough it: the fire was out, the night chilly ; so we turned in under blue blankets with a fuzz on them like moss, and, having puffed out the candle—that lived long enough to avenge its death in a houseful of villanous smoke—we turned over two or three times apiece, and, one after another, fell asleep. At the farther side of the house lay the natives, as thick as sheep in a pen, one of them a glossy black fellow, as sleek as a eunuch, born in the West Indies, but whose sands of life had been scattered on various shores. This sooty fellow twanged a quaint instrument of native workmanship, and twanged with uncommon skill. His art was the life of that savage community at the other end of the house. Again and again, during the night, I awoke and heard the tinkle of his primitive harp, mingled with the ejaculations of delight wrung from the hearts of his dusky and sleepless listeners.

Once only was that midnight festival interrupted. We all awoke suddenly and simultaneously, though we scarcely knew why; then the dog began to mouth horribly. My blanket-fellows—beds we had none—knew there was mischief brewing, and rushed out with their guns cocked. Presently the dog came in from the brush, complaining bitterly, and one of the miners shot at a rag fluttering among the bushes. In the morning we found a horse gone, and a couple of bullet-holes in a shirt spread out to dry. As soon as the excitement was over, we returned to the blankets and the floor. The eunuch tuned his harp anew and, after a long while, dawn looked in at the uncurtained window, with a pale, gray face, freckled with stars.

Kahéle saw it as soon as I did, and was up betimes. I fancy he slept little or none that night, for he was fond of music, and especially fond of such music as had made the last few hours more or less hideous. Everybody rose with the break of day, and there was something to eat long before sunrise, after which our caravan, with new vigor, headed for the summit.

Wonderful clouds swept by us ; sometimes we were lost for a moment in their icy depths. I could scarcely see the tall ears of my mule when we rode into those opaque billows of vapor that swept noiselessly along the awful heights we were scaling. It was a momentary but severe bereavement, the loss of those ears and the head that went with them, because I cared not to ride saddles that seemed to be floating in the air. What was Prince Firouz Schah to me, or what was I to the Princess of Bengal, that I should do this thing !

There are pleasanter sensations than that of going to heaven on horseback ; and we wondered if we should ever reach the point where we could begin to descend again to our natural level, and talk with people infinitely below us just then. Ten thousand perpendicular feet in the air ; our breath short ; our animals weak in the knees ; the ocean rising about us like a wall of sapphire, on the top of which the sky rested like a cover—we felt as though we were shut in an exhausted receiver, the victims of some scientific experiment for the delectation of the angels. We were at the very top of the earth. There was nothing on our side of it nearer to Saturn than the crown of our heads. It was deuced solemn, and a trifle embarrassing. It was as though we were personally responsible for the planet during the second we happened to be uppermost in the universe. I felt unequal to the occasion in that thin, relaxing atmosphere. The special guide, I knew, would shirk this august investiture, as he shirked everything else, save only the watchful care of my collapsing *porte-monnaie*. Kahéle, perhaps, would represent us to the best of his ability—which was not much beyond an amazing capacity for food and sleep, coupled with cheek for at least two of his size. There is danger in delay, saith the copybook; and while we crept slowly onward toward the rim of the crater, the sun rose, and we forgot all else save his glory. We had reached the mouth of the chasm. Below us yawned a gulf whose farther walls seemed the outlines of some distant island, within whose depths a sea of cloud was satisfied to ebb and flow, whose billows broke noiselessly at the base of the sombre walls among whose battlements we clung like insects. I wonder that we were not dragged into that awful sea, for strange and sudden gusts of wind swept past us, coming from various quarters, and rushing like heralds to the four corners of the heavens. We were far above the currents that girdle the lower earth, and seemed in a measure cut off from the life that was past. We lived and breathed in cloud-land. All our pictures were of vapor; our surroundings changed continually. Forests laced with frost; silvery, silent seas; shores of agate and of pearl; blue, shadowy caverns; mountains of light, dissolving and rising again transfigured in glorious resurrection, the sun tingeing them with infinite color. A flood of radiance swept over the mysterious picture—a deluge of blood-red glory that came and went like a blush; and then the mists faded and fled away, and gradually we saw the deep bed of the

crater, blackened, scarred, distorted — a desert of
ashes and cinders shut in by sooty walls; no tinge
of green, no suggestion of life, no sound to relieve
the imposing silence of that literal death of Nature.
We were about to enter the guest-chamber of the
House of the Sun. If we had been spirited away
to the enchanted cavern of some génie, we could not
have been more bewildered. The cloud-world had
come to an untimely end, and we were left alone
among its blackened and charred ruins. That ma-
gician, the sun, hearing the approach of spies, had
transformed his fairy palace into a bare and uninviting wilderness. But we were destined to explore
it, notwithstanding; and our next move was to dis-
mount and drive our unwilling animals over into the
abyss. The angle of our descent was too near the
perpendicular to sound like truth, in print. I will
not venture to give it; but I remember that our
particular guide and his beast were under foot, while
Kahéle and his beast were overhead, and I and my
beast, sandwiched between, managed to survive the
double horror of being buried in the *débris* that
rained upon us from the tail end of the caravan, and
slaying the unfortunate leaders ahead with the multitude of rocks we sent thundering down the cliff.
A moving avalanche of stones and dust gradually
brought us to the bed of the crater, where we offered
thanks in the midst of an ascending cloud of cinders,
every soul of us panting with exhaustion, and oozing
like a saturated sponge. The heat was terrific;
shelter there was none: L——'s coffee was all that

saved us from despair. Before us stretched miles
and miles of lava, looking like a scorched pie-crust;
two thousand feet above us hung heavy masses of
baked masonry, unrelieved by any tinge of verdure.
To the windward there was a gap in the walls,
through which forked tongues of mist ran in, but
curled up and over the ragged cliffs, as though the
prospect were too uninviting to lure them farther.
It behooved us to get on apace, for life in the deserted House of the Sun was, indeed, a burden, and
moreover there was some danger of our being locked
in. The wind might veer a little, in which case an
ocean of mist would deluge the crater, shutting out
light and heat, and bewildering the pilgrim so that
escape were impossible. The loadstone bewitched
the compass in that fixed sea, and there were no
beacons and no sounding signals to steer by. Across
the smooth, hard lava occasional traces of a trail
were visible, like scratches upon glass. Close to the
edges of this perilous path yawned chasms. Sometimes the narrow way led over a ridge between two
sandy hollows, out of which it was almost impossible
to return, if one false step should plunge you into
its yielding vortex. There was a long pull toward
afternoon, and a sweltering camp about three P.M.,
where we finished L——'s lunch, and were not half
satisfied. Even the consoling weed barely sustained
our fainting spirits, for we knew that the more tedious portion of the journey was yet to come.

The windward vestibule wound down toward the
sea, a wild gorge through which the molten lava had

poured its destructive flood. There it lay, a broad, uneven pass of dead, black coals—clinkers as ragged and sharp as broken glass—threaded by one beaten track a few inches in breath. To lose this trail were to tear the hoofs from your suffering beasts in an hour or two, and to lacerate your own feet in half the time. Having refreshed ourselves on next to nothing, we pressed forward. Already the shadows were creeping into the House of the Sun, and as yet we had scarcely gained the mouth of the pass. As we rode out from the shelter of a bluff, a cold draught struck us like a wave of the sea. Down the bleak, winding chasm we saw clouds approaching, pale messengers that travel with the trade-wind and find lodgement in the House of the Sun. They were hastening home betimes, and had surprised us in the passage. It was an unwelcome meeting. Our particular guide ventured to assume an expression of concern, and cautiously remarked that we were *pilikia*—that is, in trouble! For once he was equal to an emergency; he knew of a dry well close at hand; we could drop into it and pass the night, since it was impossible to feel our way out of the crater through clouds almost as dense as cotton. Had we matches? No. Had we dry sticks? Yes, in the well, perhaps. Kahéle could make fire without phosphorus, and we could keep warm till morning, and then escape from the crater as early as possible. After much groping about, in and out of clouds, we found the dusty well and dropped into it. Ferns—a few of them—grew about its sides;

a dwarfed tree, rejoicing in four angular branches as full of mossy elbows as possible, stood in the centre of our retreat, and at the roots of this miserable recluse the Kanakas contrived to grind out a flame by boring into a bit of decayed wood with a dry stick twirled rapidly between their palms. Dead leaves, dried moss, and a few twigs made a short-lived and feeble fire for us. Darkness had come upon the place. We watched the flaming daggers stab the air fitfully, and finally sheathe themselves for good. We filled our shallow cave with smoke that drove us into the mouth of it, from time to time, to keep from strangulation. We saw our wretched beasts shaking with cold; we saw the swift, belated clouds hurrying onward in ghostly procession; we could do nothing but shudder and return to our dismal bed. No cheerful cricket blew his shrill pipe, like a policeman's whistle; the sea sang not for us with its deep, resounding voice; the Hawaiian harp was hushed. A stone, loosened by some restless lizard, rattled down the cliff; a goat, complaining of the cold, bleated once or twice. The wind soughed; the dry branches of our withering tree sawed across each other; these were our comforters during that almost endless night.

Once the heavens were opened to us. Through a rent in the clouds we saw a great shoulder of the cliff above us, bathed in moonlight. A thousand grotesque shadows played over the face of it. Pictures came and went—a palimpsest of mysteries. Gargoyles leered at us from under the threatening

brows of the bluff; and a white spectre, shining
like a star, stood on the uppermost peak, voiceless
and motionless—some living creature lost in admiration of the moon. Then the sky fell on us, and we
were routed to our solitary cave.

There is a solitude of the sea that swallows up hope;
the despairing spirit hangs over a threatening abyss
of death; yet above it and below it there are forms
of life rejoicing in their natural element. But there
is a solitude of the earth that is more awful; in it
Death taunts you with his presence, yet delays to
strike. At sea, one step, and the spirit is set at liberty—the body is entombed forever. But alas!
within the deserts of the earth no sepulchre awaits
the ashes of him who has suffered, and nought but
the winds or the foul-feeding vultures shall cleanse
that bleaching skeleton where it lies.

We tried to sleep on our stony pillows. Kahéle
woke and found the guide and me dozing; later,
the guide roused himself to the discovery that
Kahéle and I were wrapped in virtuous unconsciousness. Anon I sat up among the rocks, listened to
the two natives breathing heavily, and heard the
wind sighing over the yawning mouth of our cavern.
I heard the beasts stamping among the clinkers, and
covered my head again with the damp blanket, and
besieged sleep. Then we all three started from our
unrefreshing dreams, and lo! the clouds were rising
and fleeing away, and a faint rosy light over the
summit-peaks looked like sunrise; so we rose and
saddled the caravan, and searched about us for the

lost trail. Hour after hour we drew nearer to the mouth of the crater. Our progress was snail-like ; each one of us struck out for himself, having lost confidence in the cunning of the other. From small elevations we took our reckoning, and he who got the farthest toward the sea lifted up his voice in triumph, and was speedily joined by the rest of the party.

At last we came upon the bluffs that overhang the green shores of the island. We were safely out of the Sun's Tabernacle, but not yet free to pass into the lowly vales of the earth. Again and again we rode to the edges of the cliffs, whose precipitous walls forbade our descent. Sometimes we clung to the bare ribs of the mountain, where a single misstep might have sent us headlong into the hereafter. Frequently we rejoiced in a discovery that promised well ; but anon a sheltered chasm unveiled its hideous depths, or an indigo-jungle laid hold of us and cut us off in that direction.

Below us lay the verdant slopes of Kaupo. From their dried-grass houses flocked the natives, looking like ants and their hills. They watched us for hours with amused interest. Now and then they called to us with faint and far-off voices—suggestions that were lost to us, since they sounded like so many bird-notes floating in the wind. All day we saw the little village lying under us temptingly peaceful and lazy. Clouds still hung below us ; some of them swept by, pouring copious drops, that drove our audience within doors for a few moments ; but the

rain was soon over, the sun shone brighter than
ever, the people returned to watch us, and the day
waned. We surprised flock upon flock of goats in
their rocky retreats; but they dispersed in all directions like quicksilver, and we passed on. About
dusk we got into the grassy land, and thanked God
for deliverance.

Here Kahéle's heart rejoiced. Here, close by the
little chapel of Kaupo, he discovered one whom he
proclaimed his grandfather; though, judging from
the years of the man, he could scarcely have been
anything beyond an uncle. I was put to rest in a
little stone cell, where the priests sleep when they
are on their mission to Kaupo. A narrow bed, with
a crucifix at the foot of it, a small window in the
thick wall, with a jug of water in the corner thereof,
and a chair with a game-leg, constituted the furnish-
ment of the quaint lodging. Kahéle rushed about
to see old friends—who wept over him—and was
very long absent, whereat I waxed wroth, and berated him roundly; but the poor fellow was so
charmingly repentant that I forgave him all, and
more too, for I promised him I would stay three
days, at least, with his uncle-grandfather, and gave
him his universal liberty for the time being.

From the open doorway I saw the long sweep of
the mountains, looking cool and purple in the twilight. The ghostly procession of the mists stole in
at the windward gap; the after-glow of the evening
suffused the front of the chapel with a warm light,
and from above the chapel-door the statue of the

Virgin—a little faded with the suns of that endless summer, a little mildewed with the frequent rains—looked down upon us with a smile of welcome. Some youngsters, as naked as day-old nestbirds, tossed a ball into the air; and when it at last lodged in the niche of the Virgin, they clapped their hands, half in merriment and half in awe, and the games of the evening ended. Then the full moon rose; a cock crew in the peak of the chapel, thinking it daybreak, and the little fellows slept, with their spines curved like young kittens. By and by the moon hung, round and mellow, beyond the chapel cross, and threw a long shadow in the grass; and then I went to my cell and folded my hands to rest, with a sense of blessed and unutterable peace.

THE CHAPEL OF THE PALMS

OH, the long suffering of him who threads a narrow trail over the brown crust of a hill where the short grass lies flat in tropical sunshine! On one side sleeps the blue, monotonous sea; on the other, crags clothe themselves in cool mist and look dreamy and solemn.

The boy Kahéle, who has no ambition beyond the bit of his foot-sore mustang, lags behind, taking all the dust with commendable resignation.

As for me, I am wet through with the last shower; I steam in the fierce noonday heat. I spur Hoké the mule into the shadow of a great cloud that drifts lazily overhead, and am grateful for this unsatisfying shade as long as it lasts. I watch the sea, swinging my whip by its threadbare lash like a pendulum—the sea, where a very black rock is being drowned over and over by the tremendous swell that covers it for a moment; but somehow the rock comes to the surface again, and seems to gasp horribly in a deluge of breakers. That rock has been drowning for centuries, yet its struggle for life is as real as ever.

I watch the mountains, cleft with green, fern-cushioned chasms, where an occasional stream

silently distills. Far up on a sun-swept ledge a
white, scattering drift, looking like a rose-garden
after a high wind, I know to be a flock of goats
feeding. But the wind-dried and sunburnt grass
under foot, the intangible dust that pervades the
air, the rain-cloud in the distance, trailing its banners of crape in the sea as it bears down upon us—
these are what fret me a little, and make life a burden for the time being; so I spur my faithless Hoké
up a new ascent as forbidding as any that we have
yet come upon, and slowly and with many pauses
creep to the summit.

Kahéle, "the goer," belies his name, for he
loiters everywhere and always; yet I am not sorry.
I have the first glimpse of Wailua all to myself. I
am not obliged to betray my emotion, which is a
bore of the worst sort.

Wailua lies at my feet—a valley full of bees
butterflies and blossoms, the sea fawning at the
mouth of it, the clouds melting over it; waterfalls
gushing from numerous green corners; silver-white
phaëtons floating in mid-air, at a loss to choose between earth and heaven, though evidently a little inclined earthward, for they no sooner drift out of
the bewildering bowers of Wailua than they return
again with noticeable haste.

Down I plunge into the depths of the valley, with
the first drops of a heavy shower pelting me in the
back; and under a great tree, that seems yearning
to shelter somebody, I pause till the rain is over.

Anon the slow-footed Kahéle arrives, leaking all

over, and bringing a peace-offering of *ohias*, the native apple, as juicy and sweet as the forbidden fruits
of Paradise.   As for these apples, they have a solitary
seed, like a nutmeg, a pulp as white as wax, a juice
flavored with roses, and their skin as red as a peony
and as glossy as varnish.   These we munch and
munch while the forest reels under the impetuous
avalanches of big rain-drops, and our animals tear
great tufts of sweet grass from the upper roadside.

Is it far to the chapel, I wonder.   Kahéle thinks
not—perhaps a *pari* or two distant.   But a *pari*, a
cliff, has many antecedents ; and I feel that some
dozen or so of climbs, each more or less fatiguing,
still separate me from the rest I am seeking, and
hope not to find until I reach the abode of Père Fidelis, at the foot of the cross, as one might say.

The rain ceases.   Hoké once more nerves himself
for fresh assaults upon the everlasting hills.   Kahéle drops behind as usual, and the afternoon
wanes.

How fresh seems the memory of this journey !
yet its place is with the archives of the past.   I
seem to breathe the incense of orange-flowers and to
hear the whisper of distant waterfalls as I write.

It must have been toward sunset—we were
threading the eastern coast, and a great mountain
filled the west—but I felt that it was the hour when
day ends and night begins.   The heavy clouds
looked as though they were still brimful of sunlight,
yet no ray escaped to gladden our side of the
world.

Finally, on the brow of what seemed to be the last hill in this life, I saw a cross—a cross among the palms. Hoké saw it, and quickened his pace: he was not so great an ass but he knew that there was provender in the green pastures of Père Fidelis, and his heart freshened within him.

A few paces from the grove of palms I heard a bell swing jubilantly. Out over the solemn sea, up and down that foam-crested shore, rang the sweet Angelus. One may pray with some fervor when one's journey is at an end. When the prayer was over I walked to the gate of the chapel-yard, leading the willing Hoké, and at that moment a slender figure, clad all in black, his long robes flowing gracefully about him, his boyish face heightening the effect of his grave and serene demeanor, his thin, sensitive hands held forth in hearty welcome—a welcome that was almost like a benediction, so spiritual was the love which it expressed—came out, and I found myself in the arms of Père Fidelis, feeling like one who has at least been permitted to kneel upon the threshold of his Mecca.

Why do our hearts sing *jubilate* when we meet a friend for the first time? What is it within us that with its life-long yearning comes suddenly upon the all-sufficient one, and in a moment is crowned and satisfied? I could not tell whether I was at last waking from a sleep or just sinking into a dream. I could have sat there at his feet contented; I could have put off my worldly cares, resigned ambition, forgotten the past, and, in the blessed tranquillity of

15

that hour, have dwelt joyfully under the palms with him, seeking only to follow in his patient footsteps until the end should come.

Perhaps it was the realization of an ideal that plunged me into a luxurious revery, out of which I was summoned by *mon père*, who hinted that I must be hungry. Prophetic father! hungry I was indeed.

Mon père led me to his little house with three rooms, and installed me host, himself being my ever-watchful attendant. Then he spoke: "The lads were at the sea, fishing: would I excuse him for a moment?"

Alone in the little house, with a glass of claret and a hard biscuit for refreshment, I looked about me. The central room, in which I sat, was bare to nakedness: a few devotional books, a small clock high up on the wall, with a short wagging pendulum, two or three paintings, betraying more sentiment than merit, a table, a wooden form against the window, and a crucifix, complete its inventory. A high window was at my back; a door in front opening upon a veranda shaded with a passion-vine; beyond it a green, undulating country running down into the sea; on either hand a little cell containing nothing but a narrow bed, a saint's picture, and a rosary. Kahéle, having distributed the animals in good pasturage, lay on the veranda at full length, supremely happy as he jingled his spurs over the edge of the steps and hummed a native air in subdued falsetto, like a mosquito.

Again I sank into a revery. Enter *mon père* with apologies and a plate of smoking cakes made of eggs and batter, his own handiwork ; enter the lads from the sea with excellent fish, knotted in long wisps of grass ; enter Kahéle, lazily sniffing the savory odors of our repast with evident relish ; and then supper in good earnest.

How happy we were, having such talks in several sorts of tongues, such polyglot efforts toward socia-bility—French, English, and native in equal parts, but each broken and spliced to suit our dire neces-sity ! The candle flamed and flickered in the land-breeze that swept through the house—unctuous waxen stalactites decorated it almost past recog-nition ; the crickets sang lustily at the doorway ; the little natives grew sleepy and curled up on their mats in the corner ; Kahéle slept in his spurs like a born muleteer. And now a sudden conviction seized us that it was bedtime in very truth ; so *mon père* led me to one of the cells, saying " Will you sleep in the room of Père Amabilis ? " Yea, verily, with all humility ; and there I slept after the benediction, during which the young priest's face looked almost like an angel's in its youthful holiness, and I was afraid I might wake in the morning and find him gone, transported to some other and more lovely world.

But I didn't. Père Fidelis was up before day-break. It was his hand that clashed the joyful An-gelus at sunrise that woke me from my happy dream ; it was his hand that prepared the frugal but appetizing meal; he made the coffee, such rich, black, aromatic coffee as Frenchmen alone have the faculty of producing. He had an eye to the welfare of the animals also, and seemed to be commander-in-chief of affairs secular as well as ecclesiastical; yet he was so young!

There was a day of brief incursions mountainward, with the happiest results. There were welcomes showered upon me for his sake; he was ever ministering to my temporal wants, and puzzling me with dissertations in assorted languages.

By happy fortune a Sunday followed, when the Chapel of the Palms was thronged with dusky worshippers; not a white face present but the father's and mine own, yet a common trust in the blessedness of the life to come struck the key-note of universal harmony, and we sang the *Magnificat* with one voice. There was something that fretted me in all this admirable experience: Père Fidelis could touch neither bread nor water until after the last mass. Hour by hour he grew paler and fainter spite of the heroic fortitude that sustained his famishing body.

"*Mon père,*" said I, "you must eat, or go to heaven betimes." He would not. "You must end with an earlier mass," I persisted. It was impossible: many parishioners came from miles away; some of these started at daybreak, as it was, and they would be unable to arrive in season for an earlier mass. Excellent martyr! thought I, to offer thy body a living sacrifice for the edification of these

savage Christians! At last he ate, but not until
appetite itself had perished. Then troops of children gathered about him clamoring to kiss the hand
of the priestly youth; old men and women passed
him with heads uncovered, amazed at the devotion
of one they could not hope to emulate.

Whenever I referred to his life, he at once led me
to admire his fellow-apostle, who was continually in
his thoughts. Père Amabilis was miles away, repair-
ing a chapel that had suffered somewhat in a late gale;
Père Amabilis would be so glad to see me; I must
not fail to visit him; and for fear of some mischance,
Père Fidelis would himself conduct me to him.

The way was hard—deep chasms to penetrate,
swift streams to be forded, narrow and slippery
trails to be threaded through forest, swamp, and
wilderness. These obstacles separated the devoted
friends, but not for long seasons. Père Fidelis
would go to him whom he had not laid eyes on for
a fortnight at least.

The boy Kahéle was glad of companionship; one
of the small fishers, an acolyte of the chapel, would
accompany us, and together they could lag behind,
eating *ohias* and dabbling in every stream.

A long day's journey followed. We wended our
way through jungles of *lauhala*, with slim roots in
the air and long branches trailing about them like
vines; they were like great cages of roots and
branches in a woven snarl. We saw a rocky point
jutting far into the sea. "Père Amabilis dwells
just beyond that cape," said my companion, fondly;

and it seemed not very far distant ; but our pace
was slow and wearisome, and the hours were sure to
distance us. We fathomed dark ravines whose
farther walls were but a stone's throw from us, but
in whose profound depths a swift torrent rushed
madly to the sea, threatening to carry us to our destruction—green, precipitous troughs, where the tide
of mountain-rain was lashed into fury, and with its
death-song drowned our voices and filled our animals with terror.

Now and then we paused to breathe, man and
beast panting with fatigue ; sometimes the rain
drove us into the thick wood for shelter ; sometimes
a brief deluge, the offspring of a rent cloud at the
head of the ravine, stayed our progress for half an
hour, until its volume was somewhat spent and
the stream was again fordable. Here we talked
of the daily miracles in nature. Again and again
the young fathers are called forth into the wilderness to attend on the sick and dying. Little
chapels are hidden away among the mountains and
through the valleys ; all these must be visited in
turn. Their life is an actual pilgrimage from chapel
to chapel, which nothing but physical inability may
interrupt.

At one spot I saw a tree under which Père Fidelis
once passed a tempestuous night. On either side
yawned a ravine swept by an impassable flood.
There were no houses within reach. On the soaked
earth, with a pitiless gale sweeping over the land,
from sunset to sunrise he lay without the consola-

tion of one companion. Food was frequently
scarce : a few limpets, about as palatable as parboiled
shoe-leather, a paste of roast yams and water, a lime
perhaps, and nothing besides but lumpy salt from
the sea-shore.

While we were riding, a herald met us bearing a
letter for *mon père*. It was a greeting from Père
Amabilis, who announced the chapel as rapidly near-
ing its complete restoration. Père Fidelis fairly wept
for joy at this intelligence, and burst into a panegyric
upon the unrivalled ingenuity of his spiritual asso-
ciate. We were sure to surprise him at work, and
this trifling episode seemed to be an event of some
importance in the isolated life they led.

At sunset we passed into the open vale of Wai-
luanui, and saw the chapel looking fresh and tidy
on the slope of the hill toward the sea. Two waterfalls that fell against the sunset flashed like falling
flame, and a soft haze tinged the slumberous solitudes of wood and pasture with the dream-like loveliness of a picture. There seemed to be but one
sound audible—the quick, sharp blows of a hammer.
Père Fidelis listened with eyes sparkling, and then
rode rapidly onward.

Behold ! from the chapel wall, high up on a scaf-
folding of boughs, his robes gathered about him,
his head uncovered, and hammer in hand, Père
Amabilis leaned forth to welcome us. The hammer fell to the earth. Père Amabilis loosened his
skirts and clasped his hands in unaffected rapture.
We were three satisfied souls, asking for nothing

beyond the hem of that lonely valley in the Pacific.

Of course there was the smallest possible house that could be lived in, for our sole accommodation, because but one priest needed to visit the district at a time, and a very young priest at that. A tiny bed in one corner of the room was thought sufficient, together with two plates, two cups, and a single spoon. Luxuries were unknown and unregretted.

"Well, father, what have you at this hotel ?" said Père Fidelis as we came to the door of the cubby-house.

"Water," replied our host, with a grave tone that had an undercurrent of truth in it.

But we were better provided for. Within an hour's time a reception took place : native parishioners came forth to welcome Père Fidelis and the stranger, each bringing some voluntary tribute—a fish, a fowl lean enough to quiet the conscience of Père Fidelis, an egg or two, or a bunch of taro.

Long talks followed ; the news of the last month was discussed with much enthusiasm, and some few who had no opportunity of joining in the debate gave expression to their sentiments through such speaking eyes as savages usually are possessed of.

The welcome supper-hour approached. Willing hands dressed a fowl ; swift feet plied between the spring and the kettle swung over the open camp-fire ; children danced for very joy before the door of the chapel, under the statue of the Virgin, whose head was adorned with a garland of living flowers. The shadows deepened ; stars seemed to cluster over the valley and glow with unusual fervor ; the crickets sang mightily—they are always singing mightily over yonder ; supper came to the bare table with its meagre array of dishes ; and, since I was forced to have a whole plate and a bowl, as well as the solitary spoon, for my sole use, the two young priests ate together from the same dish and drank from the same cup, and were as grateful and happy as the birds of the air under similar circumstances.

A merry meal, that ! For us no weak tea, that satirical consoler, nor tea whose strength is bitterness, an abomination to the faithful, but *mon père's* own coffee, the very aroma of which was invigorating; and then our friendly pipes out under the starlight, where we sat chatting amicably, with our three heads turbaned in an aromatic Virginian cloud.

I learned something of the life of these two friends during that social evening. Born in the same city in the north of France, reared in the same schools, graduated from the same university, each fond of life and acquainted with its follies, each in turn stricken with an illness that threatened death, together they came out of the dark valley with their future consecrated to the work that now absorbs them, the friendship of their childhood increasing with their years and sustaining them in a remote land, where their vow of poverty seems almost like a sarcasm, since circumstance deprives them of all luxuries.

"Do you never long for home? do you never regret your vow?" I asked.

"Never!" they answered; and I believe them. "These old people are as parents to us; these younger ones are as brothers and sisters; these children we love as dearly as though they were our own. What more can we ask?"

What more, indeed? With the rain beating down upon your unsheltered heads, and the torrents threatening to ingulf you; faint with journeyings; an hungered often; weak with fastings; pallid with prayer —what more *can* you ask in the same line? say I.

Père Fidelis coughed a little, and was somewhat feverish. I could see that his life was not elastic: his strength was even then failing him.

"Père Amabilis is an artisan: he built this house, and it is small enough; but some day he will build a house for me but six feet long and *so* broad," said Père Fidelis, shrugging his shoulders; whereat Père Amabilis, who looked like a German student with his long hair and spectacles, turned aside to wipe the moisture from the lenses, and said nothing, but laid his hand significantly upon the shoulder of his friend, as if imploring silence. Alas for him when those lips are silent forever!

I wondered if they had no recreation.

"O yes. The poor pictures at the Chapel of the Palms are ours, but we have not studied art. And then we are sometimes summoned to the farther side of the island, where we meet new faces. It is a great change."

For a year before the arrival of Père Amabilis, who was not sooner able to follow his friend, Père Fidelis was accustomed to go once a month to a confessional many miles away. That his absence might be as brief as possible, he was obliged to travel night and day. Sometimes he would reach the house of his confessor at midnight, when all were sleeping : thereupon would follow this singular colloquy in true native fashion. A rap at the door at midnight, the confessor waking from his sleep.

Confessor. "Who's there?"

Père Fidelis. "It is I!"

Conf. "Who is I!"

Père F. "Fidelis!"

Conf. "Fidelis who?"

Père F. "Fidelis kahuna pule!" (Fidelis the priest.)

Conf. "Aweh!" (An expression of the greatest surprise.) "*Entre*, Fidelis kahuna pule."

Then he would rise, and the communion that followed must have been most cheering to both, for *mon père* even now is merry when he recalls it.

These pilgrimages are at an end, for the two priests confess to one another : conceive of the fellowship that hides away no secret, however mortifying!

The whole population must have been long asleep before we thought of retiring that night, and then arose an argument concerning the fittest occupant of the solitary bed. It fell to me, for both were against me, and each was my superior. When I protested, they held up their fingers and said, "Remember, we are your fathers and must be obeyed." Thus I was driven to the bed, while mine hosts lay on the bare floor with saddles for pillows.

It was this self-sacrificing hospitality that hastened my departure. I felt earth could offer me no nobler fellowship—that all acts to come, however gracious, would bear a tinge of selfishness in comparison with the reception I had met where least expected.

I am thankful that I had not the heart to sleep well, for I think I could never have forgiven myself had I done so. When I woke in the early part of the night, I saw the young priests bowed over their breviaries, for I had delayed the accustomed offices of devotion, and they were fulfilling them in peace at last, having me so well bestowed that it was utterly impossible to do aught else for my entertainment.

Once more the morning came. I woke to find Père Amabilis at work, hammer in hand, sending his nails home with accurate strokes that spoke well for his trained muscle. Père Fidelis was concocting coffee and directing the volunteer cooks, who were seeking to surpass themselves upon this last meal we were to take together. In an hour *mon père* was to start for the Chapel of the Palms, while I wended my way onward through a new country, bearing with me the consoling memory of my precious friends. I can forgive a slight and forget the person who slights me, but little kindnesses probe me to the quick. I wonder why the twin fathers were

so very careful of me that morning! They could
not do enough to satisfy themselves, and that
made me miserable; they stabbed me with tender
words, and tried to be cheerful with such evident
effort that I couldn't eat half my breakfast, though,
as it was, I ate more than they did—God forgive
me!—and altogether it was a solemn and a memorable meal.

A group of natives gathered about us seated upon
the floor; it was impossible for Père Fidelis to
move without being stroked by the affectionate
creatures who deplored his departure. Père Amabilis insisted upon adjusting our saddles, during
which ceremony he slyly hid a morsel of cold fowl
in our saddle-bags.

That parting was as cruel as death. We shall
probably never see one another again; if we do, we
shall be older and more practical and more worldly,
and the exquisite confidence we have in one another
will have grown blunt with time. I felt it then as I
know it now—our brief idyl can never be lived over
in this life.

Well, we departed; the corners of our blessed
triangle were spread frightfully. Père Fidelis was
paler than ever; he caught his breath as though
there wasn't much of it, and the little there was
wouldn't last long; Père Amabilis wiped his spectacles and looked utterly forsaken; the natives stood
about in awkward, silent groups, coming forward,
one by one, to shake hands, and then falling back
like so many automatons. Somehow, genuine grief

is never graceful; it forgets to pose itself; its muscles are perfectly slack and unreliable.

The sea looked gray and forbidding as it shook its shaggy breakers under the cliff; life was dismal enough. The animals were unusually wayward, and once or twice I paused in despair under the prickly sunshine, half inclined to go back and begin over again, hoping to renew the past; but just then Hoké felt like staggering onward, and I began to realize that there are some brief, perfect experiences in life that pass from us like a dream, and this was one of them.

In the proem to this idyl I seem to see two shadowy figures passing up and down over a lonesome land. Fever and famine do not stay them; the elements alone have power to check their pilgrimage. Their advent is hailed with joyful bells; tears fall when they depart. Their paths are peace. Fearlessly they battle with contagion, and are at hand to close the pestilential lips of unclean death. They have lifted my soul above things earthly, and held it secure for a moment. From beyond the waters my heart returns to them. Again at twilight, over the still sea, floats the sweet Angelus; again I approach the chapel falling to slow decay; there are fresh mounds in the churchyard, and the voice of wailing is heard for a passing soul. By and by, if there is work to do, it shall be done, and the hands shall be folded, for the young apostles will have followed in the silent footsteps of their flock. Here endeth the lesson of the Chapel of the Palms.

KAHELE

FROM a bluff, whose bald forehead jutted a thousand feet into the air, and under whose chin the sea shrugged its great shoulders, Kahéle, my boy—that delightful contradiction, who was always plausible, yet never right—Kahéle and I looked timidly over into the sunset valley of Méha. The "Valley of Solitude" it was called; albeit, at that moment, and with half an eye, we counted the thirty grass-lodges of the village, and heard the liquid tongues of a trio of waterfalls that dived head-first into the groves at the farther end of the valley, where the mountains seemed to have opened its heart wide enough to let a rivulet escape into the sea. But the spot was a palpable and living dream, and no fond rivulet would go too hastily through it; so there was a glittering sort of monogram writ in water, and about it the village lodges were clustered in a very pleasing disorder.

The trail dropped down the cliff below us in long, swinging zigzags, and wound lazily through the village; crossed the stream at the ford; dipped off toward the sea, as though the beach, shining like coarse gold, were a trifle too lovely to be passed without recognition, and then it climbed laboriously

up the opposite cliff, and struck off into space.   In
ten seconds a bird might have spanned the deep
ravine, and caught as much of its loveliness as we ;
but we weren't birds, and, moreover, we had six
legs apiece to look after, so we tipped off from the
dizzy ridge that overhung the valley of Méha to the
north, and gradually descended into the heat and
silence of the place, that seemed to make a picture
of itself when we first looked down upon it from our
eyry.

We found the floor of the valley very solemn and
very lovely, when we at last got down into it.   Three
youngsters, as brown as berries, and without any
leaves upon them, broke loose from a banana-orchard
and leaped into a low *hou*-tree as we approached.
They were a little shy of my color, pale-faces being
rare in that vicinity.   Two women who were washing at the ford—and washing the very garments
they should have had upon their backs—discovered
us, and plunged into the stream with a refreshing
splash, and a laugh apiece that was worth hearing,
it was so genuine and hearty.   Another youngster
hurried off from a stone-wall like a startled lizard,
and struck on his head, but didn't cry much, for he
was too frightened.   A large woman lay at full
length on a broad mat, spread under a *pandanus*,
and slept like a turtle.   I began to think there were
nothing but women and children in the solitary
valley, but Kahéle had kept an eye on the reef, and,
with an air of superior intelligence, he assured me
that there were many men living about there, and

they, with most of the women and children, were then out in the surf, fishing.

"To the beach, by all means!" cried I; and to the beach we hastened, where, indeed, we found heaps of cast-off raiment, and a hundred footprints in the sand. What would Mr. Robinson Crusoe have said to that, I wonder! Across the level water, heads, hands, and shoulders, and sometimes half-bodies, were floating about, like the *amphibia*. We were at once greeted with a shout of welcome, which came faintly to us above the roar of the surf, as it broke heavily on the reef, a half-mile out from shore. It was drawing toward the hour when the fishers came to land, and we had not long to wait before, one after another, they came out of the sea like so many mermen and mermaids. They were refreshingly innocent of etiquette—at least, of our translation of it; and, with a freedom that was amusing as well as a little embarrassing, I was deliberately fingered, fondled, and fussed with by nearly every dusky soul in turn. "At last," thought I, "fate has led me beyond the pale of civilization; for this begins to look like the genuine article."

With uncommon slowness, the mermaids donned more or less of their apparel, a few preferring to carry their robes over their arms; for the air was delicious, and ropes of sea-weed are accounted full dress in that delectable latitude. Down on the sand the mermen heaped their scaly spoils—fish of all shapes and sizes, fish of every color; some of them throwing somersaults in the sand, like young ath-

16

letes ; some of them making wry faces, in their last
agony ; some of them lying still and clammy, with
big, round eyes like smoked-pearl vest-buttons set
in the middle of their cheeks ; all of them smelling
fish-like, and none of them looking very tempting.
Small boys laid hold on small fry, bit their heads
off, and held the silver-coated morsels between their
teeth, like animated sticks of candy. There was a
Fridayish and Lent-like atmosphere hovering over
the spot, and I turned away to watch some youths
who were riding surf-boards not far distant—agile,
narrow-hipped youths, with tremendous biceps and
proud, impudent heads set on broad shoulders, like
young gods. These were the flower and chivalry of
the Méha blood, and they swam like young porpoises, every one of them.

There was a break in the reef before us ; the sea
knew it, and seemed to take special delight in rushing upon the shore as though it were about to devour sand, savages, and everything. Kahéle and I
watched the surf-swimmers for some time, charmed
with the spectacle. Such buoyancy of material
matter I had never dreamed of. Kahéle, though
much in the flesh, could not long resist the temptation to exhibit his prowess, and having been offered
a surf-board that would have made a good lid to his
coffin, and was itself as light as cork and as smooth
as glass, suddenly threw off his last claim to respect-
ability, seized his sea-sled, and dived with it under
the first roller which was then about to break above
his head, not three feet from him. Beyond it, a

second roller reared its awful front, but he swam
under that with ease; at the sound of his "open
sesame," its emerald gates parted and closed after
him. He seemed some triton playing with the elements, and dreadfully "at home" in that very
wet place. The third and mightiest of the waves
was gathering its strength for a charge upon the
shore. Having reached its outer ripple, again Kahéle dived and reappeared on the other side of the
watery hill, balanced for a moment in the glassy
hollow, turned suddenly, and, mounting the towering monster, he lay at full length upon his fragile
raft, using his arms as a bird its pinions—in fact,
soaring for a moment with the wave under him. As
it rose, he climbed to the top of it, and there, in the
midst of foam seething like champagne, on the
crest of a rushing sea-avalanche about to crumble
and dissolve beneath him, his surf-board hidden in
spume, on the very top bubble of all, Kahéle danced
like a shadow. He leaped to his feet and swam in
the air, another Mercury, tiptoeing a heaven-kissing
hill, buoyant as vapor, and with a suggestion of invisible wings about him—Kahéle transformed for a
moment, and for a moment only; the next second
my daring sea-skater leaped ashore, with a howling
breaker swashing at his heels. It was something
glorious and almost incredible; but I saw it with
my own eyes, and I wanted to double his salary on
the spot.

Sunset in the valley of Méha. The air full of
floating particles, that twinkled like diamond-dust;

the great green chasm at the head of the valley illuminated by one broad bar of light shot obliquely through it, tipped at the end with a shower of white rockets that fringed a waterfall, and a fragment of rainbow like a torn banner. That deep, shadowy ravine seemed, for a moment, some mystery about to be divulged; but the light faded too soon, and I never learned the truth of it. The sea quieter than usual; very little sound save the rhythmical vibration of the air, that suggested flowing waters and quivering leaves; the lights shifted along the upper cliffs; a silver-white tropic-bird sailed from cloud to cloud, swiftly and noiselessly, like a shooting-star. A delicious moment, but a brief one; soon the sun was down, and the deepening shadows and gathering coolness set all the valley astir.

Camp-fires were kindled throughout the village; column after column of thin blue smoke ascended in waving spirals, separating at the top in leaf-shaped clouds. It was like the spiritual resurrection of some ancient palm-grove; and when the moon rose, a little later, flooding the Vale of Solitude with her vague light, the illusion was perfected; and a group of savages, scenting the savory process of their supper, sat, hungry and talkative, under every ghostly palm. Clear voices ascended in monotonous and weird recitative; they chanted a monody on the death of some loved one, prompted, perhaps, by the funereal solemnity of the hour; or sang an ode to the moon-rise, the still-flowing river, or the valley of Méha, so solitary in one sense, though by no means alone in its loneliness.

Kahéle patronized me extensively. I was introduced to camp after camp, and in rapid succession repeated the experiences of a traveller who has much to answer for in the way of color, and the peculiar cut of his garments. I felt as though I were some natural curiosity, in charge of the robustious Kahéle, who waxed more and more officious every hour of his engagement; and his tongue ran riot as he descanted upon my characteristics, to the joy of the curious audiences we attracted.

Some hours must have passed before we thought of sleep. How could we think of it, when every soul was wide awake, and the time alone seemed to pass us by unconsciously? But Kahéle finally led me to a chief's house, where, under coverlets of *kapa*, spiced with herbs, and in the midst of numerous members of the household, I was advised to compose my soul in peace, and patiently await daylight. I did so, for the drowsy sense that best illustrates the tail-end of a day's journey possessed me, and I was finally overcome by the low, monotonous drone of a language that I found about as intelligible as the cooing of the multitudinous pigeon. The boy sat near me, still descanting upon our late experiences, our possible future, and the thousand trivial occurrences that make the recollections of travel forever charming. The familiar pipe, smoked at about the rate of three whiffs apiece, circulated freely, and kept the air mildly flavored with tobacco; and night, with all that pertains to it, bowed over me as, in an unguarded moment, I surrendered to its narcotizing touch.

There was another valley in my sleep, like unto the one I had closed my eyes upon, and I saw it thronged with ancients. No white face had yet filled those savage and sensuous hearts with a sense of disgust which, I believe, all dark races feel when they first behold a bleached skin. Again the breathless heralds announced the approach of a king, and the multitudes gathered to receive him. I heard the beating of the tom-toms, and saw the dancers ambling and posing before his august majesty, who reclined in the midst of a retinue of obsequious retainers. The spearsmen hurled their spears, and the strong men swung their clubs; the stone-throwers threw skilfully, and the sweetest singers sang long *méles* in praise of their royal guest. A cry of fear rent the air as a stricken one fled toward the city of refuge; the priests passed by me in solemn procession, their robes spotted with sacrificial blood. War-canoes drew in from the sea, and death fell upon the valley. I heard the wail for the slaughtered, and saw the grim idols borne forth in the arms of the triumphant; then I awoke in the midst of that dream-pageant of savage and barbaric splendor.

It was still night; the sea was again moaning; the cool air of the mountain rustled in the long thatch at the doorway; a ripe bread-fruit fell to the earth with a low thud. I rose from my mat and looked about me. The room was nearly deserted; someone lay swathed like a mummy in a dark corner of the lodge, but of what sex I knew not— probably one who had outlived all sensations, and perhaps all desires; a rush, strung full of oily *kukui* nuts, flamed in the centre of the room, and a thread of black smoke climbed almost to the peak of the roof; but, falling in with a current of fresh air, it was spirited away in a moment.

I looked out of the low door: the hour was such a one as tinges the stoutest heart with superstition; the landscape was complete in two colors—a moist, transparent gray, and a thin, feathery silver that seemed almost palpable to the touch. Out on the slopes near the stream reclined groups of natives, chatting, singing, smoking, or silently regarding the moon. I passed them unnoticed; dim paths led me through guava jungles, under orange-groves, and beside clusters of jasmine, overpowering in their fragrance. Against the low eaves of the several lodges sat singers, players upon the rude instruments of the land, and glib talkers, who waxed eloquent, and gesticulated with exceeding grace. Footsteps rustled before and behind me; I stole into the thicket, and saw lovers wandering together, locked in each other's embrace, and saw friends go hand-in-hand, conversing in low tones, or perhaps mute, with an impressive air of the most complete tranquillity. The night-blooming cereus laid its ivory urn open to the moonlight, and a myriad of crickets chirped in one continuous jubilee. Voices of merriment were wafted down to me; and, stealing onward, toward the great meadow by the stream, where the sleepless inhabitants of the valley held high carnival, I saw the most dignified chiefs of Méha sporting like children, while the children capered like imps, and the whole community seemed bewitched with the glorious atmosphere of that particular night.

Who was the gayest of the gay, and the most lawless of the unlawful? My boy, Kahéle, in whom I had placed my trust, and whom, until this hour at least, I had regarded as a most promising specimen of the reorganized barbarians.

Perhaps it was all right; perhaps I had been counting his steps with too much confidence; they might have been simply a creditable performance, the result of careful training on the part of his tutors. I am inclined to think they were! At any rate, Kahéle went clean back to barbarism that night, and seemed to take to it amazingly. I said nothing; I thought it wiser to seem to hold the reins, though I held them loosely, than to try to check the career of my half-tamed domestic, and to find him beyond my control; therefore I sat on one side taking notes, and found it rather jolly on the whole.

The river looked like an inky flood with a broken silver crust; canoes floated upon its sluggish tide like long feathers; swimmers plied up and down it, now and then " blowing," whale-fashion, but slipping through the water as noiselessly as trout. I could scarcely tell which was the more attractive—Nature, so fragrant and so voluptuous, or man, who had become a part of Nature for the hour, and was very unlike man as I had been taught to accept him.

Not till dawn did the dance or the song cease; not till everybody was gray and fagged, and tongues had stopped wagging from sheer exhaustion. I returned to my mats long ere that, to revolve in my mind plans for the following day.

It was evident that Kahéle must at once quit the place, or go back to barbarism and stick there. I didn't care to take the responsibility of his return to first principles, and so ordered the animals saddled by sunrise. At that delicious moment, the youngster lay like one of the Seven Sleepers, whom nothing could awaken. Everybody in the village seemed to be making up his lost sleep, and I was forced to await the return of life before pressing my claims any further.

The scorching noon drew on; a few of the sleepers awoke, bathed, ate of their cold repast, and slept again. Kahéle followed suit; in the midst of his refreshment, I suggested the advisability of instant departure; he hesitated. I enlarged upon the topic, and drew an enticing picture of the home-stretch, with all the endearing associations clustering about its farther end; he agreed to everything with a sweet and passive grace that seemed to compensate me for the vexations of the morning.

I went to the river to bathe while the beasts were being saddled, and returned anon to find Kahéle sound asleep, and as persistent in his slumbers as

ever. The afternoon waned ; I began to see the fitness of the name that had at first seemed to me inappropriate to the valley : everybody slept or lazed
during the hot hours of the day, and a census-taker
might easily have imagined the place a solitude. At
sunset there was more fishing and more surf-swimming. It seemed to me the fish smelt stronger, and
the swimmers swam less skilfully than on the evening previous ; possibly it was quite as pretty a spectacle as the one that first charmed me, but blessings
are bores when they come out of season.

Night drew on apace ; the moon rose, and the inhabitants pretended to rest, but were shortly mag-
netized out of their houses, where they danced till
daybreak. The sweets of that sort of thing began
to cloy, and I resolved upon immediate action. Kahéle was taken by the ears at the very next sunrise,
and ordered to get up the mules at once. He was
gone nearly all day, and came in at last with a pitiful air of disappointment that quite unmanned me ;
his voice, too, was sympathetic, and there was something like a tear in his eye when he assured me that
the creatures had gone astray, but might be found
shortly—perhaps even then they were approaching ;
and the young scamp rose to reconnoitre, glad, no
doubt, of an excuse for escaping from my natural
but ludicrous discomfiture. It is likely that my boy
Kahéle would have danced till doomsday, had I not
shown spleen. It is as likely, also, that the chief
and all his people would have helped him out in it,
had I not offered such reward as I thought sufficient

to tempt their greed ; but, thank Heaven, there is an
end to everything !

On the morning of the fourth day, two travellers
might have been seen struggling up the face of the
great cliff that walls in the valley of Méha to the
south. The one a pale-face, paler than usual, urging
on the other, a dark-face, darker than was its wont.
Never did animals so puzzle their wits to know
whether they were indeed desired to hasten forward,
or to turn back at the very next crook in the trail.
We were at big odds, Kahéle and I ; for another
idol of mine had suddenly turned to clay, and,
though I am used to that sort of thing, I am never
able to bear it with decent composure. On we
journeyed, working at cross-purposes, and getting
nearer to the sky all the while, and finally losing
sight of the bewitching valley that had demoralized
and so nearly divorced us ; getting wet in the damp
grasses on the highlands, and sometimes losing ourselves for a moment in the clouds that lie late on the
mountains ; seeing lovely, narrow, and profound
vales, wherein the rain fell with a roar like hail ;
where the streams swelled suddenly like veins, and
where often there was no living creature discernible,
not even a bird ; where silence brooded, and the
world seemed empty.

A very long day's journey brought us out of the
green and fertile land that lies with its face to the
trade-wind ; there the clouds gather and shed their
rains ; but all of the earth lying in the lee of the
great central peak of the island is as dust and ashes

—unwatered, unfruitful, and uninteresting, save as
a picture of deep and dreadful desolation. No wonder that Kahéle longed to tarry in the small Eden of
Méha, knowing that we were about to journey into
the deserts that lie beyond it. No wonder that the
shining shores of the valley beguiled him, when he
knew that henceforth the sea would break upon long
reaches of black lava, as unpicturesque as a coal-
heap, the path along which was pain, and the way-
sides anguish of spirit ; where fruit was scarce, and
water brackish, and every edible dried and deceit-
ful.

Having slept the sleep of the just—for I felt that
I had done what I could to reclaim my backsliding
Kahéle—I awoke on a sabbath morning that presented a singular spectacle. Its chief features were
a glittering, metallic-tinted sea, and a smoking plain
backed by naked sand-hills. The low brush, scattered thinly over the earth, tried hard to look green,
but seldom got nearer to it than a dusty gray. Evidently there was no sap in those charred twigs, for
they snapped like coral when you tested their pli-
ancy. A few huts, dust-colored and ragged, were
scattered along the trail ; they had apparently lost
all hope, and paused by the wayside, to end their
days in despair.

The *halé-pulé*, or prayer-house, chief of the forlorn huts, by virtue of extraordinary hollowness and
a ventilation that was only exceeded by all out-of-
doors—this prayer-house, or church, was thrown
open to the public, and, to my amazement, Kahéle

suggested the propriety of our attending worship, even before the first conch had been blown from the rude door by the deacon himself.

We went along the chalky path that led to the front of the house, and sat in the shelter of the eaves for an hour or more. Seven times that conch was blown, and on each occasion the neighborhood responded, though stingily; a few worshippers would issue out of the wilderness and draw slowly toward us. One or two men came on horseback, and were happy in their mood, exhibiting the qualities of their animals on the flats before us. Some came on foot, with their shoes in hand; the shoes were carefully put on at the church door, but put off again a few moments after entering the rustic pews. Dogs came, about one for every human; these lay all over the floor, or mounted the seats, or were held in the arms of the congregation, as the case might be. Children came and played a savage version of leap-frog in the lee of the church, but they were bleak-looking youngsters, not at all like the little human vegetables that flourished in the genial atmosphere of the valley of Méha.

The conch was blown again; the most melancholy sound that ever issued from windy cavity floated up and down that disconsolate land, and seemed to be saying, in pathetic gusts, "Come to meeting! Come to meeting!" Probably everyone that could come had come; at any rate no one else followed, and, after a decent pause, the services of the morning were begun. The brief interval of ominous silence that preceded the opening was enlivened by the caprices of a fractious horse, and at least two stampedes of the canine persuasion, at which time the dogs seemed possessed of devils, and were running down in a body toward the sea, but thought better of it, and stole noiselessly back again, one after the other, just in season for the opening prayer, to which they entered with a low-comedy cast of countenance, and a depressed tail.

That prayer bubbled out of the savage throat like a clear fountain of vowels. The dignity of the man was impressive, and his face the picture of devotion ; his deportment, likewise, was all that could be desired in anyone, under the circumstances. Either he was a rare specimen of the very desirable convert from barbarism, or he was a consummate actor ; I dare not guess which of the two beguiled me with his grave and euphonious prayer.

I regret to state that, during the energetic expounding of the Scriptures, a few of the congregation forgot themselves and slept audibly ; a few arose and went under the eaves to smoke ; children went down on all-fours, and crawled under the pews in chase of pups as restless and incorrigible as themselves. At a later period, someone announced an approaching schooner, and the body of the house was unceremoniously cleared, for a schooner was as rare a visitor to that part of the island as an angel to any quarter of the globe. Further ceremony was out of the question, at least until the excitement had subsided ; the parson, with philosophical com-

posure, precipitated his doxology, and we all walked
out into the dreary afternoon to watch the schooner
blowing in toward shore.

The wind was rising; white clouds scudded over
us; transparent shadows slid under us; the whole
earth seemed unstable, and life scarcely worth the
living. Along the dead shore leaped the sea, in a
careless, dare-devil fashion; hollow rocks spouted
great mouthfuls of spray contemptuously into the
air; columns of red dust climbed into the sky, reeling to and fro as they passed over the bleak desert
toward the sea on the opposite side of the island.
These dust-chimneys were continually moving over
the land so long as the wind prevailed, which was
for the rest of that afternoon, to my certain knowledge. In fact, the gale increased every hour; sheets
of spray leaped over the rocky barriers of the shore
and matted the dry grass, that hissed like straw
whenever a fresh gust struck it.

One tattered cocoa-palm, steadfast in its mission,
though the living emblem of a forlorn hope, wrestled
with the tempest that threw all its crisp and rattling
leaves over its head like a pompon, and fretted it
till its slender neck twisted as though it were being
throttled. The thatched house seemed about to
go to pieces, and every timber creaked in agony;
yet we gathered in its lee, and awaited the slow approach of the schooner. Near shore she put about,
and seemed upon the point of scudding off to sea
again. For a moment our hearts were in our
throats; we were in danger of missing the sensa-

tion of the season : new faces, new topics of conversation, and, perhaps, something good to eat, sent
thither by Providence, who seldom forgets his children in the waste places, though I wonder that he
lets them lose themselves so often.

The schooner rocked on the big rollers for half
an hour ; a small boat put off from her, with some
dark objects seated in it ; out on the great rollers
the little shallop rocked, sometimes hidden from
view by an intervening wave, sometimes thrown
partly out of the water as it balanced for a moment
on the crest of a breaker, but gradually drawing in
toward a bit of beach, where there was a possible
chance of landing, in some shape or other. A few
rods from shore, three dusky creatures deliberately plunged overboard and swam toward us. We
rushed in a body to welcome them—two women,
old residents of the place, who came out of the sea
wailing for joy at their safe return to a home no
more inviting than the one whose prominent features I have sought to reproduce. Down they sat,
not three feet from the water, that bubbled and
hissed along the coarse sand, and lifted up their
voices in pitiful and impressive monotones, as they
recounted in a savagely poetic chant their various
adventures since they last looked upon the beloved
picture of desolation that lay about them.

The third passenger—a youngster—came to land
when he had got tired of swimming for the fun of
it, and, once more upon his native heath, he seemed
at a loss to know what to do next, but suffered him-

self to be vigorously embraced by nearly everybody
in sight, after which he joined his companions with
placid satisfaction, and capered about as naturally
as though nothing unusual had happened.

Off into the windy sea sped the small schooner,
bending to the breeze as though it were a perpetual miracle that brought her right-side-up every
once in a while.   Back to the deserted prayer-house
our straggling community wended its way; everything that had been said before was said again, with
embellishments.   It was beginning to grow tiresome.
I longed to plunge into the desert that stretched
around, seeking some possible oasis where the fainting spirit might reassure itself that earth was beautiful and life a boon.

Kahéle agreed with me that this sort of thing
was growing tiresome.   He knew of a good place
not many miles away; we could go there and sleep.
It presented a church and a good priest, and other
inducements of an exceedingly proper and unexcep-
tionable character.   The prospect, though uninviting, was sufficient to revive me for the moment, and
during that moment we mounted, and were blown
away on horseback.   The wind howled in our ears;
sand-clouds peppered us heavily; small pebbles and
grit cut our faces; heavier gusts than usual changed
earth, sea, and sky into temporary chaos.   The day
waned, so did our spirits, so did the life of our poor
beasts.   In the distance, the church of Kahéle's
prophecy stood out like a small rock in a land than
which no land I wot of can be wearier.   The sun

17

fell toward the sea ; the wind subsided, though it was still lusty and disagreeable.

We entered the church, having turned our disheartened beasts into paddock, and found a meagre and late afternoon session, seated upon mats that covered the earthen floor. A priest strove to kindle a flame of religious enthusiasm in our unnatural hearts, but I fear he sought in vain. The truth was, we were tired to death ; we needed wholesome soup, savory meats, and steaming vegetables, to humanize us. I didn't want to be a Christian on an empty stomach. The wind began to sigh, after its passion was somewhat spent ; sand sifted over the matting with a low hiss; and the dull-red curtains, that stretched across the lower half of the windows, flapped dolefully. Overhead, the wasps had hung their mud baskets, and the gray atmosphere of everything was depressing in the extreme. Service was soon over ; the people departed across the windy moors, with much fluttering of gay garments. A horse stood at pasture, with his head down, his back to the wind, and his tail glued to his side — a picture of sublime resignation. A high mound, with a sandstone sepulchre built on the face of it, cut off half of the very red sunset, while a cactus-hedge, starred with pale pink blossoms, ran up a low hill, and made silhouette pictures against the sky.

I turned to watch a large butterfly, blown over in the late gale—stranded, as it were, at the church-porch, and too far gone to set sail again ; a white sea-bird wheeled over me in big circles, and screamed faintly; something fell in the church with a loud echo—a prayer-book, probably; and then the priest came out, fastened the door of the deserted sanctuary, and the day's duties were done. We had nothing to do but follow him to his small frame dwelling, where the one little window to the west seemed to be set with four panes of burnished gold, and some homely household shrubs in his garden-plat shivered, and blossomed while they shivered, but looked like so many widows and orphans, the whole of them.

At the hospitable board life began afresh. Another day and we should again approach the borders of the earthly paradise that glorified the opposite side of the island. Kahéle's eyes sparkled; my heart leaped within me; I felt that there was a charm in living, after all; and the moment was a critical one, for had the lad begged me to return with him to the beguilements of barbarism, I think it possible that I might have consented. But he didn't! He was the pink of propriety, and an honor to his progenitors. He said a brief grace before eating, prayed audibly before retiring, was patient to the pitch of stupidity, and amiable to the verge of idiocy.

At last I began to see through him. Another four-and-twenty hours, and he would be restored to the arms of his guardians; the sweet lanes of Lahaina would again blossom before him; and all that he thought to be excellent in life would know him as it had known him only a few weeks before. It was time that he had again begun to walk the straight path, and he knew it. He was Kahéle, the

two-sided ; Kahéle, the chameleon, whose character
and disposition partook of the color of his surroundings ; who was pious to the tune of the
church-bell, yet agile as any dancer of the lascivious *hula* at the thump of the tom-tom. He was a
representative worthy of some consideration ; a
typical Hawaiian whose versatility was only excelled by the plausibility with which he developed
new phases of his kaleidoscopic character. He was
very charming, and as diverting in one *rôle* as
another. He was, moreover, worthy of much praise
for his skill in playing each part so perfectly that to
this hour I am not sure which of his dispositions he
excelled in, nor in which he was most at home.

Kahéle, adieu ! I might have upbraided thee for
thy inconstancy, had I not been accused of that same
myself. I might have felt some modicum of contempt for thee, had thy skin been white ; but under
the cover of thy darkness sin hid her ugliness, and
thy rich blood leaped to many generous actions that
a white-livered sycophant might not aspire to. I
can but forgive all, and sometimes long a little to
live over the two sides of you—extremes that met
in your precious corporosity, and made me contented with a changeful and sometimes cheerless
pilgrimage ; for I knew, boy, that if I went astray,
you would meet me upon the highest moral grounds ;
and, though I could not rely upon you, somehow
you came to time when least expected, and filled me
with admiration and surprise—a sentiment which
time and absence only threaten to perpetuate.

KAHÉLE'S FOREORDINATION

WHY does experience profit us nothing? I
have asked myself this question a thousand
times, and I repeat it now, as I hold in my hand a
rare copy of a sometime obsolete volume entitled
"South Sea Idyls." That book contains the chron-
icles of my emotional adolescence. It was written in
the first flush of youth. It is too true not to be discredited, and it has invariably been discredited by
the wrong readers in the wrong stages of the narrative. The volume contains experiences in three
episodes, respectively entitled:

"The House of the Sun."

"The Chapel of the Palms."

"Kahéle."

There is naked truth enough in these chapters to
flood a well. I know this better than anyone else,
and in proof of it I triumphantly refer the reader
to the valedictory, which was written in the days of
my enthusiasm, while the almond tree flourished, ere
the stars were darkened, and before the grasshopper
had become a burden and all the daughters of music
were brought low! After my third rhapsody, entitled "Kahéle," that soft-eyed savage discreetly
took his leave.

Time and absence did their work effectually. I returned to the metropolis of the Pacific. A letter followed me couched in appalling English. In it I detected the delicate aroma of the grape-blossoms of Lahaina. In spirit I walked again among pepper groves, and sunned my soul beside the palmfringed sea. It was a message of love from my savage, and my heart leaped within me as I recalled the fascinating, inconsistent past. I replied cordially, and set sail for other shores. The whole world lay between us. We stood with the soles of our feet turned toward one another; and, had we ascended at that moment, our spirits could never have met in the wide universe. Fortunate fate! we both survive, and I have lived to prove myself a prophet in my own country, where, thank heaven! honors are easy. Once more I drifted back to the land of my adoption. Seven years stretched between me and the glimmering past. I thought of it as of a dream; I dreamed of it as of a thought— not a semblance of reality remained. Listen to the sequel.

One morning I was summoned from my late breakfast by the postman, who, with the polite discretion which has distinguished him from the first hour of our acquaintance, begged me to open a letter which was inscribed to—

"*Mr. Charles Stoodard, California.*"

It was subdirected to an innumerable lock-box which does not exist. I broke the seal and saw at a glance that the document was unmistakably mine. No one but a savage could have written it; no one but a boned savage stuffed with missionary teachings; one whose meat and drink, whose food and raiment, whose staff of life, whose First Reader, Second Reader, Third Reader, and Speller, and History, and Romance, has been the New Testament; one who has oiled the gospel according to St. John in the crown of his hat, and has rolled cigarettes with the Song of Songs; who has stormed the school-room ceiling with Scriptural wads; in brief, a native Hawaiian scripturist. Moreover, his name followed the scrip, which I copy word for word:

"PORT GAMBLE, Kitsap County, W. T.

"MR. CHARLES STUDARD, ESQ.—DEAR SIR: I am very glad to see you my Dear Lord of Our Saviour Jesus Christ. Amenn. This is the first letter I sent to you my Dear. I remember you for the year One thousand Eight hundred and seventy one—before we are to gone Circuit the Island of Maui—and gone to Kaupo—from Kaupo to Hana and see the two Rev Father Priests. I am your young servant Kahéle. I live to [left] Honolulu on the last day of July and come here with my Both [which is Boss, with a palpable lisp] and then my Both he dead. I had nothing to do here—no one to keep my life—if you please to give me some job then I stay with you for five year. If you see this letter you teregraph for me. This is our second letter to you—[mark with what royal condescension he recalls our former correspondence] because you write me one letter to Lahaina.

"Your young servant,

"KAHÉLE."

It was all his own ; the tropical luxuriance of language, the impressive majesty of the opening paragraph, the indiscriminate use of the letters *l* and *r*—a characteristic of the Hawaiian tongue—the painful imitation of a difficult language, seldom spoken with much care, and in his case caught wholly by ear. What did I do ? I telegraphed him within the hour to work his passage down to my arms by the first vessel that met his eye. All was forgiven on the instant ; I pictured that starving prodigal skipping like the young unicorn on receipt of my reply.

I imagined the dusky fellow in the hour of his deliverance, and impatiently awaited his arrival. "No sail from day to day." By and by came a second letter, evidently from the same hand—a flesh-colored envelope, not without blemish, bearing this fragmentary address :

> "*Mr. Charles W. Stodd.*"

By this time he had come to the edge of the envelope, and he stopped short in his tracks. Within, the unhappy scribe continued his heroic struggle with the perplexing intricacies of my name :

"MR. CHARLES WARREN STODDER—*Aloha nui oe:* I received your tergraph on thirteen of this month ; when I open it and read my heart is very much of joyful. I wait for the steamer, when he come Seattle then I go to your home. Now, my Dear Both [still lisping] I have no news to tell you about the golden chain of love between you and me.

> "Your young servant,
>> "KAHÉLE."

Again I awaited the arrival of my young servant,
and thought of him a thousand times, storm-tossed
upon the wintry seas, heart-sick, home-sick, sighing
for the fragrant winds that visit so lightly the green
seclusion of his native vales. Once more the faithful postman entered with a letter and a smile ; the
envelope smaller than usual, hence the following
address :

> "*Mr. Charles Warren S.,*
> "*S. F., Calf.*"

And within, the latest effort of this tireless nomen-
clator :

> "WASHINGTON TERRITORY.

"MESSIEURS CHAS. WARREN STOD :
[Age cannot wither, nor custom stale, his infinite variety!]

"SIR : This is the third letter I sent to you, my
Dear Sir. I leave the Puget Sound on the eigh-
teen of December, A.D. 1878. I go to Seat [Seat-
tle] on the steamer Alida, and see the Captain of
Dakota, the Maill steamer of San Francisco. I tell
him I want to work my passage from Seat to S. F.
He tell me no. I stay in Seat two days. On the
twenty-two of Decem. I coming to Tacoma till this
time I write this letter. If you please—in love for
your servant—to send me ten dollars inside letter for
me to pay my passage. If I stay with you I pay you
my owe.   Your servant,
                                            "KAHÉLE."

He no longer called himself my "young servant ; "
he seemed to have grown old in the vain attempt to
reach a haven of rest. This touched me to the quick.
Ten dollars are but as a feather in the balance when

there is a soul to save. In hot haste I purchased a ticket, and it was forwarded with a line of solace to the companion of my brighter days. Once more I watched and waited. From my window on the hill I signalled every passing sail. The hours lagged. What if the poor fellow, prematurely aged, had already dropped into the greedy grave that seemed yawning at his feet? What if the means of his deliverance never reached him, but fell by chance into the hands of some worthless straggler who might at any moment cross my threshold and attempt to palm upon me a forged identity? Seven years added to the infant Kahéle might be equal to almost anyone. How was I to detect a fraud unless it were of another color, which, please heaven, it was not to be?

With the dusk, one windy eve, shrouded in cold sea-fog, the picture of desolation, Kahéle stood in the doorway. He was changed. He was a strapping fellow of one and twenty, scantily clad as to his upper works, but bearing himself with an air of decayed elegance, and wearing conspicuously a pair of nobby boots, with tapering hoodlum heels. He had evidently been a swell. He blushed with reference to his flannel shirt, his overalls, his shocking-bad hat. There could be no doubt that this was the youngster who persuaded me in the barbarian days, who wooed me in the "House of the Sun," beguiled me in the "Chapel of the Palms," and distracted me in the third chapter of his career—a chapter that is dignified with his mellifluous name. The ambrosial locks distilling the faint fragrance of cocoanut oil; the

mild eyes, with their ingenuous glance, the slightly
depressed nose, the proud, sensuous lip, now mantled
with gosling-down—it was he without the shadow of a
doubt. To put him at his ease I extended to him the
freedom of the town, and he began the new life by immediately going through my wardrobe like a million
moths. There was little for him to do but to look interesting. To be sure, he surveyed the city, and gave
me official returns each evening, after dinner. He
drew maps of the streets ; had names and numbers
at his tongue's end ; inspected the chief public buildings, and passed judgment upon them with the
obtrusive confidence of a circumnavigator, though
I am proud to state that the Palace Hotel staggered
him—he confessed to me that it was finer in some
respects than anything in Honolulu. He reverenced
Woodward's Garden, in common with the masses ;
enjoyed the drama ; revelled in the church. He aspired night and day. In confidential moments he
broke to me his plans for a future, that seemed to
him boundless in its capability. After a *fête* at
Woodward's he longed to enter the arena. The
drama inspired him with dreams of the stage. As
for the Sacrifice of the Mass, he more than once
talked seriously of studying for the priesthood, and
even asked me how much it would cost—he always
counted the cost, an example too seldom followed
by his betters. A delicious melancholy seized him
whenever he inclined to the novitiate, but his ambition was boundless, and I think he preferred a
roving commission—one that would admit of his aid-

ing the propagation of the faith by easy stages in
every quarter of the habitable globe.

It was about this time that life began to pall.
The youth missed his kindred, and mourned for
them.   Our talks were all of the past.   We lived
over the riotous days, and renewed our prilgrimages
until there was no valley left unvisited, no stone un-
turned.   He chanted his legendary songs in mellow
gutturals ; sat in the sunshine of the deep bay-win-
dow ; looked off upon the ships in the harbor, and
asked the price of them.   His wage was oftenest
spent in fruit-stalls, though on one occasion he returned to me with a small casket of jewels, which
he had purchased at the street-corner, under a torchlight, for fifteen cents.   Then it occurred to me that
some of his people must be within reach, and I sent
him forth to take the city census.   Day after day
he stood on Market Street, watching for Kanakas ;
night after night he returned again, empty-handed,
plunged in black despair.

At last he caught one on the fly, a mariner, one of
a "forec's'le" full of them.   That night there was
revelry on the water front, and the throb of the calabash quickened the feet of the Hula dancers until
daybreak, when they all ate of the national *poi* out
of one trough and slept the sleep of the just.   No
trouble now, no languishing, no weariness of spirit.
He went his way rejoicing, and returned like the
prodigal when he had wasted his portion.

I found that he had, as it were, made his entrance
into society.   He sparkled with fifteen cent jewelry,

and wore his hat over one ear. He babbled in Spanish, and casually observed that the average señorita
is as handsome as the ditto *Waihine*. He wallowed
in verbs, regular and irregular. He once said, as
in a dream, *yo amo*, and again, while his mind wandered, *nostros amúmos*. The confusion that followed
this involuntary confession was not that of a scholar.
I asked him where he had been, and why he had
sought to master a language which was little spoken
save by its inheritors. He darkened, but without a
stammer he told how his evenings were passed in
sweet communion with a select few, who, like himself, admired the melodious speech of Spain. But
where? With an innocence that threw me off my
guard, he gave me an address—Pacific Street, near
Kearney—an unsavory quarter, known as the Barbary Coast.

Still harping on his Spanish, I showed him some
papers long treasured as an heirloom in this home-
stead—certificates of stock in a fabulous Mexican
mine, from whose undiscovered bourne, so far as
heard from, no traveller returns; at all events, no living witness has gone farther than levying an assess-
ment—and lived. With the deepest interest he
studied the certificates; with the poetic fervor of his
race he built his lordly castle and peopled it with the
choicer spirits of our acquaintance. It was his wish
that we might fly at once to this glittering realm and
rest from our labors. I smiled sadly, bitterly; I
always do when a bright manhood is painted for me
by that youth in whose imperfect lexicon there is no

such word as "fail." Kahéle soothed me with savage songs. Together we groped among the evening shadows of Kearney Street, than which no respectable thoroughfare in God's world is worse lighted. It was my wish to hear the guitar touched by the skilled fingers of his friends, who are to the manner born; but ere we reached the quarter he had idealized I turned and he was gone! Like a shadow he came, like a shadow he departed.

I passed three silent, sensitive, sorrowful days. It is not well to make your idols, and to find them clay, and to prosecute the unprofitable business year after year. He returned not. No more I heard his foot upon the stair; no more I listened to his chant—its soft *cadenza* is forever hushed within my chamber. I searched the journals for casualty returns. I haunted the Morgue like a press reporter. I grew morbid and morose. Then I chanced upon his commonplace book; with the lynx-eye of a detective I studied its pages, but gained no clew to the mystery. I discovered among his effects a copy of "Spanish without a Master, on the Most Simple Principles, for Universal Self - Tuition. Price, Twenty - five Cents," "The Letter-Writer's Own Book," a broken cuff-button, and some diamond studs with the glass out—the *débris* of his jewel-case. Evidently if he fled from me, his flight was premature. Why did I suspect aught and look into the family archives to find proof of his guilt?

The mining stock was missing!

I visited the several boards in the vague fear that

I would come suddenly upon the culprit bulling the
market with his Mexico. But the Exchange was innocent of him; Pauper Alley knew him not; and
his shadow never again darkened Kearney Street, to
my knowledge. Then came another letter—the last
of the series. It was a wild scrawl, pencilled in
haste. It ran as follows:

> "CITY OF SANTA CRUZ.
>
> "I am gone to Los Angel, and to Mexico—with
> my wife. Aloha. K.
>
> "TO MR. CHARLES."

I might have known it, had I but listened to the
lessons of experience; yet doubtless it was written
in his horoscope, and I was but a means to an end.
Now dawns upon me the significance of the porten-
tous ides of May. Fool that I was, I might have
cut the net that enthralled him, and perhaps have
spared him for a costlier sacrifice. Insensible victim! Is he founding his fortune in the fastnesses
of the mineral hills? Is it well with him in his mountain stronghold? Do the torrents that pour their
silver beside his door muffle the tinkling music of
guitars, the "click" of castanets, the boom of the
hollow drum? Does he dream again of the loves of
the Barbary Coast, chief of whom is his Circe?

Yet am I proud of this climax, for did I not write
of him years ago, to wit: "He was Kahéle, the
two-sided; Kahéle, the chameleon, whose character
and disposition partook of the color of his surroundings; who was pious to the tune of the church-bell,

yet agile as any dancer of the lascivious *Hula* at the thump of the tom-tom. He was a representative worthy of some consideration ; a typical Hawaiian, whose versatility was only excelled by the plausibility with which he developed new phases of his kaleidoscopic character. He was very charming, and as diverting in one *rôle* as another. He was, moreover, worthy of much praise for his skill in playing each part so perfectly that to this hour I am not sure which of his dispositions he excelled in, nor in which he was most at home."

He went, therefore, to the devil : that the words of the prophet might be fulfilled. But what does it matter to me so long as I have my experiences over and over, and outlive them one and all ! Come, daisies and buttercups—the more the merrier ; spice my dull life with at least this variety, and let me agonize or let me die :

For I am of those Azras who, when they love, must perish !

And I'm awfully used to it.

LOVE-LIFE IN A LANAI

IT was the witching hour of sunset, and we sat at dinner, with tearful eyes, over the Commodore's curry. You see the Commodore prided himself on the strength of this identical dish, and kept a mahogany-tinted East-Indian steward for the sole sake of his skill in concocting the same.

We dined, as usual, in the Commodore's unrivalled *Lanai*—the very thought of which is a kind of spiritual feast to this hour—and while we sat at his board we heard for the twentieth time the monotonous recital of his adventures by flood and field. Like most sea-stories, his narratives were ever fresh, as though they had been stowed away in brine, were fished out of the vasty deep expressly for the occasion, and put to soak again in their natural element as soon as we had tasted their quality.

The Commodore was a roaring old sea-dog, who had been cast ashore somewhere in the early part of the century; and finding himself in quarters more comfortable than his wildest fancy dared to paint, he resolved to end his amphibious days on that strip of shining beach, and nevermore lose sight of land until he should slip his cable for the last time, and sail into undiscovered seas. Meanwhile he entertained

his friends at Wai-ki-ki, a kind of tropical Long
Branch a few miles out of Honolulu; and the grace
with which he introduced Jack-ashore to the dreamy
twilight of his *Lanai* is one of Jack's deathless memories.   We met the Commodore in the interesting
character of Jack-ashore, and with uncovered heads
and hearts full of emotion entered the *Lanai*.

And now for a word to the uninitiated concerning the *Lanai* in question.   Off there in the Pacific,
under the vertical sun, all shadow is held at a pre-
mium.   There are stationary caravans of cocoa-trees,
that seem to be looking for their desert-home—
weird, slender trees, with tattered plumes, and a
hopeless air about them, as though they were born
to sorrow, but meant to make the best of it.   Still,
these fine old palms cast a thin shadow, about the
size and shape of a colossal spider, and there is no
comfort in trying to sit in it.   Of course, there are
other trees with more foliage, and vines that run
riot and blossom themselves to death ; but somehow
the sharp arrows of sunshine dart in and sting a
fellow in an unpleasant fashion, and nothing short
of a good thatch is to be relied upon.   So out from
the low eaves of the Commodore's cottage, on the
seaward side, there was a dense roof of leaves and
grass, that ran clear to the edge of the sea, and
looked as though it wanted to go farther ; but the
Commodore knew it was useless to attempt to roof
over that institution.   There was a leafy tapestry
hanging two feet below the roof on the three sides
thereof and from the floor of the enclosure rose a

sort of trellis of woven rushes that hedged us in to
the waist. There was a wicker-gate, and an open
space between the leafy stalactite and stalagmite
barricade for ventilation and view, and everywhere
there was a kind of semi-twilight that seemed
crammed full of dreams and delicious indolence—
and this is the Hawaiian *Lanai!*

Of course, the Commodore always dined in his
Lanai. It was like taking curry on the quarter-deck
of the *What - you - call - her,* in the dead calm of the
Indian seas; and when that mahogany steward entered with turban and mock-turtle—he always
looked to me like a full-blooded snake-charmer—I
had the greatest difficulty in restraining myself, for
it seemed to me incredible that any Jack-ashore
could dine in a *Lanai* with his Excellency, and not
rise between each savory course to make a dozen
profound *salaams* to the fattish gentleman at the
head of the table, who was literally covered with
invisible naval buttons—and the hallucination increased as the dinner-courses multiplied.

At this stage—just as the snake-charmer was entering with something that seemed to have come
to an untimely end in wine-sauce—at this stage the
Commodore turned to us as though he were about
to give some order that we might disregard at the
peril of our lives—these sea-dogs never quite out-
grow that sort of thing. "Gentlemen," said he,
casting a watchful and suspicious eye over the
weather-bow, "there is to be a *Luou*—a native feast
—in the adjoining premises. Will you do me the

honor to accompany me thither after we have lighted our cigars?"

I forget what answer we made; but then dinner was well on toward dessert, and our answer was immaterial. We had our orders, couched in courteous language, and we were thankful for this consideration; moreover, we were wild to see a native feast! There is a peculiar charm in obeying our superiors, when we happen, by some dispensation of Divine Providence, to be exactly of the same mind.

Black coffee was offered us, in cups of the pattern of gulls' eggs. By this time all the sky was saffron, all the sea a shadow of saffron, and in the golden haze that lay between, a schooner with a piratical slant to her masts swam by, beyond the foam that hissed along the reef. It was a wonderful picture, but it came in between the courses of the Commodore's dinner as though it were nothing better than a panel-painting in the after-cabin of the *What-you-call-her*. However, as she swung in toward the mouth of the harbor and passed a bottle of Burgundy in safety, but seemed in imminent danger of missing stays abreast of an enormous pyramid of fruit—from the Commodore's point of sight, you know—the old gentleman lost his temper and gave an order in such peremptory terms that I cheerfully refrain from reproducing it on this occasion. To cover our confusion we immediately adjourned to the native feast.

Hawaiian feast-days are not set down in the calendar. Somebody's child has a birthday, or there is a new house that needs christening ; or perhaps a church is in want, and the feast can net a hundred or two dollars for it—since all the eatables in such cases are donated, and the eaters enter to the feast with the payment of one dollar per head. Our feast was not sanctified ; a chief of the best blood was in the humor to entertain his friends, countrymen, and lovers. We belonged to the first order ; or, rather, the Commodore was his friend, and we speedily became as friendly as possible. As we entered the premises, it appeared to us that half the island was under cover ; for limitless *Lanais* seemed to run on to the end of time in bewitching vistas. Numberless lanterns swung softly in the evening gale. A multitude of white-robed native girls passed to and fro, with that inimitable grace which I have always supposed Eve copied from the serpent and imparted to her daughters, who still affect the modern Edens of the earth. Young Hawaiian bloods clad in snow-white trousers and ballet-shirts, with wreaths of *mailné* around their necks and ginger-flowers in their hair, grouped themselves along the evergreen corridors, and looked unutterable things without any noticeable effort on their part.

Through the central corridor, under a long line of lanterns, was spread the corporeal feast, and on either side of it, in two ravenous lines, sat, tailor-fashion, the hungry and the thirsty. It is useless to attempt an idealization of the Hawaiian eater. He simply devours whatever suits his palate, as though he were a packing-case that needed filling,

and the sooner filled the more creditable the performance. But the amount of filling that he is equal
to is the marvel ; and the patient perseverance of
the man, so long as there is a crumb left, is something that I despair of reconciling with any known
system of physiology. The mastication began early
in the afternoon. It was 8 P.M. when we looked in
upon the orgy, and the bones were not all picked,
though they seemed likely to be before midnight.

"Will you eat?" said the host. It was not etiquette to decline, and we sat at the end of the
Lanai, with nameless dishes strewn about us in
hopeless confusion. We dipped a finger into pink
poi, and took a pinch of baked dog. We had limpets with rock-salt ; kukui-nuts roasted and pulver-
ized ; and the pale, quivering bits of fish-flesh, not
an hour dead, and still cool with the native coolness
of the sea. It was a fishful feast anyway ; and not
even the fruits or the flowers could entirely alleviate
the inward agony consequent upon a morsel of
raw fish, swallowed to please our host.

There was music at the farther end of the palm-
leaf pavilion, and thither we wended our way. The
inner court was festooned with flags, and covered
with a large mat. Upon the mat sat, or reclined,
several chiefesses. I am never able to account for
the audacious grace of these women, who throw
themselves upon the floor and stretch their supple limbs like tigresses, with a kind of imperial
scorn for your one-horse proprieties. Their volumi-
nous light garments scarcely concealed the ample

curves of their bodies, and the marvellous creatures
seemed to be breathing to slow music, while their
slumberous eyes regarded us with a gentle indifference that was more tantalizing than any other species of coquetry that I have knowledge of.

At one side of the enclosure sat a group of musicians, twanging upon native harps, and beating the
national calabash. Song after song was sung, pipe
after pipe was smoked, and bits of easy and playful conversation filled the intervals. The evening
waned. The eaters and drinkers were still unsatisfied, because the eatables and drinkables were not
exhausted ; but the moon was high and full, and the
reef moaned most musically, and seemed to invite
us to the shore.

The great charm of a native feast is the entire absence of all formality. Every man is privileged to
seek whom his heart may most desire, and every
woman may receive him or reject him as her spirit
prompts. We noticed that the Commodore was uneasy. He was as plump as a seal, and the crowd
oppressed him. We resolved to get the old gentleman out of his misery, and proposed an immediate
adjournment to the beach. The inner court was
soon deserted, and our little party—which now embraced, figuratively, several magnificent chiefesses,
as well as the primitive Hawaiian orchestra—moved
in silence toward the sea. The long, curving beach
glistened and sparkled in the moonlight. The sea,
within the reef, was like a tideless river, from whose
pellucid depths, where the coral spread its wilder-

ness of branches, an unearthly radiance was reflected.
A fleet of slender canoes floated to and fro upon the
water, and beyond them the creaming reef flashed
like a girdle of silver, belting us in from all the
world.

The crowning luxury of savage life is the multitudinous bondsman who anticipates your every wish,
and makes you blush at your own poverty of inven-
tion by his suggestions of unimagined joys. Mats
—broad, sweet, and clean—lay under foot, and served
our purpose better than Persian carpets. The sea
itself fawned at our feet, and all the air was shining
and soft as though the moon had dissolved in an
ecstasy, and nothing but a snap of cold weather
could congeal her again. Wherever we lay, pillows
were mysteriously slipped under our heads, and the
willingest hands in the world began an involuntary
performance of the *lomi lomi*. Let me not think
upon the *lomi-lomi*, for there is none of it within
reach ; but I may say of it, that, before the skilful
and magnetic hands of the manipulator are folded,
every nerve in the body is seized with an intense
little spasm of recognition, and dies happy. A
dreamless sleep succeeds, and this is followed by an
awakening into new life, full of proud possibilities.

We were *lomi-lomied* to the murmurs of the reef,
and during the intervals of consciousness saw an impromptu rehearsal of the "Naiad Queen," in operatic
form. The dancing girls, being somewhat heated,
had plunged into the sea, and were complaining to
the moon in a chorus of fine harmonies. History

does not record how long their sea-song rang across the waters. I know that we dozed, and woke to watch a silver sail wafted along the vague and shadowy distance like a phantom. We slept again, and woke to a sense of silence, broken only by the unceasing monody of the reef; slept and woke yet again in the waning light, for the moon had sunk to the ragged rim of an old crater, and seemed to have a large piece bitten out of her glorious disk. Then we broke camp by the shore—for the air was a trifle chilly—and withdrew into the seclusion of the Commodore's *Lanai*, where we threw ourselves into hammocks and swung until daybreak.

In those days we fed on lotus-flowers. Jack-ashore lives for the hour only, and the very air of such a latitude breathes enchantment. I believe we bathed before sunrise, and then went regularly to bed and slept till noon. Such were the Commodore's orders, and this is our apology. There was a breakfast about 1 P.M., at which we were permitted to appear in undress. The Commodore set the example by inviting us to the table in an extraordinary suit of cream-colored silk, that was suggestive of *pajamas*, but might have been some Oriental regalia especially designed for morning wear. He looked like a ship under full sail rocking good-naturedly in a dead calm. The Commodore was excessively formal at first sight—that is, just before breakfast—but his heart warmed toward mankind in general, and his guests in particular, as the meal progressed. Some people never are themselves until they have broken their fast ; they are so cranky, and seem to lack ballast.

The snaky steward sloughed his clothes twice a day. He was a slim, noiseless, gliding fellow at breakfast, but he was positively gorgeous at dinner. Of course, the Commodore had ordered this nice distinction in the temporal affairs of his servant, for he kept everything about the place in ship-shape, even to the flying of his private signal from sunrise to sunset at the top of a tall staff, that rivalled the royal ensign floating from a similar altitude not a quarter of a mile distant. His Majesty has a summer palace in Wai-ki-ki, and it has been whispered that the Commodore refused to recognize him, and never dipped his colors as the King cantered by in a light buggy drawn by a span of spanking bays.

After breakfast the cribbage-board was produced, and for three mortal hours the Commodore kept his peg on the steady march. At cribbage the old gentleman was expected to lose his temper. He stormed with the arrogance of a veteran card-player, than whom no man is supposed to make himself more disagreeable on short notice. Lieutenant Blank was usually the victim, but he deserved it. The true story of Lieutenant Blank—his name is suppressed out of consideration for his family—is so common in tropical seaports that I do not hope in this epitome to offer anything novel. The Lieutenant was a typical Jack-ashore. He had twice the mail that came to the rest of us, and he read his love-letters to the mess with a gusto. He boasted

fresh victims in every port, and gloried in his lack
of principle. It did not surprise me at all that the
Lieutenant had *shaken* his mother. In fact, under
the circumstances, I think his mother would have
been justified in shaking him, if she could have got
her hands on him. In the love-light of the Commodore's *Lanai*, life was very precious to this particular Jack-ashore. To him a *Lanai* was a city of refuge,
provided by an all-wise Commodore for those fascinating lieutenants who were pursued by the chief
women of the tribe; yet he loved to loiter without the
walls during the off-hours from cribbage. No man
so relished the *lomi-lomi*; no man, except the native-
born, so clamored for the *hula-hula*; and no man,
not even the least of these, forgot himself to the same
alarming extent whenever there was the slightest
provocation.

Of course, he met a chiefess and surrendered; of
course, he meant in time to crush the heart that pul-
sated with the blood-royal. He simpered and tried
to turn semi-savage, and was simply ridiculous. He
made silly speeches in the worst possible Hawaiian,
and afforded unlimited amusement to the women,
who are wiser in their dark skins than the children
of light. He tried to eat *poi*, and ruined his linen.
He suffered himself to be wreathed and garlanded,
until he was the picture of a sacrificial calf. He
gave gifts, and babbled in his sleep. But in the
hour when his triumph seemed inevitable he was
beautifully snubbed by his supposed victim. The
sirens of Scylla are a match for any mariner who

sails with unwadded ears. The Lieutenant cannot hope to hear the last of that adventure, though the subject is never broached by himself.

If we had dwelt a thousand years with the Commodore, and sipped the elixir of life from the gourd that hung by the door of the wine-closet, I suppose we should have had the same daily and nightly experiences to go through with, barring a slight variation in the little matter of moonshine. But there were orders superior to the Commodore's, since he was off active duty, and these orders demanded our reappearance on shipboard at an early hour of the day following. There was a farewell round of everything that had been introduced during our brief stay at Wai-ki-ki—dances, songs, sea-baths, and flirtations. The moon rose later, and was but a shadow of her former self; but the stars burned brightly, and we could still trace the noiseless flight of the solitary sail that passed like a spirit over the dusky sea.

I know that in after years, whenever I come within sound of surf under the prickly sunshine, my fancy will conjure up a picture of that grass cottage on the slope of a dazzling beach, and the portly form of the old Commodore stowed snugly in the spacious hollow of a bamboo settee, drawn up on the stocks, as it were, for repairs, with a bandanna spread over his face and a dark-eyed crouching figure beside him fighting mosquitoes with a tuft of parrot-feathers. No wonder that a body-guard of some kind was necessary, for I believe that the old Commodore's veins ran nothing but wine, and mosquitoes are good tasters.

The picture would not be complete without the attendant houris, and with their image comes an echo of barbarous chants and the monotonous thump of the tom-tom; of swaying figures; of supple wrists; of slender, lascivious hands tossed skilfully in the air, seeking to interpret their pantomimic dances, and doing it with remarkable freedom and grace. I shall hear that one song, like an echo eternally repeated—the song that was sung by all the lips that had skill to sing, in every valley under the Hawaiian sun. I remember it as a refrain that was first raised in Honolulu, but for the copyright of which the respective residents of Hawaii and Nihau would willingly lay down their lives with the last words of the song rattling in their throats.

"*Poli-anu*," or "Cool-bosom," is a fair specimen of the ballad literature of Hawaii, and the following free translation will perhaps give a suggestion of the theme. "*Poli-anu*" is sung by the old and decrepid, the lame, the halt, and the blind, as well as by the merest children. I have heard it carolled by a solitary boy tending goats upon the breezy heights of Kaupo. I have listened to it in the market-place, where a chorus of a dozen voices held the customer entranced. In the high winds of the middle channel the song is raised, as the schooner lays over at a perilous angle, and ships water enough to dampen the ardor of most singers. It is sung in the church-porch, by the brackish well in the desert, under the moonlit palms, and everywhere else. It cheers the midnight vigil of the prisoner, and makes glad the

heart of the sorrowful. It is altogether useful as well
as ornamental, and the Hawaiian who does not number among his accomplishments the ability to sing
"*Poli-anu*" tolerably well, is unworthy of the name.

POLI-ANU.

Bosom, here is love for you,
  O bosom cool as night !
How you refresh me as with dew—
  Your coolness gives delight.

Rain is cold upon the hill,
  And water in the pool,
Yet all my frame is colder still
  For you, O bosom cool.

Face to face beneath a bough
  I may not you embrace,
But feel a spell on breast and brow
  While sitting face to face.

Thoughts in absence send a thrill
  Like touch of sweeter air :
I sought you, and I seek you still,
  O bosom cool and fair !

That is all of it ; but your Hawaiian turns back
and begins over again, until he has enough.

I suppose it is no breach of confidence on my part
to state that the gorgeous old Commodore is dead.
There was nothing in his *Lanai* life to die of, except
an accident, and in course of time he met with one.
I forget the nature of it, but it finished him.   There
was wailing for three mortal days in the solemn

shadow of the *Lanai;* and then one of the large, motherly looking creatures, with numberless gauzy folds in a dress that fell straight from her broad shoulders, moved in. After three days of feasting, all vestiges of the Commodore's atmosphere had disappeared from the premises. I fancy she always felt at home there, although she was never known to open her lips in the presence of the Commodore's guests. Life was a little more intense after that. The snaky steward disappeared, without any sort of warning. I have always believed that he crawled under some rock, and laid himself away in a coil; that he will sleep for a century or so, then come out in his real character, and astonish the inhabitants with his length and his slimness.

Lieutenant Blank survives, and sails the stormy seas on a moderate salary, the major portion of which he turns into naval buttons. I hear from him once in a dog's age. He is first at Callao, with a daily jaunt into Lima; then at one of the South Sea paradises; next at Australia, or in the China Sea; and in the future—heaven knows where! He vibrates between the two hemispheres, working out his time, and believing himself supremely happy. I doubt not that he is happy, being about as selfish as men are made.

As for myself, I am a landsman. After all that is said, the sea is rather a bore, you know; but I do not forget the dreamy days of calm in the flowering equatorial waters, nor the troubled days of storm. There are a thousand-and-one trifling events in the

fragmentary experiences of the seafarer that are of
more importance than this stray leaf, but perhaps
none that will serve my purpose better. For this
yarn is as fine-drawn as the episodes in an out-of-
the-way port—with nothing but the faint odor of
its fruits a little overripe, of its flowers a little over-
blown, and a general sense of uncomfortable warmth,
to give it individuality. I have found these experiences excellent memories ; for though the dull
" waits" between the acts and the sluggishness of
the action at best are a little dreary at times, they are
forgotten, together with most disagreeable matter.
I'll warrant you, Lieutenant Blank, strutting his little
hour between-decks, or in the fleeting moments of
the delectable " dog-watch," muses upon the past.
When he has aroused the fever in his blood, and can
no longer hold his tongue, he heaves an ominous
sigh, knits his brows, and, in a voice that quivers
with unaffected emotion, he whispers to the marines
the beguiling romance of his *Love-life in a Lanai.*

IN A TRANSPORT

A LITTLE French *aspirant de marine*, with an incipient mustache, said to me, confidentially, "Where you see the French flag you see France!" We were pacing to and fro on the deck of a transport that swung at anchor off San Francisco, and, as I looked shoreward for almost the last time—we were to sail at daybreak for a southern cruise—I hugged my Ollendorf in despair, as I dreamed of "French in six easy lessons," without a master, or a tolerable accent, or anything, save a suggestion of Babel and a confusion of tongues at sea.

Thanaron, the aspirant in question, embraced me when I boarded the transport with my baggage, treated me like a long-lost brother all that afternoon, and again embraced me when I went ashore toward evening to take leave of my household. There was something so impulsive and boyish in his manner that I immediately returned his salute, and with considerable fervor, feeling that kind Heaven had thrown me into the arms of the exceptional foreigner who would, to a certain extent, console me for the loss of my whole family. The mystery that hangs over the departure of any craft that goes by wind is calculated to appal the landsman; and when the date of sailing is fixed the best thing he can do is to go aboard in season and compose his soul in peace. To be sure, he may swing an anchor for a day or two, in full sight of the domestic circle that he has shattered; but he is spared the repetition of those last agonies, and cuts short the unravelling hours just prior to a separation which are probably the most unsatisfactory in life.

Under cover of darkness a fellow can do almost anything, and I concluded to go on board. There was a late dinner and a parting toast at home, and those ominous silences in the midst of a conversation that was as spasmodic and disconnected and unnatural as possible. There was something on our minds, and we relapsed in turn and forgot ourselves in the fathomless abysses of speculation. Someone saw me off that night—someone who will never again follow me to the sea, and welcome me on my return to earth after my wandering. We sauntered down the dark streets along the city front, and tried to disguise our motives, but it was hard work. Presently we heard the slow swing of the tide under us, and the musty odor of the docks regaled us; one or two shadows seemed to be groping about in the neighborhood, making more noise than a shadow has any right to make.

Then came the myriad-masted shipping, the twinkling lights in the harbor, and a sense of ceaseless motion in waters that never can be still. We did not tarry there long. The boat was bumping her

bow against a pair of slippery stairs that led down
to the water, and I entered the tottering thing that
half sunk under me, dropped into my seat in the
stern, and tried to call out something or other as
we shot away from the place, with a cloud over my
eyes that was darker than night itself, and a cloud
over my heart that was as heavy as lead. After that
there was nothing to do but climb up one watery
swell and slide down on the other side of it, to
count the shadow-ships that shaped themselves out
of chaos as we drew near them, and dissolved again
when we had passed; while the oars seemed to
grunt in the row-locks, and the two jolly tars in
uniform—they might have been mutes, for all I
know—swung to and fro, to and fro, dragging
me over the water to my "ocean bride"—I think
that is what they call a ship, when the mood is on
them!

She did look pretty as we swam up under her.
She looked like a great *silhouette* against the steel-
gray sky; but within was the sound of revelry, and
I hastened on board to find our little cabin blue with
smoke, which, however, was scarcely dense enough
to muffle the martial strains of the *Marseillaise*, as
shouted by the whole mess.

Thanaron—my Thanaron—was in the centre of
the table, with his curly head out of the transom—
not that he was by any means a giant, but we were
all a little cramped between-decks—and he was
leading the chorus with a sabre in one hand and the
head of the Doctor in the other. Without the sup-

port of the faculty he would probably not have ended his song of triumph as successfully as he ultimately did, when Nature herself had fainted from exhaustion. It was the last night in port, a few friends from shore had come to dine, and black coffee and cognac at a late hour had finished the business.

If there is one thing in this world that astonishes me more than another, it is the rapidity with which some people talk in French. Thanaron's French, when he once got started, sounded to me like the well-executed trill of a *prima donna*, and quite as intelligible. The joke of it was, that Frenchmen seemed to find no difficulty in understanding him at his highest speed. On the whole, perhaps, this fact astonishes me more than the other.

Dinner was as far over as it could get without beginning again and calling itself breakfast; so the party broke up in a whirlwind of patriotic songs, and, one by one, we dropped our guests over the side of the vessel until there was none left, and then we waved them a thousand adieus, and kept up the last words as long as we could catch the faintest syllable of a reply. There were streaks of dull red in the east by this time, and the outlines of the city were again becoming visible. This I dreaded a little; and when our boat had returned and everything was put in ship-shape, I deliberately dropped a tear in the presence of my messmates, who were overcome with emotion at the spectacle; and, having all embraced, we went below, where I threw myself, with some caution, into my hammock and slept until broad daylight.

I did not venture on deck again until after our first breakfast—an informal one, that set uneasily on the table, and seemed inclined to make its escape from one side or the other. Of course we were well under way by this time. I was assured of the fact by the reckless rolling of the vessel and the strange and unfamiliar feeling in my stomach, as though it were some other fellow's stomach, and not my own. My legs were a trifle uncertain; my head was queer. Everybody was rushing everywhere and doing things that had to be undone or done over again in the course of the next ten minutes. I concluded to pace the deck, which is probably the correct thing for a man to do when he goes down to the sea in ships, and does business—you could hardly call it pleasure—on great waters.

I went up the steep companion-way, and found a deck-load of ropes, and the entire crew—dressed in blue flannel, with broad collars—skipping about in the most fantastic manner. It was like a ballet scene in "L'Africaine," and highly diverting—for a few minutes! From my stronghold on the top stair of the companion-way I cast my eye shoreward. The long coast ran down the horizon under a broadside of breakers that threatened to ingulf the continent; the air was gray with scattering mist; the sea was much disturbed and of that ugly, yellowish green tint that signifies soundings. Overhead, a few sea-birds whirled in disorder, shrieking as though their hearts would break. It looked ominous, yet I felt it my duty, as an American under the shadow of the tricolor, to keep a stiff upper lip —and I flatter myself that I did- so. Figuratively speaking, I balanced myself in the mouth of the companion-way, with a bottle of claret in one pocket and a French roll in the other, while I brushed the fog from my eyes with the sleeve of my monkey-jacket, and exclaimed with the bard, "My native land, good-night."

It was morning at the time, but I did not seem to care much. In fact, time is not of the slightest consequence on shipboard. So I withdrew to my hammock, and having climbed into it in safety ended the day after a miserable fashion that I have deplored a thousand times since, during the prouder moments of my life.

A week passed by—I suppose it was a week, for I could reckon only seven days, and seven nights of about twice the length of the days—during that interval; yet I should, in the innocence of my heart, have called it a month without a moment's hesitation. We arose late in the morning—those of us who had a watch below; ate a delightfully long and narrow breakfast, consisting of an interminable procession of dishes in single file; paced the deck and canvassed the weather; went below to read, but talked instead; dined as we had breakfasted, only in a far more elaborate and protracted manner, while a gentle undercurrent of side-dishes lent interest to the occasion. There was a perpetual

stream of conversation playing over the table, from
the moment that heralded the soup until the last
drop of black coffee was sopped up with a bit of dry
bread. By the time we had come to cheese, everybody felt called upon to say his say, in the face of
everybody else. I alone kept my place, and held it
because the heaviest English I knew fell feebly to
the floor before the thunders of those five prime
Frenchmen, who were flushed with enthusiasm and
good wine. I dreamed of home over my cigarette,
and tried to look as though I were still interested
in life, when, Heaven knows, my face was more like
a half-obliterated cameo of despair than anything
human. Thanaron, my foreign affinity, now and
then threw me a semi-English nut to crack, but by
the time I had recovered myself—it is rather embarrassing to be assaulted even in the most friendly
manner with a batch of broken English—by the
time I had framed an intelligible response, Thanaron
was in the heat of a fresh argument, and keeping
up a running fire of small shot that nearly floored
the mess.

But there is an end even to a French dinner, and
we ultimately adjourned to the deck, where, about
sunset, everybody took his station while the *Angelus* was said. Then twilight, with a subdued kind
of skylarking in the forecastle, and genteel merriment amidships, while *Monsieur le Capitaine* paced
the high quarter-deck with the shadow of a smile
crouching between the fierce jungles of his intensely
black side-whiskers. Ah, sir, it was something to

be at sea in a French transport with the tricolor flaunting at the peak ; to have four guns with their mouths gagged, and oilcloth capes lashed snugly over them ; to see everybody in uniform, each having the profoundest respect for those who ranked a notch above him, and having, also, an ill-disguised contempt for the unlucky fellow beneath him ! This spirit was observable from one end of the ship to the other, and, sirs, we had a little world of our own revolving on a wabbling axis between the stanch ribs of the old transport *Chevert*.

We were bound for Tahiti, God willing and the winds favorable ; and the common hope of ultimately finding port in that paradise is all that held us together through thick and thin. We might wrangle at dinner, and come to breakfast next morning with bitterness in our hearts ; we might sink into the bottomless pit of despond ; we might revile *Monsieur le Capitaine* and *Monsieur le Cuisinier*, including in our anathemas the elements and some other things ; they (the Frenchmen) might laugh to scorn the great American people—and they did it, two or three times—and I, in my turn, might feel a secret contempt for Paris, without having the power to express the same in tolerable French, so I felt it and held my tongue. Even Thanaron gave me a French shrug now and then that sent the cold shivers through me ; but there was sure to come a sunset like a sea of fire, at which golden hour we were marshalled amidships, and stood with uncovered heads and the soft light playing over us, while the littlest French boy in the crew said the evening prayer with exceeding sweetness—being the youngest, he was the most worthy of saying it—and then we all crossed ourselves, and our hearts melted within us.

There was something in the delicious atmosphere, growing warmer every day, and something in the delicious sea, that was beginning to rock her floating gardens of blooming weed under our bows, and something in the aspect of *Monsieur le Capitaine*, with his cap off and a shadow of prayer softening his hard, proud face, that unmanned us; so we rushed to our own little cabin and hugged one another, lest we should forget how when we were restored to our sisters and our sweethearts, and everything was forgiven and forgotten in one intense moment of French remorse.

Who took me in his arms and carried me the length of the cabin in three paces, at the imminent peril of my life? Thanaron! Who admired Thanaron's gush of nature, and nearly squeezed the life out of him in the vain hope of making their joy known to him? Everybody else in the mess! Who looked on in bewilderment, and was half glad and half sorry, though more glad than sorry by half, and wondered all the while what was coming next? Bless you, it was I! And we kept doing that sort of thing until I got very used to it, and by the time we sighted the green summits of Tahiti, my range of experience was so great that nothing could touch me further. It may be that we were not governed by the laws of ordinary seafarers. The *Chevert* was shaped a little like a bath-tub, with a bow like a duck's breast, and a high, old-fashioned quarter-deck, resembling a Chinese junk with a reef in her stern. Forty bold sailor-boys, who looked as though they had been built on precisely the same model and dealt out to the government by the dozen, managed to keep the decks very clean and tidy, and the brass-work in a state of dazzling brightness. The ship was wonderfully well ordered. I could tell you by the sounds on deck, while I swung in the comfortable seclusion of my hammock, just the hour of the day or night, but that was after I had once learned the order of events. There was the Sunday morning inspection, the Wednesday sham naval battle, the prayers night and morning, and the order to shorten sail each evening. Between times the decks were scrubbed and the whole ship reno-vated ; sometimes the rigging was darkened with drying clothes, and sometimes we felt like ancient mariners, the sea was so oily and the air so hot and still. There was nothing stirring save the sea-birds, who paddled about like tame ducks, and the faint, thin thread of smoke that ascended noiselessly from the dainty rolls of tobacco in the fingers of the en-tire ship's crew. In fact, when we moved at all in these calm waters, we seemed to be propelled by forty-cigarette power, for there was not a breath of air stirring.

It was at such times that we fought our bloodless battles. The hours were ominous ; breakfast did

not seem half a breakfast, because we hurried
through it with the dreadful knowledge that a conflict was pending, and possibly—though not probably—we might never gather at that board again;
for a naval engagement is something terrible, and
life is uncertain in the fairest weather. Breakfast is
scarcely over when the alarm is given, and with the
utmost speed every Frenchman flies to his post.
Already the horizon is darkened with the Prussian
navy, yet our confidence in the staunch old *Chevert*,
in each particular soul on board, and in our undaunted leader—*Monsieur le Capitaine*, who is even
now scouring the sea with an enormous marine
glass that of itself is enough to strike terror to the
Prussian heart—our implicit confidence in ourselves
is such that we smilingly await the approach of the
doomed fleet. At last they come within range of
our guns, and the conflict begins. I am unfortunately compelled to stay beneath the hatches. A
sham battle is no sight for an inexperienced landsman to witness; and, moreover, I would doubtless
get in the way of the frantic crew, who seem resolved to shed the last drop of French blood in behalf of *la belle France*.

Marine engagements are, as a general thing, a
great bore. The noise is something terrific; ammunition is continually passed up through the transom
over our dinner-table, and a thousand feet are rushing over the deck with a noise as of theatrical
thunder. The engagement lasts for an hour or two.
Once or twice we are enveloped in sheets of flame.

We are speedily deluged with water, and the conflict is renewed with the greatest enthusiasm.
Again, and again, and again, we pour a broadside
into the enemy's fleet, and always with terrific effect.
We invariably do ourselves the greatest credit, for,
by the time our supplies are about exhausted, not a
vestige of the once glorious navy of Prussia remains
to tell the tale. The sea is, of course, blood-stained
for miles around. The few persistent Prussians
who attempt to board us are speedily despatched,
and allowed to drop back into the remorseless waves.
A shout of triumph rings up from our triumphant
crew, and the play is over.

Once more the hatches are removed ; once more
I breathe the sweet air of heaven, for not a grain of
powder has been burned through all this fearful
conflict ; once more my messmates rush into our
little cabin and regale themselves with copious
draughts of absinthe, and I am pressed to the proud
bosom of Thanaron, who is restored to me without
a scar to disfigure his handsome little body. I grew
used to these weekly wars, and before we came in
sight of our green haven there was not a Prussian
left in the Pacific. It is impossible that any nation,
though they be schooled to hardships, could hope to
survive such a succession of disastrous conflicts. On
the whole, I like sham battles; they are deuced ex-
citing, and they don't hurt.

How different, how very different those sleepy
days when we were drifting on toward the Marque-
sas Islands ! The silvery phaëtons darted overhead

like day-stars shooting from their spheres. The sea-
weed grew denser, and a thousand floating things—
broken branches with a few small leaves attached,
the husk of a cocoa-nut, or straws such as any dove
from any ark would be glad to seize upon—these
gave us ample food for speculation. "Piloted by
the slow unwilling winds," we came close to the
star-lit Nouka Hiva, and shortened sail right under
its fragrant shadow. It was a glorious night.
There was the subtile odor of earth in the warm
faint air, and before us that impenetrable shadow
that we knew to be an island, yet whose outlines
were traceable only by the obliterated stars.

At sunrise we were on deck, and looking westward
saw the mists melt away like a veil swept from
before the face of a dusky Venus just rising from
the waves. The island seemed to give out a kind
of magnetic heat that made our blood tingle. We
gravitated toward it with an almost irresistible impulse. Something had to be done before we yielded
to the fascinations of this savage enchantress. Our
course lay to the windward of the southeastern
point of the land ; but, finding that we could not
weather it, we went off before the light wind and
drifted down the northern coast, swinging an hour
or more under the lee of some parched rocks, eying
the "Needles"—the slender and symmetrical peaks,
so called—and then we managed to work our way
out into the open sea again, and were saved.

Valleys lay here and there, running back from the
shore with green and inviting vistas ; slim waterfalls

made one desperate leap from the clouds and buried themselves in the forests hundreds of feet below, where they were lost forever. Rain-clouds hung over the mountains, throwing deep shadows across the slopes that, but for this relief, would have been too bright for the sentimental beauty that usually identifies a tropical island.

I happened to know something about the place, and marked every inch of the scorching soil as we floated past groves of rose-wood, sandal-wood, and a hundred sorts of new and strange trees, looking dark and velvety in the distance; past strips of beach that shone like glass, while beyond them the cocoa-palms that towered above the low brown huts of the natives seemed to reel and nod in the intense meridian heat. A moist cloud, far up the mountain, hung above a serene and sacred haunt, and under its shelter was hidden a deep valley, whose secret has been carried to the ends of the earth; for Herman Melville has plucked out the heart of its mystery, and beautiful and barbarous Typee lies naked and forsaken.

I was rather glad we could not get any nearer to it, for fear of dispelling the ideal that has so long charmed me. Catching the wind again, late in the afternoon, we lost the last outline of Nouka Hiva in the soft twilight, and said our prayers that evening as much at sea as ever. Back we dropped into the solemn round of uneventful days. Even the sham-battles no longer thrilled us. In fact, the whole affair was a little too theatrical to bear frequent rep-

etition. There was but one of our mess who could
muster an episode whenever we became too stagnant
for our health's good, and this was our first officer
—a tall, slim fellow, with a warlike beard, and very
soft, dark eyes, whose pupils seemed to be floating
aimlessly about under the shelter of long lashes.
His face was in a perpetual dispute with itself, and
I never knew which was the right or the wrong side
of him. B—— was the happy possessor of a tight
little African, known as Nero, although I always
looked upon him as so much Jamaica ginger. Nero
was as handsome a specimen of tangible darkness as
you will sight in a summer's cruise. B—— loved
with the ardor of his vacillating eyes, yet governed
with the rigor of his beard. Nero was consequently
prepared for any change in the weather, no matter
how sudden or uncalled for. In the equatorial seas,
while we sailed to the measure of the Ancient Mariner, B—— summoned Nero to the sacrifice, and,
having tortured him to the extent of his wits, there
was a reconciliation more ludicrous than any other
scene in the farce. It was at such moments that
B——'s eyes literally swam, when even his beard
wilted, while he told of the thousand pathetic eras
in Nero's life, when he might have had his liberty,
but found the service of his master more beguiling;
of the adventures by flood and field, where B——
was distinguishing himself, yet at his side, through
thick and thin, struggled the faithful Nero. Thus
B—— warmed himself at the fire his own enthusiasm had kindled on the altar of self-love, and every

moment added to his fervor. It was the yellow fever, and the cholera, and the small-pox, that were
powerless to separate that faithful slave from the
agonizing bedside of his master. It was shipwreck
and famine, and the smallest visible salary, that
seemed only to strengthen the ties that bound them
the one to the other. Death—cruel death—alone
could separate them ; and B—— took Nero by the
throat and kissed him passionately upon his sooty
cheek, and the floating eyes came to a stand-still
with an expression of virtuous defiance that was calculated to put all conventionalities to the blush.
We were awed by the magnanimity of such conduct,
until we got thoroughly used to it, and then we
were simply entertained. We kept looking forward
to the conclusion of the scene, which usually followed in the course of half an hour. B—— having
fondled Nero to his heart's content, and Nero having become somewhat bored, there was sure to arise
some mild disturbance, aggravated by both parties,
and B——, believing he had endured as much as any
Frenchman and first officer is expected to endure
without resentment, suddenly rises, and, seizing
Nero by the short, wiry moss of his scalp, kicks him
deliberately from the cabin, and returns to us, bursting with indignation. This domestic equinox we
soon grew fond of ; and, having become familiar with
all its signals of approach, we watched with agreeable interest the inevitable climax. It was well for
Nero that Nature had provided against any change
of color in his skin, for he must have borne the

sensation of his chastisement for some hours, though he was unable to give visible expression of it. By and by came B——'s own private birthday. Nothing had been said of it at table, and, in fact, nothing elsewhere, that I remember; but Nero, who had survived several of those anniversaries, bore it in mind, and our dinner was something gorgeous—to look at! Unhappily, certain necessary ingredients had been unavoidably omitted in the concocting of the dessert, ornamental pastry not being set down in our regular bill of fare; but B—— ate of pies that were built of chips, and of puddings that were stuffed with sawdust, until I feared we should be called upon to mourn the loss of a first officer before morning.

Moreover, B—— insisted that everything was unsurpassed; and, Heaven be thanked! I believe the pastry could easily lay claim to that distinction. At any rate, never before or since have I laid teeth to such a Dead Sea dessert. At this point, B—— naturally called Nero to him and thanked him, with moist and truthful eyes, and the ingenuous little Jamaican dropped a couple of colorless tears that would easily have passed for anybody's anywhere. For this mutual exhibition of sentiment everyone of us was duly grateful, and we never afterward scorned B—— for his eccentricities, since we knew him to be capable of genuine feeling. Moreover, he nearly died of his birthday feast, yet did not once complain of the unsuspecting cause of all his woe; who was at his side night and day, anticipating all

20

his wishes, and deploring the unaccountable misfortunes of his master.

So the winds blew us into the warm south latitudes. I was getting restless. Perhaps we had talked ourselves out of legitimate topics of conversation, and were forcing the social element. It was tedious beyond expression, passing day after day within sound of the same voices, and being utterly unable to flee into never so small a solitude, for there was not an inch of it on board. Swinging at night in my hammock between decks, wakefully dreaming of the future and of the past, again and again I have stolen up on deck, where the watch lay in the moonlight, droning their interminable yarns and smoking their perpetual cigarettes—for French sailors have privileges, and improve them with a considerable grace.

It was at such times that the wind sung in the rigging, with a sound as of a thousand swaying branches full of quivering leaves—just as the soft gale in the garden groves suggests pleasant nights at sea, the vibration of the taut stays, and the rush of waters along the smooth sides of the vessel. A ship's rigging is a kind of sea-harp, played upon by the four winds of heaven.

The sails were half in moonlight and half in shadow. Every object was well defined, and on the high quarter-deck paced Thanaron, his boyish figure looking strangely picturesque, for he showed in every motion how deeply he felt the responsibility of his office. There was usually a faint light in

the apartments of *Monsieur le Capitaine*, and I
thought of him in his gold lace and dignity, poring
over a French novel, or cursing the light winds. I
used to sit upon the neck of a gun—one of our
four dummies, that were never known to speak
louder than a whisper—lay my head against the
moist bulwarks, and listen to the half-savage chants
of the Tahitian sailors who helped to swell our
crew. As we drew down toward the enchanted
islands they seemed fairly bewitched, and it was
with the utmost difficulty that they could keep their
mouths shut until evening, when they were sure to
begin intoning an epic that usually lasted through
the watch. Sometimes a fish leaped into the moonlight, and came down with a splash ; or a whale
heaved a great sigh close to us, and as I looked over
the bulwarks I would catch a glimpse of the old fellow just going down, like a submerged island. Occasionally a flying-fish — a kind of tangible moon-
beam—fell upon deck, and was secured by one of
the sailors ; or a bird, sailing about with an eye to
roosting on one of our yards, gave a plaintive, ominous cry, that was echoed in falsetto by two or three
voices, and rung in with the Tahitian cantata of island
delights. Even this sort of thing lost its charm after
a little. Thanaron could not speak to me, because
Thanaron was officer of the deck at that moment, and
Thanaron himself had said to me, "Order, Monsieur, order is the first law of France !" I had always supposed that heaven had a finger in the making of that law—but it is all the same to a Frenchman.

Most sea-days have a tedious family resemblance, their chief characteristic being the almost total absence of any distinguishing feature. Fair weather and foul ; sunlight, moonlight, and starlight ; moments of confidence ; oaths of eternal fidelity ; plans for the future long enough to crowd a century uncomfortably ; relapses, rows, recoveries ; then, after many days, the water subsided, and we saw land at last.

Land, God bless it ! Long, low coral reefs, with a strip of garden glorifying them ; rocks towering out of the sea, palm-crowned, foam-fringed ; wreaths of verdure cast upon the bosom of the ocean, forever fragrant in their imperishable beauty ; and beyond and above them all, gorgeous and glorious Tahiti.

On the morning of the thirty-third day out there came a revelation to the whole ship's company. A faint blue peak was seen struggling with the billows ; presently it seemed to get the better of them, growing broader and taller, but taking hours to do so. The wind was stiff, and the sea covered with foam ; we rolled frightfully all day. Our French dinner lost its identity. Soup was out of the question ; we had hard work to keep meat and vegetables from total wreck, while we hung on to the legs of the table with all our strength. How the old *Chevert* "bucked," that day, as though conscious that for months to come she would swing in still waters by the edge of green pastures, where any such conduct would be highly inappropriate.

Every hour the island grew more and more beautiful, as though it were some lovely fruit or flower, swiftly and magically coming to maturity. A central peak, with a tiara of rocky points, crowns it with majesty, and a neighboring island of great beauty seems its faithful attendant. I do not wonder that the crew of the *Bounty* mutinied when they were ordered to make sail and turn their backs on Tahiti; nor am I surprised that they put the captain and one or two other objectionable features into a small boat, and advised them to continue their voyage if they were anxious to do so; but as for them, give them Tahiti, or give them worse than death—and, if convenient, give them Tahiti straight, and keep all the rest for the next party that came along.

As soon as we were within hailing distance the pilot came out and took us under his wing. We kissed the hand of a citizen of the new world, and, for the first time since losing sight of the dear California coast, dismissed it from our minds. There was very little wind right under the great green mountains, so the frigate *Astrea* sent a dozen boats to tow us through the opening in the reef to our most welcome anchorage. No Doge of Venice ever cruised more majestically than we, and our sea-pageant was the sensation of the day.

"Click-click" went the anchor-chains through the hawse-holes, down into a deep, sheltered bowl of the sea, whose waters have never yet been ruffled by the storms that beat upon the coral wall around it. Along the crescent shores trees dropped their yellow leaves into the water, and tried their best to

bury the slim canoes drawn up among their roots.
Beyond this barricade of verdure the eye caught
glimpses of every sort of tropical habitation imaginable, together with the high roofs and ponderous
white walls of the French Government buildings.
The foliage broke over the little town like a green
sea, and every possibility of a good view of it was
lost in the inundation. Above it towered the sublime crest of the mountain, with a strip of cloud
about its middle in true savage fashion. Perpetual
harvest lay in its lap, and it basked in the smile of
God.

Twilight, fragrant and cool ; a fruity flavor in the
air, a flower-like tint in sea and sky, the ship's boat
waiting to convey us shoreward. . . . O Thanaron, my Thanaron, with your arms about my neck,
and B——'s arms about you, and Nero clinging to
his master's knees—in fact, with everybody felicitat-
ing every other body, because it was such an evening as descends only upon the chosen places of the
earth, and because, having completed our voyage in
safety, we were all literally in a transport!

A PRODIGAL IN TAHITI

L ET this confession be topped with a vignette done in broad, shadowless lines and few of them—something like this:

A little, fly-blown room, smelling of garlic; I cooling my elbows on the oily slab of a table (breakfast for one), and looking through a window at a glaring whitewashed fence high enough to shut out the universe from my point of sight. Yet it hid not all, since it brought into relief a panting cock (with one leg in a string), which had so strained to compress itself into a doubtful inch of shade that its suspended claw clutched the air in real agony.

Having dazzled my eyes with this prospect, I turned gratefully to the vanities of life that may be had for two francs in Tahiti. *Vide* bill of fare: One fried egg, like the eye of some gigantic Albino; potatoes hollowed out bombshell fashion, primed with liver-sausage, very ingenious and palatable; the naked corpse of a fowl that cared not to live longer, from appearances, yet looked not happy in death.

Item: Wonder if there *is* a more ghastly spectacle than a chicken cooked in the French style; its knees drawn up on its breast like an Indian mummy,

while its blue-black, parboiled, and melancholy visage tearfully surveys its own unshrouded remains.
After a brief season of meditation I said, and I trust
I meant it, "I thank the Lord for all these blessings." Then I gave the corpse of the chicken
Christian burial under a fold of the window curtain,
disposed of the fried eye of the Albino, and transformed myself into a mortar for the time being,
taking potato-bombshells according to my calibre.

There was claret all the while and plenty of butterless roll, a shaving of cheese, a banana, black
coffee and cognac, when I turned again to dazzle
myself with the white fence, and saw with infinite
pity—a sentiment perhaps not unmixed with a suspicion of cognac or some other temporary human-
izing element—I saw for a fact that the poor cock
had wilted, and lay flat in the sun like a last year's
duster. That was too much for me. I wheeled toward the door where gleamed the bay with its
lovely ridges of light; canoes drifting over it drew
the eye after them irresistibly; I heard the ship-
calkers on the beach making their monotonous clatter, and the drone of the bareheaded fruit-sellers
squatted in rows, chatting indolently, with their
eyes half shut. I could think of nothing but bees
humming over their own sweet wares.

About this time a young fellow at the next table,
who had scarcely a mouthful of English at his command, implored me to take beer with him; imply-
ing that we might, if desirable, become as tight as
two bricks. I declined, much to his admiration.

he regarding my refusal as a clear case of moral courage, whereas it arose simply and solely from my utter inability to see his treat and go him one better.

A grown person in Tahiti has an eating hour allotted to him twice a day, at 10 A.M. and 5 P.M. My time being up, I returned to the store in an indifferent frame of mind, and upon entering the presence of my employer, who had arrived a moment before me, I was immediately covered with the deep humiliation of servitude and withdrew to an obscure corner; while Monsieur and some naval guests took absinthe unblushingly, which was, of course, proper enough in them. Call it by what name you will, you cannot sweeten servility to my taste. Then why was I there and in bondage? The spirit of adventure that keeps life in us, yet comes near to worrying it out of us now and then, lured me with my handful of dollars to the Garden of the Pacific. "You can easily get work," said someone who had been there and didn't want it. If work I must, why not better there than here? thought I; and the less money I take with me the surer am I to seek that which might not attract me under other circumstances. A few letters which proved almost valueless; an abiding trust in Providence, afterward somewhat shaken, I am sorry to state, which convinces me that I can no longer hope to travel as a shorn lamb; considerable confidence in the good feeling of my fellow-men, together with the few dollars above referred to—comprised my all when I set foot on the leaf-strewn and shady beach of Papeete.

Before the day was over I saw my case was almost hopeless ; I was one too many in a very meagre congregation of foreigners. In a week I was desperate, with poverty and disgrace brooding like evil spirits on either hand. Every ten minutes someone suggested something which was almost immediately suppressed by the next man I met, to whom I applied for further information. Teach, said one : there wasn't a pupil to be had in the dominion. Clerkships were out of the question likewise. I might keep store, if I could get anything to put in it ; or go farther, as someone suggested, if I had money enough to get there. I thought it wiser to endure the ills I had than fly to others that I knew not of. In this state I perambulated the green lanes of Papeete, conscious that I was drawing down tons of immaterial sympathy from hearts of various nationalities, beating to the music of regular salaries in hard cash, and the inevitable ringing of their daily dinner-bell ; and I continued to perambulate under the same depressing avalanches for a fortnight or more—a warning to the generation of the inexperienced that persists in sowing itself broadcast upon the edges of the earth, and learns too late how hard a thing it is to take root under the circumstances.

One gloomy day I was seized in the market-place and led before a French gentleman who offered me a bed and board for such manual compensation as I might be able to give him in his office during the usual business hours, namely, from daybreak to some time in the afternoon, unless it rained, when business was suspended, and I was dropped until fair weather should set that little world wagging again.

I was invited to enter into the bosom of his family, in fact, to be *one* of them, and no single man could ask to be more; to sit at his table and hope for better days, in which diversion he proposed to join me with all his soul.

With an emotion of gratitude and a pang at being thus early a subject of charity, I began business in Papeete, and learned within the hour how sharper than most sharps it is to know only your own mother-tongue when you're away from home.

Nightly I walked two hot and dusty miles through groves of bread-fruit and colonnades of palms to my new master's. I skirted, with loitering steps, a placid sea whose crystalline depths sheltered leagues and leagues of sun-painted corals, where a myriad fish, dyed like the rainbow, sported unceasingly. Springs gushed from the mountain, singing their song of joy; the winds sang in the dark locks of the sycamore, while the palm-boughs clashed like cymbals in rhythmical accompaniment; glad children chanted their choruses, and I alone couldn't sing, nor hum, nor whistle, because it doesn't pay to work for your board, and settle for little necessities out of your own pocket, in any latitude that I ever heard of.

We lived in a grove of ten thousand cocoa-palms
crowning a hill-slope to the west.   How all-sufficient
it sounds as I write it now, but how little I cared
then, for many reasons !   My cottage had prior tenants, who disputed possession with me—winged
tenants who sought admission at every cranny
and frequently obtained it in spite of me ; these
were not angels, but hens.   My cottage had been a
granary until it got too poor a receptacle for grains,
and a better shelter left it open to the barn-fowls
until I arrived.   They hated me, these hungry
chickens ; they used to sit in rows on the window-
sill and stare me out of countenance.   A wide bed-
stead, corded with thongs, did its best to furnish my
apartment.   A narrow, a very narrow and thin
ship's mattress, that had been a bed of torture for
many a sea-sick soul before it descended to me ; a
flat pillow like a pancake ; a condemned horse-
blanket contributed by a good-natured Kanack who
raked it from a heap of refuse in the yard, together
with two sacks of rice, the despair of those hens in
the window, were all I could boast of.   With this
inventory I strove (by particular request) to be one
of those who were comfortable enough in the château adjoining.   Summoned peremptorily to dinner, I entered a little latticed *salon*, connected with
the château by a covered walk, discovered Monsieur seated at table and already served with soup
and claret ; the remainder of the company helped
themselves as they best could ; and I saw plainly
enough that the family bosom was so crowded al-

ready, that I might seek in vain to wedge myself
into any corner of it, at least until some vacancy
occurred.

After dinner, sat on a sack of rice in my room,
while it grew dark and Monsieur received calls;
wandered down to the beach at the foot of the hill
and lay a long time on a bed of leaves, while the
tide was out and the crabs clattered along shore and
were very sociable. Natives began to kindle their
evening fires of cocoa-nut husks; smoke, sweet as
incense, climbed up to the plumes of the palm-trees
and was lost among the stars. Morsels of fish and
bread-fruit were offered me by the untutored savage, who welcomed me to his frugal meal and desired that I should at least taste before he broke his
fast. Canoes shot out from dense, shadowy points,
fishers standing in the bows with a poised spear in
one hand; a blazing palm branch held aloft in the
other shed a warm glow of light over their superb
nakedness. Bathed by the sea, in a fresh, cool
spring, and returned to my little coop, which was
illuminated by the glare of fifty floating beacons;
looking back from the door I could see the dark
outlines of the torch-bearers and hear their signal
calls above the low growl of the reef a half-mile
farther out from shore. It was a blessing to lie
awake in my little room and watch the flicker of
those fires; to think how Tahiti must look on a
cloudless night from some heavenly altitude—the
ocean still as death, the procession of fishermen
sweeping from point to point within the reef, till

the island, flooded with starlight and torchlight, lies like a green sea-garden in a girdle of flame.

A shrill bell called me from my bed at dawn. I was not unwilling to rise, for half the night I lay like a saint on the tough thongs, having turned over in sleep, thereby missing the mattress entirely. Made my toilet at a spring on the way into town ; saw a glorious sunrise that was as good as break-fast, and found the whole earth and sea and all that in them is singing again while I listened and gave thanks for that privilege. At 10 A.M. I went to breakfast in the small restaurant where I have sketched myself at the top of this chronicle, and whither we may return and begin over again if it please you.

I was about to remark that probably most melan-choly and homesickness may be cured or alleviated by a wholesome meal of victuals ; but I think I won't, for, on referring to my note-book, I find that within an hour after my return to the store I was as heart-sick as ever and wasn't afraid to say so. It is scarcely to be wondered at : the sky was dark ; aboard a schooner some sailors were making that doleful whine peculiar to them, as they hauled in to shore and tied up to a tree in a sifting rain ; then everything was ominously still, as though something disagreeable were about to happen ; thereupon I doubled myself over the counter like a half-shut jack-knife, and burying my face in my hands, said to myself, "O, to be alone with Nature! her silence is religion and her sounds sweet music." After which the rain blew over, and I was sent with a hand-cart and one underfed Kanack to a wharf half a mile away to drag back several loads of potatoes. We two hungry creatures struggled heroically to do our duty. Starting with a multitude of sacks it was quite impossible to proceed with, we grew weaker the farther we went, so that the load had to be reduced from time to time, and I believe the amount of potatoes deposited by the way considerably exceeded the amount we subsequently arrived at the store with. Finding life a burden, and seeing the legs of the young fellow in harness with me bend under him in his frantic efforts to get our cart out of a rut without emptying it entirely, I resolved to hire a substitute at my own expense, and save my remaining strength for a new line of business. Thus I was enabled to sit on the wharf the rest of the afternoon and enjoy myself devising new means of subsistence and watching the natives swim.

Someone before me found a modicum of sweets in his cup of bitterness, and in a complacent hour set the good against the evil in single entry, summing up the same to his advantage. I concluded to do it myself, and did it, thus:

EVIL.	GOOD.
I find myself in a foreign land with no one to love and none to love me.	But I may do as I please in consequence, and it is nobody's business save my own.
I am working for my board	But I may quit as soon as

and lodging (no extras), and find it very unprofitable.

I feel like it, and shall have no occasion to dun my employer for back salary so long as I stop with him.

My clothes are in rags. I shall soon be without a stitch to my back.

But the weather is mild and the fig-tree flourisheth. Moreover, many a good savage has gone naked before me.

I get hungry before breakfast and feel faint after dinner. What are two meals a day to a man of my appetite?

But fasting is saintly. Day by day I grow more spiritual, and shall shortly be a fit subject for translation to that better world which is doubtless the envy of all those who have lost it by over-eating and drinking.

Nothing can exceed the satisfaction with which I read and re-read this philosophical summary, but I had relapses every few minutes so long as I lived in Tahiti. I remember one Sunday morning, a day I had all to myself, when I cried out of the depths and felt better after it. It was a real Sunday. The fowls confessed it by the indifference with which they picked up a grain of rice now and then, as though they weren't hungry. The family were moving about in an unnatural way; some people are never themselves on the Lord's day. The canoes lay asleep off upon the water, evidently conscious of the long hours of rest they were sure of having. To sum it all, it seemed as though the cover had been taken off from the earth, and the angels were sitting in big circles looking at us. Our clock had run down, and I found myself half an hour too early at mass. Some diminutive native children talked together with infinite gesticulation, like little old men. At every lag in the conversation, two or three of them would steal away to the fence that surrounded the church and begin diligently counting the pickets thereof. They were evidently amazed at what they considered a singular coincidence, namely, that the number of pickets, beginning at the front gate and counting to the right, tallied exactly with the do. do. beginning at the do. do. and counting to the left; while they were making repeated efforts to get at the heart of this mystery, the priest rode up on horseback, dismounted in our midst, and we all followed him into chapel to mass.

A young Frenchman offered me holy water on the tips of his fingers, and I immediately decided to confide in him to an unlimited extent if he gave me the opportunity. It was a serious disappointment when I found, later, that we didn't know six words in any common tongue. Concluded to be independent and walked off by myself. Got very lonesome immediately. Tried to be meditative, philosophical, botanical, conchological, and in less than an hour gave it up—homesick again, by Jove !

Strolled to the beach and sat a long time on a bit of wreck partly embedded in the sand ; consoled by the surpassing radiance of sunset, wondered how I could ever have repined, but proceeded to do

21

it again as soon as it grew dark. Some natives
drew near, greeting me kindly. They were evidently lovers; talked in low tones, deeply interested in the most trivial things, such as a leaf falling into the sea at our feet and floating stem up,
like a bowsprit; he probably made some poetic al-
lusion to it, may have proposed braving the seas
with her in a shallop as fairy-like, for both fell
a-dreaming and were silent for some time, he worshipping her with fascinated eyes, while she, wom-
an-like, pretended to be all unconscious of his admiration.

Silently we sat looking over the sea at Moorea,
just visible in the light of the young moon, like a
spirit brooding upon the waters—till I broke the
spell by saying "Good-night," which was repeated
in a chorus as I withdrew to my coop and found my
feathered guests had beaten in the temporary barricade erected in the broken window, entered, and
made themselves at home during my absence—a
fact that scarcely endeared the spot to me. Next
morning I was unusually merry; couldn't tell why,
but tried to sing as I made my toilet at the spring;
laughed nearly all the way into town, saying my
prayers, and blessing God, when I came suddenly
upon a horse-shoe in the middle of the road. Took
it as an omen and a keepsake; horse-shoes aren't
shed everywhere nor for everybody. I thought it
the prophecy of a change, and at once cancelled my
engagement with my employer without having set
foot into his house farther than the dining-room,

or made any apparent impression upon the adamantine bosom of his family.

After formally expressing my gratitude to Monsieur for his renewed offers of hospitality, I turned myself into the street, and was once more adrift in the world. For the space of three minutes I was wild with joy at the thought of my perfect liberty. Then I grew nervous, began to feel unhappy, nay, even guilty, as though I had thrown up a good thing. Concluded it was rash of me to leave a situation where I got two meals and a mattress, with the privilege of washing at my own expense. Am not sure that it wasn't unwise, for I had no dinner that afternoon; and having no bed either, I crept into the veranda of a house to let and dozed till daybreak.

There was but one thing to live for now, namely, to see as much of Tahiti as possible, and at my earliest convenience return like the prodigal son to that father who would doubtless feel like killing something appropriate as soon as he saw me coming. I said as much to a couple of Frenchmen, brothers, who are living a dream-life over yonder, and whose wildest species of dissipation for the last seven years has been to rise at intervals from their settees in the arbor, go deliberately to the farther end of the garden, and eat several mangoes in cold blood.

To comprehend Tahiti, a man must lose himself in forests whose resinous boughs are knotted with ribbons of sea-grass; there, overcome by the music of sibilant waters sifting through the antlers of the

coral, he is supposed to sink upon drifts of orange-
blossoms, only to be resuscitated by the spray of an
approaching shower crashing through the green
solitudes like an army with chariots—so those
brothers said, with a mango poised in each hand;
and they added that I should have an official document addressed to the best blood in the kingdom,
namely, Forty Chiefs of Tahiti, who would undoubtedly entertain me with true barbarian hospitality,
better the world knows not. There was a delay for
some reason; I, rather impatient, and scarcely hoping to receive so graceful a compliment from head-
quarters, trudged on alone with a light purse and
an infinitesimal bundle of necessities, caring nothing for the weather nor the number of miles cleared
per day, since I laid no plans save the one, to see as
much as I might with the best grace possible, keeping an eye on the road for horse-shoes. Through
leagues of verdure I wandered, feasting my five
senses and finding life a holiday at last. There
were numberless streams to be crossed, where I
loafed for hours on the bridges, satisfying myself
with sunshine. Not a savage in the land was freer
than I. No man could say to me, " Why stand ye
here idle?" for I could continue to stand as long as
I liked and as idly as it pleased me in spite of him!
There were bridgeless streams to be forded; but
the Tahitian is a nomad continually wandering from
one edge of his fruitful world to the other; moreover, he is the soul of peace toward men of good-
will; I was invariably picked up by some bare-

backed Hercules, who volunteered to take me over the water on his brawny brown shoulders, and could have easily taken two like me. It was good to be up there while he strode through the swift current, for I felt that he was perfectly able to carry me to the ends of the earth without stopping, and that sense of reliance helped to reassure my faith in humanity.

As I wandered, from most native houses came the invitation to enter and eat. Night after night I found my bed in the corner of some dwelling whither I had been led by the master of it, with unaffected grace. It wasn't simply showing me to a spare room, but rather unrolling the best mat and turning everything to my account so long as it pleased me to tarry. Sometimes the sea talked in its sleep not a rod from the house; frequently the mosquitoes accepted me as a delicacy and did their best to dispose of me. Once I awoke with a headache, the air was so dense with the odor of orange-blossoms.

There was frequently a strip of blue bay that ebbed and flowed languidly and had to be lunched with; or a very deep and melodious spring, asking for an interview, and, I may add, always getting it. I remember one miniature castle built in the midst of a grassy Venice by the shore. Its moats, shining with gold-fish, were spanned with slender bridges; toy fences of bamboo enclosed the rarer clumps of foliage; and there was such an air of tranquillity pervading it I thought I must belong there. Something seemed to say, "Come in." I went in, but

left very soon; the place was so fairy-like, I felt as
though I were liable to step through it and come
out on some other side, and I wasn't anxious for
such a change.

I ate when I got hungry a very good sort of a
meal, consisting usually of a tiny piglet cooked in
the native fashion, swathed in succulent leaves and
laid between hot stones till ready for eating; bread-
fruit, like mashed potato, but a great deal better;
orange-tea and cocoa-milk—surely enough for two
or three francs.   Took a sleep whenever sleep came
along, resting always till the clouds or a shadow
from the mountain covered me so as to keep cool
and comfortable.   Natives passed me with saluta-
tions.   A white man now and then went by barely
nodding, or more frequently eying me with suspicion and giving me as much of his dust as he found
convenient.   In the wider fellowship of nature I
forswore all blood relations and blushed for those
representatives of my own color as I footed it right
royally.   Therefore I was enabled to scorn the fellow who scorned me while he flashed the steel hoofs
of his charger in my face and dashed on to the village we were both approaching with the dusk.

What a spot it was!   A long lane as green as a
spring meadow, lying between wall-like masses of
foliage whose deep arcades were frescoed with blossoms and festooned with vines.   It seemed a path-
way leading to infinity, for the blood-red bars of
sunset glared at its farther end as though Providence had placed them there to keep out the un-

regenerated. Not a house visible all this time, nor a human, though I was in the heart of the hamlet. Passing up the turf-cushioned road I beheld on either hand, through a screen of leaves, a log spanning a rivulet that was softly singing its monody; at the end of each log the summer-house of some Tahitian, who sat in his door smoking complacently. It was a picture of still life with a suggestion of possible motion; a village to put into a greenhouse, water, and keep fresh forever. Let me picture it once more—one mossy street between two babbling brooks, and every house thereof set each in its own moated wilderness. This was Papeali.

Like rows of cages full of chirping birds, those bamboo huts were distributed up and down the street. As I walked I knew something would cause me to turn at the right time and find a new friend ready to receive me, for it always does. So I walked slowly and without hesitation or impatience until I turned and met him coming out of his cage, crossing the rill by his log and holding out his hand to me in welcome. Back we went together, and I ate and slept there as though it had been arranged a thousand years ago; perhaps it was! There was a racket up at the farther end of the lane, by the chief's house; songs and nose-flutings upon the night air; moreover, a bonfire, and doubtless much nectar—too much, as usual, for I heard such cheers as the soul gives when it is careless of consequences, and caught a glimpse of the joys of barbarism such as even we poor Christians cannot

wholly withstand, but turning our backs think we
are safe enough. Commend me to him who has
known temptation and not shunned it, but actually
withstood it !

It was the dance, as ever it is the dance where
all the aspirations of the soul find expression in
the body; those bodies that are incarnate souls or
those souls that are spiritualized bodies, inseparable, whatever they are, for the time being. The fire
glowed fervently; bananas hung out their tattered
banners like decorations; palms rustled their silver
plumes aloft in the moonlight; the sea panted upon its sandy bed in heavy sleep; the night-blooming cereus opened its waxen chambers and gave
forth its treasured sweets. Circle after circle of
swart savage faces were turned upon the flame-lit
arena where the dancers posed for a moment with
their light drapery gathered about them and held
carelessly in one hand. Anon the music chimed
forth—a reiteration of chords caught from the
birds' treble and the wind's bass ; full and resounding syllables, richly poetical, telling of orgies and
of the mysteries of the forbidden revels in the
charmed valleys of the gods, hearing which it were
impossible not to be wrought to madness ; and the
dancers thereat went mad, dancing with infinite
gesticulation, dancing to whirlwinds of applause till
the undulation of their bodies was serpentine, and
at last in frenzy they shrieked with joy, threw off
their garments, and were naked as the moon. So
much for a vision that kept me awake till morning;

when I plodded on in the damp grass and tried
to forget it, but couldn't exactly, and never have
to this hour. Went on and on over more bridges
spanning still-flowing streams of silver, past springs
that lay like great crystals framed in moss under
dripping, fern-clad cliffs that the sun never reaches.
Came at last to a shining, whitewashed fort, on an
eminence that commands the isthmus connecting
the two hemispheres of Tahiti, where down I
dropped into a narrow valley full of wind and discord and a kind of dreary neglect that made me
sick for any other place. More refreshment for the
wayfarer, but to be paid for by the dish, and therefore limited. Was obliged to hate a noisy fellow
with too much bushy black beard and a freckled
nose, and to like another who eyed me kindly over
his absinthe, having first mixed a glass for me. A
native asked me where I was going; being unable
to give any satisfactory answer, he conducted me to
his canoe, about a mile distant, where he cut a
sapling for a mast, another for a gaff, twisted, in a
few moments, a cord of its fibrous bark, rigged a
sail of his sleeping-blanket, and we were shortly
wafted onward before a light breeze between the
reef and shore.

Three of us, with a bull-pup in the bows, dozed
under the afternoon sun. He of the paddle awoke
now and then to shift sail, beat the sea impetuously
for a few seconds, and fall asleep again. Voices
roused me occasionally, greetings from colonies of
indolent Kanacks on shore, whose business it was

to sit there till they got hungry, laughing weariness to scorn.

Close upon our larboard-bow lay one of the islands that had bewitched me as I paced the shore but a few days previous ; under us the measureless gardens of the sea unmasked a myriad imperishable blossoms, centuries old some of them, but as fair and fresh as though born within the hour. All that afternoon we drifted between sea and shore, and beached at sunset in a new land. Foot-sore and weary, I approached a stable from which thrice a week stages were despatched to Papeete.

A modern pilgrim finds his scrip cumbersome, if he has any, and deems it more profitable to pay his coachman than his cobbler.

I climbed to my seat by the jolly French driver, who was continually chatting with three merry nuns sitting just back of us, returning to the convent in Papeete after a vacation retreat among the hills. How they enjoyed the ride, as three children might ! and were quite wild with delight at meeting a corpulent *père*, who smiled amiably from his saddle and offered to show them the interior of the pretty chapel at Faaa (only three *a*'s in that word)—the very one I grew melancholy in when I was a man of business.

So they hurled themselves madly from the high seat, one after the other, scorning to touch anything so contaminating as a man's hand, though it looked suicidal, as the driver and I agreed while the three were at prayers by the altar. Whipping up over

the road townward, I could almost recognize my
own footprints left since the time I used to take
the dust in my face three mornings a week from the
wheels of that very vehicle as I footed it in to business. Passing the spring, my toilet of other days,
drawing to the edge of the town, we stopped being
jolly and were as proper as befitted travellers. We
looked over the wall of the convent garden as we
drove up to the gate, and saw the mother-superior
hurrying down to us with a cumbersome chair for
the relief of the nuns, but before she reached us
they had cast themselves to earth again in the
face of destiny, and there was kissing, crying, and
commotion as they withdrew under the gateway
like so many doves seeking shelter. When the gate
closed after them, I heard them all *cooing* at once,
but the world knows nothing further.

Where would I be dropped? asked the driver. In
the middle of the street, please you, and take half
my little whole for your ride, sir! He took it,
dropped me where we stood, and drove away, I pre-
tending to be very much at my ease. God help me
and all poor hypocrites!

I sought a place of shelter, or rather retirement,
for the air is balm in that country. There was an
old house in the middle of a grassy lawn on a by-
street; two of its rooms were furnished with a few
papers and books, and certain gentlemen who con-
tribute to its support lounge in when they have
leisure for reading or a chat. I grew to know the
place familiarly. I stole a night's lodging on its

veranda in the shadow of a passion-vine ; but, for
fear of embarrassing some early student in pursuit
of knowledge, I passed the second night on the floor
of the dilapidated cook-house, where the ants covered me. I endured the tortures of one who bares
his body to an unceasing shower of sparks ; but I
survived.

There was, in this very cook-house, a sink six feet
in length and as wide as a coffin ; the third night I
lay like a galvanized corpse with his lid off till a rat
sought to devour me, when I took to the streets and
walked till morning. By this time the president of
the club, whose acquaintance I had the honor of,
tendered me the free use of any portion of the premises that might not be otherwise engaged. With a
gleam of hope I began my explorations. Up a narrow and winding stair I found a spacious loft. It
was like a mammoth tent, a solitary centre-pole its
only ornament. Creeping into it on all-fours, I
found a fragment of matting, a dry crust, an empty
soda-bottle—footprints on the sands of time.

"Poor soul !" I gasped; "where did *you* come
from? What *did* you come for? Whither, O,
whither, have you flown ?"

I might have added, How did you manage to get
there ? But the present was so important a consideration, I had no heart to look beyond it. The next
ten nights I passed in the silent and airy apartment
of my anonymous predecessor. Ten nights I crossed
the unswept floor that threatened at every step to
precipitate me into the reading-room below. With

a faint heart and hollow stomach I threw myself upon my elbow and strove to sleep. I lay till my heart stopped beating, my joints were wooden, and my four limbs corky beyond all hope of reanimation. There the mosquito revelled, and it was a promising place for centipedes.

At either end of the building an open window admitted the tip of a banana-leaf; up their green ribs the sprightly mouse careered. I broke the backbones of these banana-leaves, though they were the joy of my soul and would have adorned the choicest conservatory in the land. Day was equally unprofitable to me. My best friends said, "Why not return to California?" Every one I met invited me to leave the country at my earliest convenience. The American consul secured me a passage, to be settled for at home, and my career in that latitude was evidently at an end. In my superfluous confidence in humanity I had announced myself as a correspondent for the press. It was quite necessary that I should give some plausible reason for making my appearance in Tahiti friendless and poor. Therefore, I said plainly, "I am a correspondent, friendless and poor," believing that any one would see truth in the face of it, with half an eye. "Prove it," said one who knew more of the world than I. Then flashed upon me the alarming fact that I couldn't prove it, having nothing whatever in my possession referring to it in the slightest degree. It was a fatal mistake that might easily have been avoided, but was too well established to be rectified.

In my chagrin I looked to the good old bishop for consolation. Approaching the Mission House through sunlit cloisters of palms, I was greeted most tenderly. I would have gladly taken any amount of Holy Orders for the privilege of ending my troublous days in the sweet seclusion of the Mission House.

As it was, I received a blessing, an autograph, and a "God-speed" to some other part of creation. Added to this I learned how the address to the Forty Chiefs of Tahiti in behalf of the foreign traveller, my poor self, had been despatched to me by a special courier, who found me not; and doubtless the *fêtes* I heard of and was forever missing marked the march of that messenger, my proxy, in his triumphal progress.

In my innocent degradation it was still necessary to nourish the inner man. There is a market in Papeete where, under one broad roof, threescore hucksters of both sexes congregate long before daylight, and, while a few candles illumine their wares, patiently await custom. A half-dozen coolies with an eye to business serve hot coffee and chocolate at a dime per cup to any who choose to ask for it. By 7 A.M. the market is so nearly sold out that only the more plentiful fruits of the country are to be obtained at any price. A prodigal cannot long survive on husks, unless he have coffee to wash them down. I took my cup of it, with two spoonfuls of sugar and ants dipped out of a cigar-box, and a crust of bread into the bargain, sitting on a bench in the market-place, with a coolie and a Kanack on either hand.

It was not the coffee nor the sugared ants that I gave my dime for, but rather the privilege of sitting in the midst of men and women who were willing to accept me as a friend and helpmate without questioning my ancestry, and any one of whom would go me halves in the most disinterested manner. Then there was sure to be some superb fellow close at hand, with a sensuous lip curled under his nostril, a glimpse of which gave me a dime's worth of satisfaction and more too. Having secreted a French roll (five cents) all hot, under my coat, and gathered the bananas that would fall in the yard so seasonably, I made my day as brief and comfortable as possible by filling up with water from time to time.

The man who has passed a grimy chop-house, wherein a frowzy fellow sat at his cheap spread, without envying the frowzy fellow his cheap spread, cannot truly sympathize with me.

The man who has not felt a great hollow in his stomach, which he found necessary to fill at the first fountain he came to, or go over on his beam-ends for lack of ballast, cannot fall upon my neck and call me brother.

At daybreak I haunted those street fountains, waiting my turn while French cooks filled almost fathomless kegs, and coolies filled pot-bellied jars, and Kanacks filled their hollow bamboos that seemed fully a quarter of a mile in length. There I meekly made my toilet, took my first course of breakfast, rinsed out my handkerchiefs and stockings, and went my way. The whole performance was embarrassing, because I was a novice and a dozen people watched me in curious silence. I had also a boot with a suction in the toe ; there is dust in Papeete ; while I walked that boot loaded and discharged itself in a manner that amazed and amused a small mob of little natives who followed me in my free exhibition, advertising my shooting - boot gratuitously.

I was altogether shabby in my outward appearance, and cannot honestly upbraid any resident of the town for his neglect of me. I know that I suffered the agony of shame and the pangs of hunger ; but they were nothing to the utter loneliness I felt as I wandered about with my heart on my sleeve, and never a bite from so much as a daw.

Did you ever question the possibility of a man's temporary transformation under certain mental, moral, or physical conditions ? There are seasons when he certainly isn't what he was, yet may be more and better than he has been, if you give him time enough.

I began to think I had either suffered this transformation or been maliciously misinformed as to my personality. Was I truly what I represented myself to be, or had I been a living deception all my days ? No longer able to identify myself as any one in particular, it occurred to me that it would be well to address a few lines to the gentleman I had been in the habit of calling "father," asking for some particulars concerning his absent son. I immediately drew up this document ready for mailing :

MOSQUITO HALL, CENTIPEDE AVENUE, PAPEETE.

DEAR SIR : A nondescript awaits identification at this office. Answers to the names at the foot of this page, believes himself to be your son, to have been your son, or about to be something equally near and dear to you. He can repeat several chapters of the New Testament at the shortest notice ; recites most of the Catechism and Commandments ; thinks he would recognize two sisters and three brothers at sight, and know his mother with his eyes shut.

He likewise confesses to the usual strawberry-mark in fast colors. If you will kindly send by return mail a few dollars, he will clothe, feed, and water himself, and return immediately to those arms which, if his memory does not belie him, have more than once sheltered his unworthy frame. I have, dear sir, the singular fortune to be the article above described.

The six months which would elapse before I could hope for an answer would probably have found me past all recognition, so I ceased crying to the compassionate bowels of Tom, Dick, and Harry, waiting with haggard patience the departure of the vessel that was to bear me home with a palpable C. O. D. tacked on to me. Those last hours were brightened by the delicate attentions of a few good souls who learned, too late, the shocking state of my case. Thanks to them, I slept well thereafter in a real bed, and was sure of dinners that wouldn't rattle in me like a withered kernel in an old nutshell.

22

I had but to walk to the beach, wave my lily hand, heavily tanned about that time, when lo! a boat was immediately despatched from the plump little corvette *Cheveret;* where the tricolor waved triumphantly from sunrise to sunset, all the year round.

Such capital French dinners as I had there, such offers of bed and board and boundless sympathy as were made me by those dear fellows who wore the gold-lace and had a piratical-looking cabin all to themselves, were enough to wring a heart that had been nearly wrung out in its battle with life in Tahiti.

No longer I walked the streets as one smitten with the plague, or revolved in envious circles about the market-place, where I could have got my fill for a half-dollar, but had neither the one nor the other. No longer I went at daybreak to swell the procession at the water-spout, or sat on the shore the picture of despair, waiting sunrise, finding it my sole happiness to watch a canoe-load of children drifting out upon the bay, singing like a railful of larks; nor walked solitarily through the night up and down the narrow streets wherein the *gendarmes* had learned to pass me unnoticed, with my hat under my arm and my heart in my throat. Those delicious moons always seduced me from my natural sleep, and I sauntered through the cocoa-groves whose boughs glistened like row after row of crystals, whose shadows were as mosaics wrought in blocks of silver.

I used to nod at the low, whitewashed "calabooses " fairly steaming in the sun, wherein Herman Melville got some chapters of " Omoo."

Over and over again I tracked the ground of that delicious story, saying to the bread-fruit trees that had sheltered him, " Shelter me also, and whoever shall follow after, so long as your branches quiver in the wind ! "

O reader of " Omoo," think of " Motoo-Otoo," actually looking warlike in these sad days, with a row of new cannons around its edge, and pyramids of balls as big as cocoa-nuts covering its shady centre.

Walking alone in those splendid nights I used to hear a dry, ominous coughing in the huts of the natives. I felt as though I were treading upon the brinks of half-dug graves, and I longed to bring a respite to the doomed race.

One windy afternoon we cut our stern hawser in a fair wind and sailed out of the harbor ; I felt a sense of relief, and moralized for five minutes without stopping. Then I turned away from all listeners and saw those glorious green peaks growing dim in the distance ; the clouds embraced them in their profound secrecy ; like a lovely mirage Tahiti floated upon the bosom of the sea. Between sea and sky was swallowed up vale, garden, and waterfall ; point after point crowded with palms ; peak above peak in that eternal crown of beauty ; and with them the nation of warriors and lovers falling like the leaf, but, unlike it, with no followers in the new season.

www.ingramcontent.com/pod-product-compliance
Lightning Source LLC
Chambersburg PA
CBHW011154090426
42740CB00018B/3386

* 9 781410 107770 *